Taliesin's Travels brings fresh significance to
one of Britain's best-loved tales.

For over a thousand years the impish Taliesin has
enthralled and enlightened people. As a farmer's son,
he is grounded in the land. Yet, because his mother is
the goddess Nature, he can travel, free as a demi-god,
throughout time and space.

Thanks to his intimate contact with spirits of place, sun
and underworld, Taliesin reveals and portrays the
interconnecting, ever-transforming essence of life. His
often painful and sometimes ludicrous adventures engage
with creation in its entirety. Transcending history, he
invites *us* to see our own millennium as a cyclical,
mythic journey so that, like him, each individual
comes to identify with the whole of creation.

With a keen sense of enjoyment, Michael Dames provides
a deep and imaginative account of the tales and poetry
associated with Taliesin. Prehistoric, Romano-British and
Christian aspects of Taliesin's persona are brought
together in a magical synthesis.

Michael Dames is well-known for is pioneering studies of
the myths and legends of the British Isles. His previous
books include *The Silbury Treasure, The Avebury Cycle,
Mythic Ireland* and *Merlin and Wales.*

Taliesin's Travels

Taliesin's Travels

A demi-god at large

Michael Dames

Heart of Albion

Taliesin's Travels: a demi-god at large
Muchael Dames

Cover design and illustration by author

ISBN 1 872883 89 3
EAN 978 1872 883 892

Published by
Heart of Albion Press
2 Cross Hill Close, Wymeswold
Loughborough, LE12 6UJ

albion@indigogroup.co.uk

Visit our Web site: www.hoap.co.uk

Printed in England by Booksprint

CONTENTS

Notes on the Welsh alphabet and pronunciation

The alphabet runs: a, b, c, ch, d, dd, e, f, ff, g, ng, h, i, j, l, ll, m, n, o, p, ph, r, rh, s, t, th, u, y, w. All these are regarded as separate letters. There is no k, q, v or z.

Pronunciation: **ch** as in Scottish 'loch', **dd** as in 'that', **f** as in English 'van', **ff** as in English 'fan', **g** as in English 'get', **h** is always sounded, **ll** pronounced as 'ch' plus 'k', aspirated, **r** is rolled , **oe** as in English 'oy', **wy** as oo-ee.

The Welsh language within the Indo-European language family: a few words of comparison.

Sanskrit	Welsh	English	Latin	French
duva	dau	two	duo	deux
trayas	tri	three	tres	trois
matar	mam	mother	mater	mere, maman
asti	oes	is	est	est
navas	newydd	new	novus	nouveau

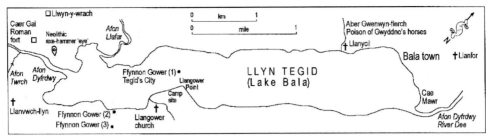

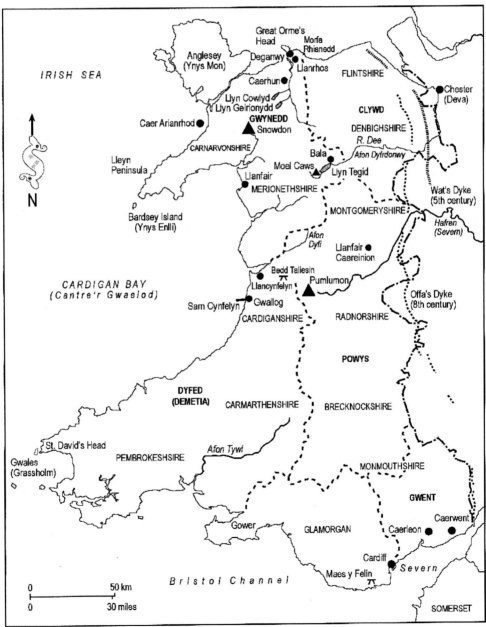

INTRODUCTION

TALIESIN'S TRAVELS is based on the Welsh folk tale named either *Hanes Taliesin,* or *Chwedl Taliesin,* both meaning 'The Story of Taliesin.' This ancient tale has been told and retold orally for more than a thousand years. The earliest surviving written version of the tale is that compiled in 1548 by the Welshman Elis Gruffydd.[1]

Two dozen manuscripts of the same story, almost identical with one another, were written during the following centuries, indicating its persistent popularity in Wales. *Taliesin's Travels* employs quotations from a nineteenth century English by Lady Charlotte Guest,[2] along with some more recent translations by P. K. Ford.[3] Their work is gratefully acknowledged.

Hanes Taliesin is fascinating partly because it comes from 'the people', rather than a literary or aristocratic elite. Through the horrors and comic twists of an entertaining narrative, this is a folk story that in Sir I. Williams opinion, evolved in North Wales in the ninth century. It takes a wry view of military heroics and the flattery of princes, while raising archaic yet timeless issues concerning human dealings with the supernatural and natural worlds.

As a demi-god, Taliesin is a half-and-half character. Straddling the sacred–profane divide, often to his own discomfort, he mixes common sense with profound mystery. As a farmer's offspring, he is known as Gwion Bach, but by this name he also serves as a British substitute for Roman Bacchus, the god of wine.

Gwion is then killed, reborn, and magically changed into a 'bright-browed' version of the Greek sun god, Apollo. Yet he keeps one foot on the ground by borrowing the name of a *mortal,* sixth century Welsh poet, Taliesin. Thus a collection of the *mythic* Taliesin's gnomic utterances and poems, found in the fourteenth century *Book of Taliesin,* is interspersed with some verses attributed to the *mortal* bard.[4]

The ten historical poems have received considerable critical attention. On the other hand, the *mythological* works in *the Book of Taliesin,* translated in 1868 by Rev Robert Williams and edited by W.F. Skene, have been largely ignored. Yet it is particularly these poems that complement and illuminate the *Chwedl Taliesin* prose tale, and serve to emphasise its relevance to our own times.

Throughout *Taliesin's Travels,* quotations from poems attributed to both of these 'Taliesins' are printed in *italic,* as are all paragraphs taken from versions of the prose tale.

Opposite above: *A view of Llanfair Caereinion, Montgomeryshire; Gwion Bach's home parish.*
Below: *Llyn Tegid (Lake Bala) to which Gwion Bach travelled.*

Both in his poetry and his folk tale, the legendary Gwion Bach-Taliesin brings things together. He mends and revitalises forgotten connections, dissolves the boundary between human and non-human, contacts the spirit in Nature, discovers the language of the Welsh landscape, rides with the sun between zenith and abyss, and joins Otherworld fires to the domestic hearth. Moreover, he places his love of the parochial in an intercontinental, indeed a world-wide context of journeyings.

In the course of his travels he encounters fairies, spirits of place, and pagan Welsh deities, some ferocious, others benign. As a born healer, he presents his experience-based knowledge in such a way as to illuminate the Indo-European sacred tradition that underlies many of Wales' legends. Given his untiring inclusiveness, he also seeks rapport with Christianity and with modern secularism.

By combining *Chwedl Taliesin's* prose with *Book of Taliesin* poetry, *Taliesin's Travels* tries to re-engage with his myth from the inside, since myth of its nature calls for complete involvement rather than detachment. Taliesin's pilgrimage involves his

2

Opposite: *Bwrdd Arthur
(Arthur's Table) in
foreground with Cadair
Bronwen (Bronwen's Chair)
on skyline; Berwyn
Mountains,
Montgomeryshire. Here the
sixth century Christian saint
who protected a hunted
hare merges with her
'nature goddess' self.*

Right: *St Melangell's twelfth
century shrine, in Pennant
Melangell
church, Montgomeryshire.
Taliesin travels through a
mythic landscape.*

own self-discovery, yet for the reader it may also lead to a renewed sense of companionship with a re-sanctified world, enjoyed with heightened appreciation.

Taliesin embodies the art of continuity. Instead of a thin present, cut off from ancestral wisdom, he advocates and demonstrates an a-historic reunion. Just as the geology of Britain is composed of rocks of many ages, which collectively give shape and character to our island, so Taliesin is equally at home among all the disparate peoples that have lived here. Confronted by racial, religious, political and chronological divisions, he absorbs these differences, and from them manages to refine a supernatural currency, legal tender to all.

As a poet, he operates in a realm where each word is rich with connotations, and where visual symbols can likewise contain whole constellations of meanings, displayed in gracefully flowing changes. Through playfulness and charm, Taliesin's adventures opens up a byway towards enchantment. He implicitly challenges us to undertake our own version of his travels, no matter where we start from, or intend to go.

CHAPTER ONE

SETTING OUT

The call

Taliesin, the central character of this story, starts out with another name, Gwion Bach, who is said to come from Llanfair Caereinion, in Montgomeryshire.[1]

Whenever his tale was read or re-told, this Gwion Bach, 'Little Gwion', was bound to abandon his 'ordinary' life. Son of a squire, he slipped away from his farmhouse home in Llanfair and squelched across the yard into a lane. But this was to be more than a short scamper through a neighbour's orchard and back. He failed to return for the usual evening meal. As dusk turned into darkness, his puzzled father listened in vain for the sound of tiny fingers twiddling the latch from the outside. A search of the neighbourhood served only to show that the son, *gwan bach*, 'little child, dear thing, darling', had vanished into legendary night.

Alone and without provisions, Gwion Bach was obliged by his *chwedl* or 'story' to head for the biggest lake in Wales, Llyn Tegid in Merionethshire.[2] Over stony ridges and across deep valleys he ran. Black cattle and wild goats watched him speed past. On the moonlit moors they glimpsed him, bobbing between clumps of heather, as he scuttled along gullies in the spongy peat. Instinct drives him to score these Berwyn Mountains with the marks of his repeatable journey, for he is an agent in the endless cycle of erosion and renewal. From the outset, the mercurial Gwion Bach helps to fashion the land that he has come to represent.

Travelling north-west from Montgomeryshire, he moved from the province of Powys into that of Gwynedd. Several miles short of his 'lake of destiny' he dropped into a ravine, to seek shelter from a squall under the creaking branches of an oak. Gwion Bach was hungry, but at that season a boy might survive on hazel nuts, mushrooms and fresh water, as did his Neanderthal predecessors in the Pont Newydd cave, Denbighshire, a quarter of a million years before. He carried their knowledge and interests in his bones.

When the rain eased, he climbed from his temporary refuge and set off again, stumbling onwards until he collapsed, overwhelmed by fatigue, against a grey boulder, criss-crossed with white quartz veins, where he fell fast asleep. There, events from many eras invaded his sleep. Some came as local place-names, whispered in a muffled chant by long-buried generations, attempting to re-vocalise.

4

They craved to be freed from a 'once only' history and hoped to find renewed life in reiterated myth. So, in his dream, Gwion had to repeat the landscape features that they named:

Nant Achlas ('Voice Valley'), Bwrdd Arthur ('Arthur's Table'), Cader Bronwen ('Bronwen's Chair'), Gwely Melangell ('Melangell's Bed'), Moel Gwylfa ('Watch Hill'), Braich y Gawres ('Arm of the Giantess'), Carnedd y Filiast, ('Cairn of the Greyhound bitch'). As they flowed from his mouth, he saw these words as sacred road signs belonging to a forgotten Highway Code.

Among those clamouring for his attention was a sixth century mortal bard from Powys (Gwion's own province), named Taliesin. Taliesin is credited with the authorship of about a dozen surviving poems.[3] Gwion Bach shuddered and groaned in his sleep, for he dreaded this real Taliesin, who had been a notable glorifier of warfare. After serving the bloodthirsty King Brochwel of Powys as his court bard, Taliesin had boasted:

> *'I sang before a famous lord in the meadows of Severn*
> *Before Brochual of Powys who loved my muse.'* [4]

Gwion Bach had good reason to fear Taliesin, for barely three centuries after that poet's death, the Welsh had converted the man into an immortal demi-god. Consequently, a supernatural wraith named 'Taliesin' now stalked the land, looking for a host body to infiltrate and take over. He had his eye on Gwion Bach as a likely victim.

When Gwion awoke, he found himself already entangled in lines of verse snatched from the historic Taliesin's sixth century past – a dangerous time and place, saturated with violence. Indeed, whenever Gwion turned to History he heard 'ancestral voices prophesying war.'[5]

Llywarch Hen

Slaughter was a way of life in the Brythonic territories North of Hadrian's Wall, in Cumbria, and throughout Wales. While reflecting on this, Gwion had walked to within sight of an ancient house that epitomised the obsession with conflict. It was called Plas Rhiwaedog, 'Bloody Brow Hall.' It still stands near a hollow known as *Pwll y celanydd*, 'Pit of the corpses', less than half a mile from Llyn Tegid. From the safety of a *pabell* or 'tent' pitched across the River Dee at Llanfor, another sixth century poet, Llywarch Hen, who had already seen his twentyfour sons killed in battle, urged his sole adopted son, Cynddelw, to attack the Saxons at Plas Rhiwaedog:[6]

Llywarch orders: 'Defend Thou the brow of yonder hill', adding in an aside: 'When there is but one son left it is vain to be over-fond of him.'[7] Cynddelw duly obeyed and died in the skirmish. The Welsh word *cynndelw*, 'prototype, original pattern', marks him as the eternal warrior-god (*cyn*, 'before' and *'delw'* 'idol'), doomed to self-sacrifice at any heartless father's command.

Plas Rhiwaedog: 'Bloody-brow Hall. The early seventeenth century mansion built over the site of Llywarch Hen's last son's battle.

Subsequently, Llywarch, the aged bard, blamed himself for all these filial deaths: 'Through my tongue they have been killed.'[8] Youth had been consumed by an old man's martial fantasies. Gwion felt disgust, for Llywarch was the bard acclaimed as the father and founder of Welsh poetry, a heritage drenched in fulsome praise of futile wars.

In a similar vein the sixth century poet, Taliesin had flattered his warrior patrons, such as King Urien Rheged: '*The princes of all nations are in thrall to thee; In thy advance there is wailing... God has made thee Master in assault for fear of thy onslaught. The Loegrians [English] know it when they converse. Death have they suffered and many vexations- The burning of their homes and the taking of their attire... Without finding deliverance from Urien Rheged.*'[9]

Taliesin then lists his rewards received from Urien, ruler of Rheged, a small and unstable kingdom around the Solway Firth:

> '*He has dowered me with the mead of his glory, And has given fine lands to me in abundance, And great quantities of gifts and gold, ...And I will praise thy works until I perish.*'[10]

Yet Urien's 'works' were little more than banditry, the results of which Taliesin described:

> '*Neither field nor wood afforded shelter to aggression when it came. Like waves loud-roaring over the land I saw impetuous men in hosts; And after the morning battle, mangled flesh. I saw the throng of three regions dead... Ravens were red with the blood of men* .'[11]

Gwion Bach regarded Taliesin's 'achievement' as propaganda for political anarchy and endless horror. As a 'boy-child 'and a future man, was he, Gwion, predestined to follow this bellicose track, shared by poet, soldier and conscripted farmer, that Welsh society had trodden for centuries? He felt penned in by the same forces that had sent thousands of boys to death in battle. Prehistoric cairns and twentieth century monuments to their annihilation stood in many a Welsh parish.

'That must be my predestined fate', Gwion bitterly concluded. 'Llywarch and Taliesin's words have cancelled my dearest hopes. They have polluted the waters of Llyn Tegid, the lake of tranquillity, for which I yearn and have so naively set out to find.'

Although he was standing within sight of his Tegid objective, he was inclined to turn about and rush towards the highest mountains that he could imagine, hoping to lose himself deep within their folds. Instead, he stood firm and said aloud:

'If that Taliesin ever gets inside me, I shall try to cure his mad bellicosity. He and I may then discover a land beyond organised homicide.'

CHAPTER TWO

LLYN TEGID

The Point

When Gwion Bach eventually arrived at Llyn Tegid he worked his way along the south shore until he came to a peninsula, poking out from the lake's otherwise parallel sides. Near this promontory's tip a hand-painted sign announced:

'*Llangower Campsite*. Families and Couples Only'

Having run away from his father and lacking a mother, he had no family. Moreover, he had forgotten his alternative future name, which, if added to his first, might have qualified him as a 'couple.' Yet he decided to enter the forbidden camp and walked along the track towards Llangower Point, mumbling: 'Any of us could be the man who encounters his double.'[1]

Soon he came to a large notice board, which warned:

> 'TAKE CARE. Le Lac est froid. Der see ist kalt. Mae'r llyn yn oer. The lake is cold.'[2]

> 'Ah!' thought Gwion, 'my pilgrimage destination must be a place of international significance.' Then he read the last line: 'Depth 100 feet only 20 yards from shore.'

> A third sign, strapped to a tree, stated: 'Dogs on lead. Parking £2. Shower 50p. No noise between 11pm and 8am.'[3]

Beyond that, there was one more board. It was headed: Snowdonia National Park, and read: 'Plumes of blue-green algae have been seen here since 1995. The scum is toxic. If the water is not crystal clear do not enter. There is a risk of vomiting, diarrhoea, fever, muscular and joint pains, skin rashes and irritation. Keep pets away. See a doctor as soon as possible.'[4]

Through the alders and willows on either side of these instructions Gwion glimpsed small grey patches of the lake, twinkling slightly, like frosted glass windows, modestly concealing yet hinting at a sacred world.

Rubber tyre, suspended at Llangower Point, Llyn Tegid, 2004. 'The donated and votive things… things that are the sign of something other. Things set up, lifted up, or in whatever manner made over to the gods.' David Jones, Anathemata, *1972.*

More than that, it represented a photographic negative of a golden neck torque, or a shining halo-fruit.

From one of the trees, and suspended by a long rope, a worn-out rubber tyre dangled, slowly rotating. Immediately he saw this, Gwion Bach found his vocation. It was *to play*. This rubber ring, smoothed by active mileage, symbolised his destiny. Like him, it was a wanderer, a joy rider. More than that, it represented a photographic negative of a golden neck torque, or a shining halo-fruit, produced by the tree of life. The tyre silently mouthed Gwion a message concerning his newly revealed ambition. It signalled: 'Play, and be a god.'

With a cry of glee the child ran to the tyre, stuck his head and elbows through the ring. Then he swung, pendulum-slow, down through imagined equatorial forest and up again to tundra. The bough from which the rope was suspended creaked as his motion then gradually changed into a gyrating cone, till he found himself stirring the entire hemisphere with his rubber spoon.

'This is a good game. I have joined polar point to longest latitude, and lassoed modern and primeval together. But I should learn to acquire skill at other amusements, all games, including the 24 feats traditionally prescribed for Welsh youths of high birth.[5] If I am to match the sport of the gods, I must master every piece of their playground equipment.'

To his right he could see scores of dinghies with sails furled, settled down for imminent winter hibernation. They were beached on the grass above the pebbled shore. Was it too late in the year to expect a trip in one of them? He looked around, searching for the person in charge, who might allow him to take a boat onto the water. Finding the camp office locked, he drifted inland towards the cluster of houses near Llangower church, to ask consent from an inhabitant for his voyage.

Gwarwr at play

On passing the churchyard wall he heard two girls giggling inside the enclosure. He pushed open a stiff iron gate and saw them among the gravestones. They wore white dresses in a style that went out of fashion *circa* 1825. Together they were twirling round and round, with full skirts ballooning out as they did so, till dizzy and shrieking with laughter, both sank to the ground, whereupon their dresses slowly deflated.

'What is this game called', Gwion asked? 'Making cheeses', they answered, in English. 'Can I join in'? At this they tittered. One said: 'Of course not; it is a girls' game and you are wearing the wrong clothes. Besides, we are dead. We died of diphtheria on our Welsh excursion in July 1821. That is why we have to play here now.'

Then they slipped through a crack in the side of what Sir S.R. Glynne, Bart. described as 'a curious stone altar tomb… with a lock in front and hinges behind',[6] though it was not designed for them. The huge yew tree, growing on a mound at one end of the graveyard rustled and rearranged its branches as a wind came in from the lake. Gwion shuddered and turned pale. To recover his composure he went into the church, sat on a bench, and prayed for protection from measles and mumps to its patron saint, Gwawr. Llangower's church, parish and Point were all named after her.[7]

The Welsh word *gwawr* means 'play.' By chance he had landed in the national House of Play, but after a quick glance around the building he had to admit that it was rather dull, both inside and out. Lacking aisles, transepts, or a trace of medieval ornament, the church had been completely rebuilt in the eighteenth century and then subjected to grim 'restoration' during the Victorian era. St Gwawr had apparently been forbidden to play in her own home. Recent stained glass images of St Paul and Faith made sure of that; yet Gwion sensed that she was still there, silently repeating '*gwawr*' to herself.

Saint Gwawr (sometimes written Cowair or Cywair) is the living spirit of play. She is joined by Welsh *gwawry,* 'play, sport, diversion, frolic', along with her companion *chwarae,* 'play, amusement, drama, performance, and play of a wheel.' To these talented spirits, she adds Welsh *cywair,* meaning 'song, harmony, tune, key-note', and 'cheese rennet.'

In Wales, words often emerge as living things from favoured locations. So *gwawr* becomes St Gwawr of Llangower, to inspire and epitomise sports (both formal and spontaneous), drama, music, and the mechanical arts. Gwawr was and is mistress of

Llangower church and graveyard, dedicated to St Gwawr,
spirit of Welsh gwawr, *'play.'*

them all. Like many other pre-Christian Welsh deities and cultural prototypes, she was automatically awarded sainthood in the early medieval period.

Popular belief maintains that St Gwawr is the mother of Llywarch Hen, Wales' famously ancient poet.[8] As a future poet–in-waiting, Gwion Bach was shocked to learn of this connection and stared hard at the Llangower ground. Was he being asked to call Llywarch, that old warmonger, 'Brother'? In his senility, Llywarch had come to live at Llanfor, only three miles from Llangower.[9] This implies that Gwawr, like her son, was also a sixth century mortal. Her human identity is often conflated with that of a princess named Gwawr. She was a daughter of King Brychan Brycheiniog who ruled part of South Wales, based on modern Brecknockshire.

Like many other deceased mortals, Gwawr was subsequently drawn into myth. On her death, she was assimilated into a supernatural mythic cycle and then returned to the surface world as its perennial agent, where her task was to promote all kinds of play as modes of divine pagan ritual, persisting into Christian times. She personified and legitimised this continuity, which the people of Penllyn (as the five parishes bordering Llyn Tegid are collectively named), perpetuated with enthusiasm.

An Englishman wrote from Bala in 1770: 'If you would ask them how they spend their lives in this part of the world, they might answer 'We drink, dance and are merry.' 'I do not know a people so addicted to mirth, [though] the complexion of their country, one would imagine, could not inspire such sentiments of festivity and joy. They sing and dance not by hours but days, weeks. They are free, hospitable and

11

cheerful and always endeavouring to frame rustic jokes. The Welsh language is here spoken with the greatest classical purity. They boast of their Welsh bards'... [10]

The Methodist spoil-sport

This state of affairs continued at Llangower as in most other parts of Wales ~~till circa~~ until about 1791. Then it was attacked and all but destroyed by a single zealous advocate of Calvinistic Methodism, the Reverend Thomas Charles of Bala, who regarded the prevailing traditions as demonic and set about their elimination.[11]

He had come to Llyn Tegid in 1778 as an ordained Church deacon, but was sickened by what he correctly discerned to be the encouragement given to paganism by the churches around the lake. He therefore broke away to become an independent preacher, advocating the harsh, world-despising sixteenth century doctrines of John Calvin.

Charles later described with abhorrence the habitual 'dancing and singing to the harp that he encountered, adding 'in every corner of the town [of Bala] some sport or other went on.' Referring to Llanuwchllyn, a village at the head of Llyn Tegid, Charles complained: 'Every Sunday afternoon until dark was spent in idle amusements...[including]...*Y chwareu gamp,* a sort of sport in which all the young men of the neighbourhood had a trial of strength, and people assembled from the surrounding country to see their feats.'[12]

At first Charles was ignored, but in mid-October 1791 his belief that humanity was hopelessly depraved, because sunk in Nature's poisoned well, was suddenly accepted with hysterical enthusiasm by several young people in the area. He later recalled: 'A wild, vain young woman of this town... had such a deep sense of her lost and helpless state as to confine her to bed for three weeks, where in the greatest agony of soul distress she roared till her strength failed her. She hung... over infinite and eternal misery, justly deserved. The arrows of God stuck fast in her.'[13]

Soon he could report with satisfaction that: 'This revival of religion has put an end to all the merry meetings for dancing, singing with the harp and every kind of sinful mirth. No harps ... have been played in this neighbourhood for several months past. The craft is not only in danger but has been entirely destroyed and abolished.'[14] One incorrigible harpist was rumoured to have fed communion bread to dogs. He persisted in playing his instrument at Fach Ddeiliog in Llangower parish, where he fell into the lake and drowned. A cloud of smoke hung over the spot where he sank.[15]

Had Gwion Bach arrived at Bala on 13th June 1803, he, like the traveller Richard Fenton, might have 'been driven thence in consequence of the immense confusion expected from a great Methodist Association (Meeting). The salient mania which spreads like wildfire over the Principality, has its origin here.'[16]

Charles' movement rapidly built 1,641 chapels, 1,428 churches and opened 1,731 Sunday schools throughout Wales. Simultaneously, it demolished those milestones in the traditional year that had stood by their respective ceremonies for millennia,

The Reverend Thomas Charles stands before his chapel in Bala. The Calvinistic Methodist movement that he started here in 1791 swept away most pre-Christian customs and beliefs; yet the story of Taliesin survived.

namely the deeply rooted pagan Quarterdays known as *Gwyl Fair* (February 1st), *Calan Mai* (May Day), *Gwyl Awst* (August 1st) and *Calan Gaeaf* (November 1st).

The collapse was swift and almost total. For example, whereas in 1770 a 'Hallow E'en' bonfire flickered outside every cottage door, to mark the death of one year and birth of the next, fifty years later such fires were things of the past. *Calan Gaeaf* had been the weirdest of all the spirit nights, when the living communed with the dead and with supernatural powers. On that night Stone Age chamber tombs were visited for prophecy and guidance. Links between supernatural and natural forces were reaffirmed, so benefiting practical affairs.[17] Such rites and customs were now prohibited, denounced by ministers and disowned by the people as wicked superstition.

Reviewing the change, Gwion wondered: 'How can I survive in this new ethos, where I am plainly marked down for extermination, if not already cancelled? A corrupted playground is a dismal idea. I must find my grave.' In search of it, he climbed the churchyard mound and lay down with his head against the ancient yew tree's roots.

It was October 31st, *Calan Gaeaf*. Around his prostrate body dusk advanced and gathered the host of separate tombstones into a uniformly black family snapshot. Then a flake of yew bark fell onto his brow. He blinked and looked up. The tree's branches encircled him inside its great skirt. It was perhaps a thousand years old and still full of life. This mighty vegetable had swayed through countless bereavements and misfortunes, but had never for a moment ceased to stand for an enjoyable world, nurtured from a divine substratum.

Gwion rose. Green needles swished across his face. He patted the tree trunk as if it was a horse and whispered: 'Shall we let world-hating fanatics have the last word? I swear to you that, while I breathe, the great cause of play will not be lost.' He then spread his arms as if conducting the entire churchyard in a new choral work and bellowed: 'My ancestors! Take heart! Calvin's curse is on the wane. I foresee his empty chapels turned into Bingo halls. Beloved Gwawr will sing her numbers again on this dank earth. By St Gwawr, we *shall* play on, and for ever'!

In fact, even at the height of the Methodist era, Welsh churchyards continued to serve as venues for time-honoured sporting activities while the typically circular shape of many of these plots (the Reverend E. Owen counted fourteen in his area[18]), is evidence of their original purpose as pre-Christian sacred sites. Megaliths erected c.2000 BC, still incorporated into the churchyard wall at Ysbytty Cynfan, Ceredigion, are a further sign of continuity. Indeed, the word *llan*, now part of so many Christianised Welsh place-names, carries connotations of a pagan ritual enclosure. Thus churchyard games and major Christian festivals were often held on the same day.

Well into the nineteenth century Sunday games of fives were played against church gable ends at Cilcen and Llanelidan in Clwyd. At Clochaenog the parson regularly served as scorekeeper during important inter-parish contests.[19] A ball or stone, tossed through the air by competing factions mimed the progress of sun and moon and of the entire divinely given cosmos. In miniature, humanity played at (and with) gods. This is the aim of most religions. To this end, bands of half-naked men chased a ball of tallow-soaked wool from parish to parish across South Wales in the game of *knappan*. Similarly, the ten-pound 'feat stone' in Efenechtydd's *llan* was tossed backwards to propitiate underworld powers.

Physical, intellectual and emotional talents were combined in the *Twenty-four Feats of Skill* traditionally set as initiation rites into full Welsh manhood. These tasks included competence at chess, harp playing, along with composition and oral delivery of poetry.[20] They were viewed as demonstrations of an all-pervasive sacred harmony, and as dynamic symbols of a holy universe.

Lalita

Gwion Bach mulled over the implications of this play-world, and its inter-continental scope. For example, Lalita, alias Mahadevi, the 'Great Goddess' of Hindu tradition, is named from the Sanskrit word *lal*, 'to play, to sport, to caress, fondle, cherish, nurse and love', so adding a far-off yet welcome maternal hope for the motherless Gwion Bach.[21]

'Perhaps I shall be adopted by an Indo-European family who share the Welsh delight in music', he daydreamed, unaware that the entire Cymric nation has from the outset belonged to that diaspora and that Sanskrit *lal* is also 'the amorous musical scale, the *raga*.

Another belief of Far Eastern deities, such as Lalita and Brahma, is that 'games' must include that of universe creation and destruction, played for its own sake, without acquisitiveness or selfishness.[22] Wishing to take part in this ultimate sport, Gwion Bach looked across Llyn Tegid to the Bala Adventure and Water Sports Centre, situated near Bala town.

There, all summer long, canoeing, sailing, wind surfing and rock climbing are offered to everyone, in a mood of pure fun, with little competitive rivalry. Such engagement with the elements of wind, water and rock provides access to the primeval world of remotest ancestors, in touch with fundamental mysteries.

As Gwion stood transfixed at the water's edge he caught his own reflection, repeatedly slivered and re-assembled by the play of wavelets. Their frolickings yielded an unstable but more generous image of his usual cramped persona. Yet he drew back, nervous about playing tricks with identity.

The Bala Sports Centre advertises a 'Sphere-o-mania Ride', in which a volunteer is strapped alone into a twelve-feet diameter metal ball and launched down steep hills towards the lake. Here the latest technology and the pre-human landscape are bounced together in the mind and body of the spinning volunteer. The journey is recommended as 'An excellent activity for people looking to do something a little different.'

'If I had one ride in that Sphere-o-mania, I could re-make the whole world in microcosm', Gwion reflected, but was secretly thankful that the ride had closed for the winter, for he had no wish to break his neck. Instead he decided to find and bathe in St Gwawr's spring.

Ffynnon Gwawr and the Lake

As Thomas Pennant noted in 1771: 'beneath Llangower church flows Afon Gwawr.'[23] Gwion paddled in this stream. To this day it defines the north edge of her churchyard. About 1700 the Oxford based antiquarian Edward Lhuyd wrote of a Ffynnon Gwawr, her 'spring.' Mothers took their infants there to bathe, hoping to cure them of rickets.[24] The site is a patch of boggy ground, half a mile south of her church between the lane and the lakeside. Gwion Bach went to that spot and stooped down between tufts of rushes, but was unable to find enough to drink, far less to bathe in. The spring had been disturbed by the course of a light railway, routed along the lakeside. To compensate for the interference, a water trough was set up beside the road and declared to be an alternative Ffynnon Gwawr, while a nearby farm took up the same name, but the trough has now been removed to make room for increased motor traffic.

Gwion then heard a rumour that the original Ffynnon Gwawr was not on land at all, but lies under the deepest part of Llyn Tegid, just off Llangower Point. A stupendous overflow from that first Ffynnon Gwawr spring had caused the lake, now up to 136

Above: *Fishermen at Llyn Tegod* circa *1800, where the supernatural was often landed.*

Top right: *The shepherd-lord of Penllyn, with his wife Ceridwen, who rises from Llyn Tegid;* M. Drayton, Polyolbion, *1617.*

feet deep and four miles long, to come into being. Lakeside people say that it was 'the imperative duty of someone to place a lid over this valley bottom well each night, but one evening the task was overlooked.'[25] By morning a new lake had flooded much of the valley and inundated the city built earlier around Gwawr's primary fountain.

Another story relates how, prior to the flood, a minstrel had been told to play there at a festival, but that a bird had lured him to a hill, where he fell asleep. In the morning he awoke to find Llyn Tegid covering the city; and on the new lake's surface floated his harp. On calm days fishermen rowing or sailing near Llangower Point claim to see the chimney pots of submarine buildings. Moreover, after a severe winter, when a sudden thaw breaks the ice, the sound of bells has been heard, percolating up from the depths.[26]

Gwawr, one may suppose, stimulates these mirages, having by chance given birth to the lake itself. The visions and the water-body are her twinned offspring. For humanity, real water and imagined town are bound together by the attraction of a lost domain. The combination had drawn Gwion Bach towards the lake; and just as

Afon Gwawr, her playful stream, perpetually flowed into Llyn Tegid, so he wanted to move from land toward her submerged source.

He therefore sprinted to the lake's shore and jumped headfirst into the *kalt, froid,* waves. Thrashing, gasping and spluttering, he swam out for two hundred yards and then dived over what he presumed was the location of Gwawr's first wellhead. There he hoped to enjoy *lila par excellence,* 'the free motion or movement, regular or irregular, like the play of water in a fountain', and with an intensity and completeness far beyond the range of the surface world's experience. He would drink from that fountain of ultimate energies, the absolute play of plays.

Lost cities

Wales was largely a country of scattered rural settlements prior to the onset of the Industrial Revolution. Consequently the term *dinas,* 'city', was used rather loosely by early Welsh writers, such as the eighth century Nennius. He called both the meagre village of Llanberis and some abandoned Iron Age hill forts, such as Caer Caradoc, 'cities.'[27]

'Let us agree on one thing', a Welsh farmer said to me one morning in 1998, waving towards Caer Arianrhod, a rock in the sea, visible only at low tide, ' Caer Arianrhod is a city!' In Wales, a 'city' was, and to some extent still is, a matter of quality rather than quantity, with the highest grade being guaranteed by founders with supernatural contacts, such as Tegid Voel. He is the nominal ruler of the city lying beneath Llyn Tegid.

In one important respect his lost 'city' accords with the world's earliest urban forms. They were usually founded as temple communities, in which a human king served as consort to a goddess, who was housed in its core shrine. The prosperity of the citizens depended on the *heiros gamos* or 'divine wedding' between their monarch and the goddess.[28]

Tegid Voel belongs within this tradition. Owen's *Cambrian Biography* places him in the fifth or sixth centuries AD. As Chieftain of Penllyn, the five parishes that impinge on the lake's shore, he was destined to wed the under-lake deity. He continues to dwell with his supernatural bride in the now submerged 'temple-city' at the centre of his territory.

However, in staying permanently below the lake, Tegid abandoned his mortal self in favour of a supernatural life and is now cut off from his land-dwelling subjects. The separation was made worse by the deluge of disapproval directed at him after the arrival in Britain of Judeo-Christian monotheism, whose god Jehovah declared: 'Thou shalt have no other gods before me.'

The overflow of Gwawr's fountain effectively hid Tegid's city from Christian destruction of the kind wrought by St Germanus. That saint is reputed to have burned and obliterated the pagan King Vortigern's stronghold at Llandysul, Carmarthenshire, a fate which submergence enabled Tegid's town to avoid.

Welsh school outing to Llyn Tegid, circa *1910.*

Second flood

By the fifth century Christianity had begun to divide up Wales into its own church-based parishes. Hostility towards local deities and spirits of place was the new orthodoxy. But this gave rise to unexpected side effects among the people, namely a sense of guilt regarding their rejection of long-honoured deities, combined with a lingering sense of attachment to them.

The uneasy mood found an outlet in a rumour that Tegid might be planning revenge on those of the new faith. It was said that he could order another supernaturally induced upwelling of the lake. A chant was often repeated:

> 'Bala old the lake has had, and Bala new
> The lake will have, and Llanfor, too.'[29]

Because the surface world had become defiled by the Christian dogma of Original Sin (and its related post-Christian legacy of contempt for the natural world, which denies the sacredness contained within material phenomena), Gwawr's restorative waters were required to perform a 'counter-baptism', however superficially injurious. Her spring of primal innocence was (and is) an antidote to Calvin's curse and its nihilistic aftermath.

Robin Ddu, a sixteenth century prophet from Bangor, mistakenly announced that the next Llyn Tegid deluge would come on Bala's Fair Day, at one hour after noon. Hearing that, the entire population ran to the hills, to wait and watch. After the hour had passed uneventfully, everyone returned to business and pleasure at the Fair, while awaiting the next alarm.[30]

Llyn Tegid floods the second town of Bala, circa 1920. A local rhyme states that the lake will inundate modern Bala and the downstream village of Llanfor.

The fairies and Gwion Bach

Further hints of contact between Tegid's hermetic domain and surface reality are given by Llyn Tegid's fairies, known in Wales as 'Children of the King of the Netherworld', *Plant Rhi is Ddwfn,* or simply as *Plant Annwn.* 'Children of the Deep.'[31]

'On *Cae Mawr*, the 'Great Field', close to where the Dee leaves the lake, crowds of them were said to emerge from beneath lake's banks at night; or did, until they were driven away during the 1850s.[32] For countless human generations they had been regarded as *glan llyn y modion*, 'the lakeside means of grace', a phrase employed in extemporary prayers.

Gwion Bach had much in common with these diminutive creatures. They too were *bach,* small, and shared his preference for repeatable events. In their case, these often took the form of circle dances. Any young man caught within their spinning ring was bound to dance for a year and a day, in time with the sun's daily and annual rotation. By performing in moonlight, the *Plant Annwn* ensured that lunar cycles were not forgotten.

Like Gwion, fairies were devoted to play, and with a combination of intensity and mischievousness that mortals found disturbing. For example, Morgan ap Rhys, a Merioneth harper, was given a fairy harp, but when he touched the strings people

Left: *A man of 'early Neolithic' type, living in 1860 near Pumlumon, mid-Wales, direct descendant of an archaic racial group, according to Professor H. J. Fleure.*

Centre: *A Bronze Age arrowhead from Bugeilyn, Montgom., regarded as a supernaturally-made 'elf shot.'*

Right: *A torch-carrying Welsh elf or* pwca *(in English 'Puck'). Fairies speak up for the marginalised.*

found themselves dancing so furiously that furniture was smashed and heads broken against kitchen ceilings.

The tension between humanity and Welsh fairies accounts for their *Dynion bach Teg,* or 'Fair little Rabble' tag. The entire breed was often dismissed as *y ellylles,* 'the wicked fairies.' This term brackets them with 'elves, goblins, sprites, demons and spectres' of a mostly harmful kind, no better than blue-green algae scum.

Fairies were frequently accused of stealing human babies, snatched away by night, with a fairy 'changeling' put in its place, which the mortal foster-parents were obliged to rear.[33] With this in mind, on first arriving at the lake, Gwion Bach had steered clear of Cae Mawr. He did not want them to recognise <u>him</u> as a possible changeling and was trying to forget his own suspicions on that score, made worse by teasing from boys in his home village of Llanfair Caereinion. From behind a hedge, they would shout: 'Einion, Einion!' as he went by; or 'Taliesin is a fairy!'

They all knew the fairy story, in which Einion, who featured in the place-name, was lured into taking a fairy mistress, named Olwen. She was one of three beautiful daughters of 'a fine old lady' who Einion had met on an unintended visit to *Hud a Lledrith,* the 'land of Charm and Fantasy.' Olwen and Einion soon had a son. Their son's name was Taliesin.[34]

'But I am Gwion Bach, not Taliesin', the boy would shriek, spurting tears of shame and rage while he ran after the rapidly dispersing gang. 'I am *normal!*' he would scream, prompting further gusts of laughter from his tormentors, who took his behaviour as proof that he was not.

Gwion indeed suspected that in time he would turn into a reincarnation of the fairy half-breed Taliesin, who, like him, came from Llanfair Caereinion. Yet he shrank from such a changeling 'Taliesin' future, where he would be lost forever between worlds and two different ways of being.

Einion, his legendary forefather's name means 'anvil', Welsh *einion*. He epitomises the iron sword-wielding warrior prince of Iron Age and medieval Wales. On his block the tools of violence were forged and sharpened. Yet Einion had cohabited with an iron-hating fairy. Gwion was confused, hammered between contradictions.

All fairies detest iron. They prefer stone. Neolithic flint arrowheads, popularly termed 'fairy darts', along with stone axes, scrapers and other domestic tools of the New Stone Age, which have been found along Llyn Tegid's shore, are attributed to their skill.[35] But of metals, only gold and silver (both refined in Britain's Late Neolithic era, before 2,000 BC) are happily worn by the *Plant Annwn*.

Gwion was asked to do two jobs. He was required to act as a 'go-between', bridging the gulf between mortal and supernatural understanding. Simultaneously he had to resolve the four thousand year-old prehistoric and historic conflict between Wales' Stone Age tribes, supported by the 'fairies', versus the people of the Bronze, Iron and Plastic Ages who had ruthlessly pushed them aside.(According to the anthropologist H.J. Fleure, remnants of the Neolithic race continue to live in the remote valleys around Pumlumon, Wales' central mountain, a fairy stronghold.[36])

If called on to act as a reincarnation of the weird 'Taliesin', son of a fairy mother and a warrior forefather, Gwion would be required to deliver the communal peace that had plainly eluded them.

Indeed, according to the orally-transmitted fairy tale, first written down by Mr W. Jones in 1884, Einion and Olwen had made no attempt to explain or advocate the wider implications of their union. On the contrary, rather than present their loving bond as an exemplary model for future human-fairy relations, Einion had deceived the populace regarding Olwen's true nature. When pressed to reveal her pedigree, he replied evasively that she was from 'a very fair family', rather than admit that she was of *Y Tylwyth Teg*, 'The Fair Family', another synonym for 'fairies.'[37]

Consequently a general rapprochement, either across the sacred-profane frontier, or between the rival advocates of Stone Peace and Iron War, had yet to be attempted. Enion and Olwen had simply transmitted the challenge, via their hybrid family tree, towards him; and then disappeared.

Desperate to dodge the responsibility, Gwion Bach asked himself: 'Why should I believe any of this? It is only a fairy story.' With this dismissive remark he inadvertently answered his question, since the authentic fairy tale is passed down the human generations *because* it contains in narrative form the essence of what matters most to the society concerned. This he intuitively recognised as the truth. He was doomed to serve as a go-between, linking surface reality to the 'fairy ' otherworld under the lake.

Nevertheless, he considered searching for a half-human understudy or a foolhardy mortal willing to undertake the work in his place and wondered if a willing substitute might be found among the Welsh wizards, such as those described by J. Barnes in 1586:

'Swarms of soothsayers and enchanters profess that they walk... at night with these fairies; from who they brag they have their knowledge. They have stroken such an astonishing reverence of the fairies into the hearts of our silly people that they dare not name them without honour, calling them *bendith y mamme u dhun*, 'mothers' blessings of the human race.'[38]

Among these necromancers, ancient and modern, Gwion spotted several, better qualified than he for a descent into the underworld; yet of them not one came from Llanfair Caereinion. So he walked to Llangower Point and dived in. Twirling downwards, his ears popped and his lungs hurt. The pain threatened to crush him. As local folklore had predicted, he also heard a voice. It sang: 'Line cannot fathom me. Go, or I will swallow you up!'[39]

Other fishermen had spoken of a dragon lying coiled in that chill deep.[40] Yet although convinced that he could never act the hero, Gwion reminded himself that even in Tragedy there is often a role for a clown. With that in mind, he abandoned himself to a descent that spun him towards the city rising from Llyn Tegid's supposedly bottomless bed.

CHAPTER THREE

UNDER THE LAKE

Gwion and Cai

'Uncanny' was how Gwion Bach described Llyn Tegid's floor, when interviewed years later by a *Western Daily Mail* reporter. Asked to elaborate, the imp went on: 'The uncanny threatens accepted norms. It is something which ought to have remained secret or hidden, but which has come to light, bringing a return of the alienated, old-established familiar, yet leading to intellectual uncertainty. One does not know one's way about in the uncanny. Most folk feel out of their depth there, whereas the bottom-hugging *gwyniaid* fish, a species unique to Llyn Tegid, wanders the streets of the submerged city, clearly at home, while perch, roach and pike circulate at ease between its mansard roofs and glittering spires.' He was reading from a prepared statement.

When Gwion Bach landed on the bottom of Llyn Tegid he was surprised to see the giant Cai Hir guarding an outer gateway. 'Excuse me, but I did not expect to find you down here. I thought you were gatekeeper at Arthur's Caerleon Court in South Wales. That's what the *Peredur* text states.'[1] 'Does it? Do you believe every thing you read in medieval Welsh Romance?' the giant replied. After a pause he added: 'I'm there *and* here; why not? So where do you think *you're* going, you whipper-snapping runt? If you're looking for a theme park, you won't find one on this level.'

Hoping to befriend Cai, Gwion held out his hand, but soon regretted doing so, for the giant's handshake was searingly hot. As *Culhwch and Olwen* notes: 'when the rain was heaviest, a handbreadth before his [Cei's] hand and another behind his hand, what would be in his hand would be dry, by reason of the greatness of his heat.'[2]

'How hot your hand is', gasped Gwion. 'So would yours be, if you'd swallowed the sun every evening, as I do.' 'Are all those sunsets still in you'? 'They would be, if I didn't shit each one out at midnight. It boosts their basement fires and helps keep me regular. That's why I'm known as 'Path, son of Way.'[3] My digestive tract is second to none.' He belched.

Named as Arthur's foremost warrior in the earliest texts, Cai 'could be as 'tall' (Welsh *hir*) as the tallest tree in the forest.'[4] He had taken over the Roman fort, built between AD 75 and 80 at the head of Llyn Tegid, but abandoned in AD 130.[5] He re-named it Caer Gai after himself and made sure that the Ordnance Survey complied with the change. The fort is conveniently sited for his nocturnal duties in Tegid's underwater realm, into which his long reflection easily reaches.

Cai, alias Gai or Cei, was at home below water. It was he, who, submerged in the Menai Straits, had wrestled with and killed the enormous cat, Cath Palug, offspring of the pig Henwen. According to the Mabinogion 'Cei had this peculiarity, nine nights and nine days his breath lasted under water, nine nights and nine days would he be without sleep.'[6]

'Will you talk to me for nine days about Lord Tegid' Gwion asked? 'I seek an introduction to him and wish to be on his wavelength from the outset, if possible.'

'He won't see you. He is unsociable; a recluse. He is Tegid; from Latin *taceo,* 'to make no utterance, to be silent', which gives us Welsh *tagu,* 'to choke, strangle, throttle.' His words don't come out. It's as if he has a cobra round his neck. Not forgetting Latin *tego,* 'to place a covering over, to hide, to conceal.' I picked up a few words from the Romans before they pulled out', Cai added modestly, speaking out of character.

'Be that as it may, if you want to look on the bright side', he continued after a short pause, 'you could describe Tegid as Welsh *teg,* that is 'fair, handsome, fine, agreeable, clean, pure, just, right, equitable, reasonable, complete and entire.' As Lord of this city he has certain standards to maintain. Some claim him for the father of *Y Tylwyth Teg,* the entire 'Fair Family', but I don't hold with that. He has enough on his hands coping with that son of his.'

'Why is Tegid *voel*'? Gwion asked. '*Voel* is a mutation of Welsh *moel* said Cai, with a growing sense of authority. '*Moel* is 'bald' and 'a bare, rounded, belly-shaped hill, such as you can see reflected upside down in this lake. He is ordinary's inverted opposite.'

Tegid and sea serpent

When Cai retired to the latrine, Gwion Bach slipped through the temporarily unguarded gate into Tegid's Otherworld. There he received a second and much bigger shock – his first glimpse of Tegid Voel.

He found the chieftain sitting beside Gwawr's lake-floor fountain and looking more like a giant conger eel than either a man or a superhuman leader. He was coiled in a deep trance, dreaming of somewhere else, a place described in a genuine folk tale, set on the coast of Carnarvonshire, North Wales and recorded by Professor J. Rhys in 1882.[7]

In serpentine form, Tegid was possessed by one of 'the great dreams of the arts, which recur to haunt us with a sense of how little we know of the real dimensions of our own experience.'[8] Penllyn's lord was silent because preoccupied with 'some of those dreams that refuse to go away and remain staring at us until we confront them. They are the reality behind all ancestor worship and are part of our [own] identity.'[9]

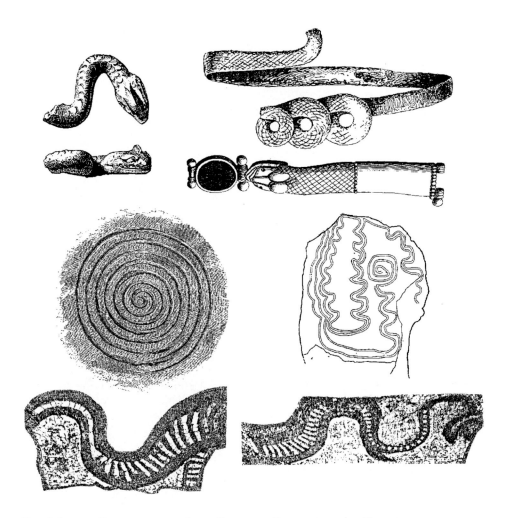

Top left: *Bronze serpent from Caerwent Roman temple, Gwent.*
Top right: *Silver snake bracelet from Penmaenmawr, Caernarvonshire and gold*
                serpent from Gogofau gold mine; Carmarthenshire.
Centre left: *Bronze Age engraved stone at Llanbedr, Merionethshire.*
Centre right: *Dreaming of snakes. Incised megalith from Bryn Celli Ddu, Anglesey.*
Bottom left and right: *Third millenium BC serpentine 'dolphins', on a Roman*
                mosaic from St Michael's Row, Chester.

So Tegid was wrapped in the snake described in a North Wales folktale. It tells how
a young man, also named Tegid, went sea fishing in a boat. He was driven by winds
to an area where the surface 'was as smooth as glass and as bright as the clearest
light… the most wonderful place he had ever seen.' Beneath the water he could
detect a most splendid country – fertile fields, dales covered with pastures, flowery
hedges, groves clad in green foliage, luxuriant forests, lazy rivers, and beautifully
ingenious mansions dotted about. The inhabitants of this country amused themselves

with all sorts of frolics. Some danced energetically to music, 'a faint echo of which, given forth by the waves, never ceased to charm his ears.'[10]

'It is strange that your King should be so enchanted by an off-shore Otherworld, when he commands one of his own, here under this lake', Gwion remarked to a passing fish. 'Are the gods never content with what they have, but must project their desires towards marine infinity?'

In fact, Tegid Voel had reached the part in his dream saga where a fishermen reports a sea-serpent, twined among coastal rocks. They tell his namesake Tegid to destroy the monster. He agrees, but on approaching the cliffs he hears a deep voice saying: 'Do not kill your sister.'

His sister is a sea serpent! The story adds that she is his twin, and that her name is Ceridwen.

That night, the fisherman Tegid returns to the rocks and calls out to his 'sister' by name. After waiting a long while she creeps towards him in her sea serpent shape. Then a weird black knight appears, who had previously murdered Tegid's father.With his unsheathed sword flaming fire, the Knight begins to chop Ceridwen into a thousand bits, but the pieces re-unite as fast as he can cut them apart, and become as whole as before.

Eventually the serpentine Ceridwen twists herself around her assailant's neck and bite him terribly on the breast. A White knight then rushes in, spears the Black knight to death and hurries off, with the sea snake coiled around his own neck.[11]

Llyn Tegid's imagined monsters

The legend goes on to say that a monster, more terrible than any seen before, now attacks the young Tegid. There is a consensus among experts in non-Christian iconography that fabulous serpents on land, in the air, or from the sea, symbolise the life force and powers of regeneration. The serpent combines a feminine swallowing capacity with a phallic shape, while its repeated shedding of skin suggests death and renewal. In Tegid's story these paired opposites are also symbolised by the black and white knights, while the sea serpent, worn around the white knight's neck, is a reminder that 'snakes combine a beneficent with an underworld role.'[12]

As Gwion stood over Tegid Voel, imploring him to wake, the chieftain's dream turned much more alarming, to judge by the violent convulsions that began to shake his entire body and made Gwion Bach realise that to be as engrossed by a story is to relive it.

The legend goes on to say that a monster more terrible than any seen before now attacks the young Tegid. It is a beast of prey, a ferocious reptile, which haunts him in a variety of guises. Sometimes it appears like an ocean, across which he has to swim, sometimes a mountain of ice, that he is obliged to scale. Then it becomes a white-hot furnace, yet the intense heat has no effect on him.[13] Thus Tegid is subjected to a trial by the elements, encountered in quick succession.

His ability to survive these extremes indicates that he is no ordinary man. Instead, he performs like a demi-god, at one with natural phenomena, even at their most destructive. On emerging successfully from these ordeals, Tegid is escorted by two Welsh gods in a search for his father's grave. They eventually find it, but all attempts to raise the corpse to new life fail. The gods then depart, but with a filial devotion, indicative of respect for ancestral power in general, Tegid decides to dwell permanently on that grave mound.

His mermaid mother sometimes comes ashore to console him, and his twin sister Ceridwen decides to live nearby, 'to make the glad gladder and the pretty prettier, and to maintain her dignity and honour in peace and tranquillity.'[14] So the story concludes.

'This' writes Professor Rhys, 'is evidently a reference to Llyn Tegid, Bala Lake, and to the legend of Taliesin.'[15] If so, the Ceridwen who is Tegid Voel's Lake Bala wife is also his twin sister!

She evidently joins him under Llyn Tegid in an incestuous union, consummated over Tegid's father's underwater tomb. Moreover, if, as vividly described in the coastal account, Ceridwen can manifest as a gigantic sea serpent, so too, presumably, can her male twin, Tegid Voel. As a serpent he is sure to be Welsh *moel,* 'bald.' No wonder that he is also famously taciturn. He has important secrets to keep beneath Llyn Tegid.

Together, Ceridwen and Tegid intertwine like the two wingless dragons often portrayed in world art, or as the inseparable strands of a double helix, now recognised as the key to every organism. Llyn Tegid's mystery is that of DNA's twinned spirals animating a single cell's watery interior, and replicating in miniature the oceanic oneness of life, in all its protean variety. Tegid Voel and Ceridwen's marriage is a united 'I will,' which also serves to bring the coast of Wales into its heartland, while exchanging salt water for sweet.

The 'pair of serpents' image remained deeply embedded in Welsh culture. A folk belief that persisted into the nineteenth century asserted that shortly before any farmer and his wife dies a pair of male and female snakes appear and then expire.[16] Rhys reminds us that at Llyn Tegid a pair of springs and their streams which flow into the lake and which were formerly named Dwyfan and Dwyfach, were probably regarded as male and female water divinities respectively.[17] They are coupled by name, by proximity to one another and by joint contribution to the *llyn.* Here water-serpents become the water itself, *and* the winged serpents that are said to frequent Penllyn.

As for Tegid and Ceridwen's incest, whereas in most human societies incest is taboo, many of the creation myths on which human societies are founded regard incest between deities as indispensable. The universe is born from such mating. Sexual union between 'First Beings' – often male-female twins, like India's Yama and Yami, or Yima and Yimak in Iran – is a recurring theme.[18] Thus the Norse god Njordr and his sister beget the deities Freyr and Freyja who marry one another, while in Cornwall Merlin cohabited with his twin sister Viviane.[19]

Left: *Morfran, son of Ceridwen and Tegid Voel, is synonymous with Welsh morfran, the 'cormorant.' Morfran was a notably good diver into 'utter darkness', as found in the abyss.*

Right: *'Morfran' as a sandstone head in Montgomery castle, carved circa AD 1300.*

'There will be slaughter, let there be the speech of Avagddu',
Book of Taliesin, *vii, 10.*

These myths point in turn to another widespread archaic belief, that the fundamental sacred nucleus of the cosmos is a double-sexed androgynous entity, which subsequently devolved into male-female twins whose reunion will, it is hoped, restore the original and undivided sanctity of the primary androgyne. In diving to the city built around Gwawr's unfathomable lake-floor spring, Gwion had alighted on a potent serpentine thread, an archetypal tale that is coiled around the entire world.

The cauldron of inspiration

Beneath Lake Bala, Tegid Voel's wife Ceridwen was worried about their son Avagddu, who was, according to all the *Chwedl Taliesin* texts: '... *the most ill favoured man in the world... [She] thought that he was not likely to be admitted among men of noble birth, by reason of his ugliness, unless he had some exalted merits or knowledge.'* [20]

Afagddu is a contraction of Welsh *y fagddu,* 'the utter darkness, extreme blackness, gloom.' In some *Hanes Taliesin* manuscripts Avagddu is the brother of Tegid's other son, named Morfran. Morfran is equally dark. He is the 'sea crow', Welsh *mor* plus *bran,* alias the deep diving, hooked-bill cormorant or 'great crow' which fishes the coasts and estuaries of Wales. It is often heard croaking and grunting, as it perches on rocks and opens umbrella-shaped wings to dry. Adopting that bird's character, the mythic Morfran was feared in tenth century Wales. 'No man placed his weapon on him at [the battle of] Camlan, so exceedingly ugly was he; all thought he was a devil's helping.' Instead of feathers, there 'was hair on him like the hair of a stag.'[21]

Avagddu was a nickname for Morfran. Therefore these 'two' sons of Tegid and Ceridwen merge into a single epitome of the abyss which contains magic truths. As one, the brothers are present at Llyn Tegid in the Welsh term for 'a water bird that dives', *Dowcars y Bala*, 'Diver of Bala.' That bird had to reach supernatural depths, for local folklore asserts that Lake Bala is bottomless. When two men in a boat tried to plummet it, an underwater voice cried out: 'Line cannot fathom me. Go, or I will swallow you up!'

It was at Llyn Tegid that Ceridwen *'resolved, according to the arts of the book of Fferyllt*, ['the Magician'], *to boil a cauldron of Inspiration and Science for her son, that his reception might be honourable because of his knowledge of the mysteries of the future state of the world.'* [22]

Allusions to the tale are made by several twelfth-to-fourteenth century Welsh poets, including Cynddelw. He implied that Morfran benefited from his mother's stew. 'May God pour forth for me authentic inspiration…as when Morfran sang the elegy for Einion.'[23] Einion, the founder of Gwion's Caereinion birthplace, was apparently a patron of Morfran, and Einion's anvil may therefore have been forged from the molton iron at the planet's core, towards which Morfran-Avagddu dived!

Regarding that inferno, Lake Bala is on the line of an active fault in the earth's crust that has produced a belt of easily eroded rocks along its line; hence the rift valley in which the *llyn* now lies.[24]

Before Gwion had time to explore these findings, Ford's translation swept him onwards:

> *'After labouring long in her arts, she* [Ceridwen] *discovered that there was a way of achieving such knowledge by the special properties of the earth's herbs and by human effort and cunning. This was the method: choose and gather certain kinds of the earth's herbs on certain days and hours.'* [Guest has: *she 'gathered every day of all charm-bearing herbs.'*] *She then 'put them all in a cauldron of water, and set the cauldron on the fire. It had to be kindled continually in order to boil the cauldron night and day for a year and a day.' After that, she would see three drops spring forth, containing all the virtues of the multitudes of the herbs.'* [25]

'And she put Gwion Bach the son of Gwreang [a name derived from the Welsh *gwreng*, 'commoner or plebeian man'], *of Llanfair in Caereinion in Powys, to stir the cauldron.'* [26] (Llywelyn Sion describes Gwion as the *'son of a squire from Llan Fair in Caer Einion.'*[27])

'That's me! She's chosen me!' cried Gwion, proud that his destiny was unfolding again. However, a blind man sitting beside him signalled Gwion to keep quiet, for

the story continues: *'and she put a blind man named Morda* (or *Dallmor Dallmaen*, 'blind and dumb', according to Sion), *to kindle the fire beneath it.'* [28]

By contrast Gruffydd's text says that after Gwion Bach had led Morda to the cauldron, he, Morda, tended and stirred it, while Ceridwen set Gwion *'to stoke the fire under the cauldron.'* She, meanwhile, was *'keeping it full of water and herbs till the end of a year and a day.'* [29]

Gruffydd takes pains to emphasise this division of labour. Water, along with the plants that drink it, is normally associated with the feminine in mythic accounting. Thus Llyn Tegid's water comes from Gwawr's well and womb. Both she and Ceridwen are divine epiphanies of our watery planet. They are ladies of the lake, doubling as a sodden Welsh *Mam Daear*, 'Mother Earth.'

Gwion Bach's essence, by contrast, is to be found in her fire. The flames that Ceridwen instructs him to kindle and tend in her lacustrine underworld he will discover again, radiating, after many trials, from within himself, as a sublime brilliance, intrinsic to his successfully refined personality.

Perhaps Ceridwen selected a blind man, Morda, to stir the cauldron partly because he could not see to steal her secret receipt. Again, having lost sight of the ordinary world, Morda is better able to absorb insights from her 'other' domain. Because Morda sits between two worlds, as a liminal figure he is named after Welsh *morfa*, 'sea-marsh', neither water nor land, but a subtle mixture of both. As Sion's Dallmor Dallmaen,[30] he is *dall*, 'blind' to *mor*, 'sea', and to *maen*, 'stone', but he compensates by developing other senses, Turning his handicap into an advantage, he finds a way to keep in touch with natural plants and supernatural realities as Ceridwen's cauldron stirrer.

Ceridwen epitomises and demonstrates this interplay of worlds. She finds her herbs here on earth, rather than in some disembodied realm, yet after dissolving them in time with this world's annual cycle in Wales, she distils, mixes, brews and makes

Opposite top left: *Spring water from the breasts of St Anne; St Anne's well effigy, Llanmihangel, Glamorgan.*

top right: *Decorated bronze hanging bowl from Cerrig y Drudion, Denbighshire; 20 cm diameter; third century BC.*

centre left: *A Romano-British goddess stirs her 'vessel of rebirth'; Low relief from Corbridge, Northumberland.*

bottom left: *Neolithic baked clay pot from Ty Isaf, Breckonshire; third millennium BC.*

bottom right: *'Ceridwen' goes plant collecting. This prehistoric megalith at Glasfryn, Carnarvonshire was, until* circa *AD 1900, regarded as a supernatural female. Repeatedly dressed as such, her face was whitewashed.*

Top: *Bronze Age bronze cauldron from Llyn Fawr, Glamorgan; 56 cm diameter.*

Bottom: *Bronze vessel from Llanycil, Llyn Tegid; 14.2 cm., Romano-British or early medieval.*

available their inner magic, as a supernatural elixir, the quintessence of her 'otherness.'

'On whatever man those three drops fell, she would see that he would be extraordinarily learned in various arts and full of the spirit of prophecy.' [31]

Gruffydd then describes the approaching climax of her labours:

> *'At that time Ceridwen took hold of Morfran, her son, and stationed him close to the cauldron to receive the drops when their hour to spring forth from the pot arrived. Then Ceridwen set her haunches down to rest.'* [32]

Gwion and Ceridwen

> *'She was asleep at the moment the three marvellous drops sprung from the cauldron, and they fell upon Gwion Bach, who had shoved Morfran out of the way. Thereupon the cauldron uttered a cry'...'Then Ceridwen woke from her sleep, like one crazed, and saw Gwion. He was filled with wisdom, and could perceive that her mood was so poisonous that she would utterly destroy him as soon as she discovered how he had deprived her son of the marvellous drops. So he took to his heels and fled.'* [33]

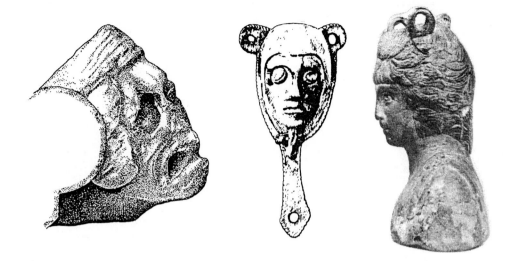

Left: *Morfran at the cauldron's lip; carved stone head, Montgomery castle, circa 1300.*

Centre: *Morda, alias Dallmor Dallmaen, the blind man, seen as a metal bucket mount from Segontium, Carnarvon.*

Right: *'Gwion Bach' as a balsarium or incense container; AD third century; (Carlisle Museum).*

Guest's translation runs:

> *'It chanced that three drops of the charmed liquor fell upon the finger of Gwion Bach. And by reason of their great heat, he put his finger to his mouth. The instant he put those marvel-working drops into his mouth, he foresaw everything that was to come, and perceived that his chief care must be to guard against the wiles of Caridwen, for great was her skill. And in very great fear he fled towards his own land.'* [34]

The 'hot finger in mouth' also features in an Irish legend telling how Finn mac Cumaill, a solar demi-god, acquired his powers. After watching a pool for seven years, Finn's teacher caught the Salmon of Knowledge, which Finn cooked, but burnt his thumb in doing so. When sucked, his thumb then gave him access to wisdom.[35]

In both cases the combination of water with fire, arranged and supervised by a superior being, is critical. So is the element of chance, followed by the infantile habit of finger or thumb sucking as a substitute for the maternal nipple. Finn's pool, Llyn Tegid, and cauldrons can all serve as 'breasts', holding the liquid from which divine wisdom is drawn.

> *Thereupon came in Caridwen and saw all the toil of the whole year was lost. And she seized a billet of wood and struck the blind Morda*

33

'Ceridwen' as a running megalith, Caernarvonshire, 1988.

> on the head until one of his eyes fell out upon his cheek. And he said, 'Wrongfully hast thou disfigured me, for I am innocent. Thy loss was not because of me.'
>
> 'Thou speakest truth' said Caridwen, 'it was Gwion Bach who robbed me'… 'And she went forth after him, running.' [36]

Ceridwens

Who was Ceridwen? Welsh folklore suggests that she could be a sea serpent living off the coast of North Wales where she was twin brother to the fisherman Tegid. That she was *also* the wife of Tegid Voel, living under Lake Bala, is confirmed by the folk tale *Chwedl Taliesin*.

Among the two dozen surviving manuscripts her name is variously spelt Ceridwen, Caridwen and Graidwen, while in early Welsh poetry she can appear as Kerritwen and Kyrridven. But despite these variations, one 'person' is consistently evoked. She owns the cauldron, the source of Welsh *awen*, 'poetic inspiration.' As to what kind of being she was, Gruffydd regards her as a human magician,*'learned in the three arts: magic, enchantment and divination'*,[37] whereas Guest says 'Caridwen is generally considered to be the Goddess of Nature of Welsh Mythology.'[38]

The last syllable of her name, *wen*, is a shortened form of Welsh *gwen*, (feminine),'white', and 'holy.' Traces of Ceridwen's sacredness cling to the ghostly figure of *Y Ladi Wen*, The White Lady' who haunted the outskirts of the industrial towns that sprang up in South Wales in the nineteenth century. She was often seen at night, wringing her hands as if in great sorrow. On one occasion a man asked her what he could do to help. She answered that if only he would hold her tightly by both hands until she told him to stop, her troubles would be over. He did so, but a barking dog caused him to turn around and lose his grip, whereupon she screamed:

'I shall be bound for another seven years'! Then she vanished. Many similar anecdotes tell of her desperation and dashed hopes.[39]

Like the after-image of a bright light, *Y Ladi Wen* sat at cross roads, by fords and in churchyards, refusing to admit that her time was nearly over. By AD 1900 her last vestiges were left to children. They knew her as a wraith, a bogie that would punish misbehaviour. They took away her power by singing her into nonsense:

'Ladi Wen on top of a tree sawing an umbrella shaft. It's one o'clock, It's two o'clock. It's time for the pigs to have dinner.' Ceridwen, the great white goddess, finished as pigs' swill.[40]

Yet to this day parts of her former good name are lodged in Welsh dictionaries. The Welsh scholar P.C. Bartrum writes that Ceridwen means 'fair and loved', from *ceredd,* 'love', *ceredig,* 'beloved, kind, loving, dear, diligent', and *ceredigedd* 'benevolence and generosity.' Likewise, 'Caridwen' relates to Welsh *cariad* 'charity, affection, sweetheart, darling,'and to *cariadol,* 'amorous, passionate', both linked to *cariad-ddyn,* 'lover, love, beloved friend.'

This is the Ceridwen who cares for her horrible son Avagddu-Morfran, and the mother who passes on her good looks both to her daughter Creirwy, and to the girls of Bala town. Tradition declares them to be the best looking young women in Wales.[41] In the *Triads,* Creirwy is accounted one of 'the three beauteous ladies of the Isle of Britain.'[42] She is *creiries,* a 'gem, jewel, greatly cherished treasure'; also *crair,* 'a holy thing, a darling, an object of love.'

As mistress of Nature, Ceridwen sees her own loving 'eye', *llygad,* in almost everything. She is *llygad y ffynnon,* 'the eye of the spring', *llygad y dydd,* 'the eye of day', and the *llygad y tan,* in the 'middle of the fire.' Many of the common flowers in her vegetable soup, such as cowslip, dandelion, wood sorrel, alkanet, stitchwort, wild pansy, herb Bennet, May weed and marsh cinquefoil, have a *llygad* or 'eye' prefix in Welsh.

These weeds return her gaze, as do the *llygadau* 'bubbles surfacing on her boiling broth', along with the 'eyes' in a millstone, a needle, and those made by the top of a pit shaft, the arch of a bridge, and even 'the mesh-holes of a net.' Ignoring our illusory 'culture-nature divide', she looks with equal intensity, inside and out, to make an active array of reciprocated intelligence. Thanks to her glance, the world that she conjures up and inhabits is a living unity, in which her divinity is pervasively immanent,

The price to be paid for Ceridwen's gift is her own destructive side, which is also contained within her name and its related vocabulary. These negative associations may have been additionally accentuated by Christian distortion of her positive aspects. For example, even her *cerydd,* 'love', has now taken on the extra meanings of 'lust, sin, and crime.'

Before the arrival of Christianity, and for long afterwards, the range and truth of super- Nature's comprehensive role, was seen in the contest between dark and light

Aspects of Ceridwen

Top left: *As 'beloved White One', both Ceridwen and her daughter Creirwy continued the white Venus figurine tradition of Roman Britain. Numerous fragments from Wales match this example, from Wallbrook, London.*

Top right: *Mother goddess feeding two infants, from Silchester Hants., second century AD. Several images of the same type have been found in 'Wales'.*

Bottom right: *Incised eye motif on an Iron Age wooden tub from Glastonbury.*

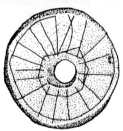 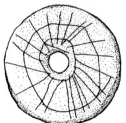

Aspects of Ceridwen

Top left: 'The Wookey Hole Witch', Somerset, a stalagmite venerated in antiquity and medieval times.

Top right: A Bala knitter; circa 1880.

Bottom: Romano-British spindle whorl from Prestatyn, Clwyd. Spinning and weaving were regarded as divinely invented crafts. The central holes, as the deity's 'eyes', supervised the work.

forces. Ceridwen was one of innumerable goddesses of day and night, and of every season, who epitomised the contrasting events and different phases in the annual and human life cycle. Thus Williams suggests a derivation of her name, based on the 'Kyrridven' name found in one medieval poem. From Welsh *cyrridfen* (*cyrrid*, 'hooked, crooked', plus *ben*, 'woman'), he turns Ceridwen into a version of *Y'r Hen Chrwchwd*, 'The Old Humpbacked.'[43] This in turn merges her with *y gwrach* or *wrach*, 'the hag' of Welsh folklore.

The Ceridwen who smashed out Morda's eye and chased Gwion Bach was feared for her rage. She was Welsh *ceryddwr*, 'rebuker' and 'corrector', who drew on her 'Graidwen' alias, derived from Welsh *graid*, 'burning fierceness', which was felt around *Calan Gaeaf* bonfires *and* in her cauldron. Such heat opened routes between human and divine worlds that were almost impassable at other times.

Poison

On Llyn Tegid's north shore, half a mile above Cai's requisitioned Roman fort, there are two '*Wrach*' place names that may help denote Ceridwen's *Calan Gaeaf* progress around the lake. A farmstead, now ruined, called *Llwyn y Wrach*, her 'grove or loin', stands a mile from *Coed Llwyn y Wrach*, the Hag's *coed*, or 'wood.'

A small Romano-British golden-bronze 'cauldron', in effect a round-bottomed bowl, was found nearby, lying six feet below the surface of the Maes y Clochydd bog.[44] It was possibly deposited there as a votive offering to Ceridwen, or her Romano-British equivalent, as part of a lake*side* setting for an annual restaging of the perennial Ceridwen-Gwion Bach incident.

This response was necessary, not least because the results of Gwion's theft were played out on the world's surface, as the *Chwedl Taliesin* texts make clear. For example, the moment Gwion Bach ran off with her 'Three Drops', a calamity occurred that affected a stream trickling into Lake Bala from its north shore parish of Llanycil. As Gruffydd writes:

> '*Thereupon the cauldron uttered a cry, and from the strength of the poison, shattered.*' [45] Guest has: '*And the cauldron burst in two, because all the liquor within it, apart from the three drops, was poisonous. So that the horses of Gwyddno Garanhir were poisoned by the water of the stream into which the liquor of the cauldron ran, and the confluence of that stream was called The Poison of the Horses of Gwyddno from that time forth.*' [46]

Opposite top: *Gwion Bach, splashed by the 'three drops', sees the cauldron burst, while Morda stokes the fire.*

bottom: *Aber Gwenwyn-fierch, the 'Poisoning of horses stream' enters Llyn Tegid at Llanycil. Here Gwyddno Garanhir's legendary steeds 'died' below the surface.*

And I know whence she emanates
And her home and her hospitality,
Her fate and her destiny
Till doomsday.

Since the poison drained into that particular stream, the cauldron and its fire, if set above the ground, were presumably sited somewhere in that rivulet's catchment area. Today the brook is still named Aber Gwenwyn-feirch, 'Poisoned-horse mouth.' After a short one and a half -mile course, this allegedly 'polluted' stream continues to trickle past Llanycil church and graveyard, before debouching into Llyn Tegid, to 'befoul' the entire sacred lake with its legendary load.

In farming terms, the steed were 'poisoned' by winter's collapsing vegetation, bereft of nutriment. In fact a large proportion of Welsh domesticated animals were slaughtered each November in anticipation of fodder shortage.

Other Welsh stories imply that Gwyddno's steeds are solar, and equipped with gilded saddles as they convey the sun across the sky. With the advance of winter, their efforts grow steadily feebler and they are ever more reluctant to leave their night 'stable' – hence, perhaps, the Welsh word *cil* or 'nook' in the Llanycil place-name.

For Gwyddno's solar steeds, the show drew to a close in November. The dregs of Ceridwen's annual brew put them down, as they all but sank behind winter's black curtains, dead to the world. Likewise, the broken and therefore emptied cauldron signified the year's funeral, just as in Antiquity the deliberate smashing of a pot marked a human death.

Ceridwen's poison symbolises the role played by putrefaction prior to Nature's renewal. The cauldron's bursting sediment acts as a prototype for countrywide dung spreading, essential to agriculture and with implications for human society as a whole. 'Rituals of purity and impurity create unity in experience', writes M. Douglas, effectively returning the incident to general use. She adds that 'reflections on dirt involve the relation of order to disorder, being to non-being, and life to death.'[47]

As for the theological implications, Leach finds that 'power is located in dirt[including] urine, faeces, saliva and sweat… If completely cleansed, I would have no interface with the outside world and therefore would be impotent. This paradox is central to a vast variety of religious practice.'[48]

By setting the cauldron's explosion above ground, at the stream's union with the holy lake, Gwion Bach's story selects just such an interface, between sacred and profane realms, where the boiling and its aftermath are shared between supernatural submarine and earthly domains. Moreover, since the lake both engenders and *reflects* the cooking, including both its fair and foul results, Llyn Tegid in its entirety serves as an enlarged 'topographical cauldron', itself synonymous with the lake goddess's living and therefore defecating body. From this perspective, Ceridwen and her pot *are* Llyn Tegid.

Opposite top: *'Ceridwen enraged', seen in* Goddess of the Green, *a painting by Alan Davie; 63 x 75 inches; 1954.*

bottom: *Gwion Bach escapes as a fish. The bottom-hugging* gwyniaid *fish of Llyn Tegid, also known as* Y Gwrach, *'The Old Wife or Hag.'*

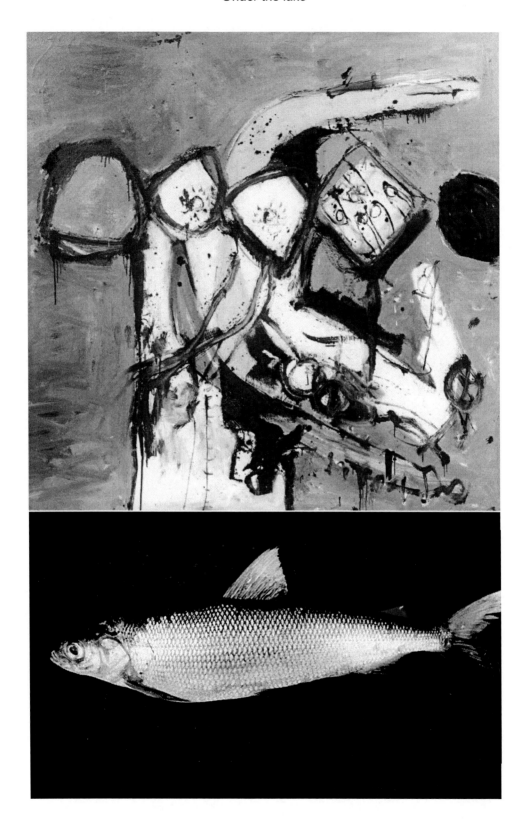

On whatever scale she appears, and in whatever manner, she remains the supreme Welsh *gwrach*, 'hag.' The word *gwrach* derives from a gloss on Old German *grua*, 'anus.' As Leach reminds us, 'Human orifices play a central role in the imagery and narratives of almost every culture, since they link seen to unseen, and interior to exterior realities.'[49] Accordingly, Welsh 'anus' is *llygad tin*, literally 'rump or bottom eye.' Some insights come through filth.

Llyn Tegid's mixture of pollution and purity was probably viewed as a four mile-long, working effigy of the supernatural female. Ceridwen occupied its waters from head to foot as a lady of the lake who *was* the lake, with Tegid as her consort. To this image, the twisting headwater rivers, Afon Twrch, Afon Dyfrdwy and Afon Lliw contribute her wildly flowing 'hair.' A narrowing of the *llyn*, between Llangower Point and Pont y Lafar on the opposite bank, creates an elegant neck. The lake's 'outflow' (Welsh *bala*), of the river Dee, corresponds to her menstrual and urine release. Granted this metabolism, the lake's Aber Gwenwyn-feirch 'orifice' is her anus, creating each winter a delta-load of gravelly faeces.

This anthropomorphic interpretation merely reiterates an attitude to landscape that was once orthodox, indeed universal, and which is by no means extinct. Britain in her entirety remains Britannia, an allegorical female who is still portrayed on our coinage. Likewise Ireland (Eire), is recognised as the island-wide deity Eriu.[50] In addition, from source to estuarine mouth, the numerous rivers of the British Isles were typically regarded as female deities. Compared with many of them, Ceridwen's Llyn Tegid body is only of middling size. By contrast, the river Dee, having run through that lake, then winds on for another seventy miles.

Yet it was not the Dee, but Llyn Tegid's Ceridwen that Gwion Bach had betrayed, and from whom he now fled. By cunning he had acquired her wisdom, but to retain and benefit from the stolen gift he had first to escape her wrath.

CHAPTER FOUR

THE PURSUIT

Transformations

> '*And she went forth after him, running. And he saw her, and changed himself into a hare and fled. But she changed herself into a greyhound and turned him. And he ran towards a river and became a fish.*' [1] So begins Gwion Bach's flight from Ceridwen. She cried out: '*Gwion the false has despoiled me.*' '*And she set out on the same road he himself had taken before, lifting her petticoats and running... in a frenzy of pursuit.*' [2]

From the start of the chase that follows, the two participants share a shape-shifting ability. Always present in Ceridwen, some of her skill enters Gwion's system. By his sudden change from hare to fish he extends Poetry's metaphor-based wizardry into physical transformation. For the Welsh, the source of that magic lay in Ceridwen and her cauldron. Having run off with the essence of its[and her] power, Gwion Bach discovers that he can summon up as many disguises as he needs in order to evade Ceridwen's attacks on him. As he would later recall:

> '*I have fled with vigour, I have fled as a frog*
> *I have fled as a crow, scarcely finding rest*
> *... I have fled as a roe into an entangled thicket*
> *... I have fled as a squirrel, that vainly hides.*' [3]

A comparable transformative ability is evident in the prehistoric Celtic metalworker, The urge to display dynamic ambiguity as a sacred attribute, capable of being read as animal, vegetable, pure pattern, or any combination of these, appears to underlie their work.

Fleeing down-stream in hare mode, Gwion remembers to give a respectful if grudging nod to Llywarch Hen, the legendary oldest Welsh poet, who sits in his '*pabell,*' or 'tent' at Llanfor, which may also be a stone circle. Five re-sited megaliths, two of which now serve as barn door posts, survive in *Pen issa'r llan* farmyard, adjoining Llanfor's church, a mile below Bala.

Llywarch is sunk in senile misery having lost his own sons, and does not respond to Gwion's greeting, though he ought to have wished the future poet 'Good Luck' as he

*Ceridwen as a greyhound,
chasing Gwion as hare.*

rushes by, for the baton of inspiration must somehow be transferred from old to young. Instead, addressing his walking stick, Llywarch complains about his own year's end descent into impotence:

> 'I am old, I am alone, I am disfigured and cold
> Before I was bent-backed I was dazzling…
> Little wooden staff, it is autumn
> Bracken is red, stalks are brown.
> I have turned away from that which I love…
> Old age is mocking me From my hair to my teeth
> And the knob which women used to love.
> … Alas that death does not come to me.'[4]

River

The end of Llywarch's old year marked the start of Gwion Bach's new, though he was afraid it might end prematurely. Ceridwen, in her Welsh *filiast* or 'greyhound bitch' guise, was by now so close that he could smell her breath. No dog runs faster than a greyhound. This one could have sprung from beneath the prehistoric mountain-top cairn, erected six miles north west of Bala, and marked *Carn y Filiast* on modern maps. She was probably a leader of the notorious *Cwn Annwn* pack, which tracked down and devoured humans.[5] 'Ceridwen', as a *filiast,* could emanate from monuments built during the third millennia BC in Wales. They are typically named *Gwal y Filiast*, 'Kennel of the Greyhound Bitch.' Ceridwen-as-dog had plenty of hunting experience.[6]

It is possible that these earth and stone barrows, together with their chambers, were designed in anthropomorphic shape. The Earth mother's perceived divinity accounts for the immense effort involved. Through five millennia, she had housed her dog inside her monumental body, along with the human dead. Wherever Gwion fled in Wales, the phantom greyhound was ready to leap from one of her many cromlech 'kennels.' Chased by this 'multiple' and archaic adversary, Gwion panicked, jumped into the nearest river and became a fish.

To his surprise, once accustomed to the current, he enjoyed the river. 'That dog will never find me down here', he reasoned; 'and how good it feels to be a fish.' With one flick of his tail he could bisect the stream of bubbles that rose from his mouth as he spoke.

Top left: *Derfel's wooden horse, at rest in Llanderfel church porch.*

Left centre: *The river Dyfrdwy, Dyfrdonwy, or Dee, seen near Llangollen.*

Bottom: *Medieval midwinter mummers in animal masks.*

Right: *The goddess of changes; bronze shield rib, found in the Thames at Wandsworth; made* circa *150 BC.*

A man had once told him that the Gaelic for 'river', *caise,* can mean 'a woman's private parts.' Therefore in mid-stream Gwion sang the Welsh monk Gildas' words: 'Britain is decked like a man's chosen bride... with lucid fountains, and abundant brooks wandering over the snow-white sands; with transparent rivers flowing in gentle murmurs and offering a sweet pledge of slumber to those who recline upon their banks.'

Then Gwion asked the river in which he lay, as she surged passed: 'What is your name'? 'Sorry; Can't stop; must get on; good bye; watch out, I'm coming, come, gone again', the river replied. Gwion drifted down stream, trying to keep pace with her, and introduced himself properly: 'How do you do? My name is Gwion Bach. I am from Llanfair Caereinion in Powys. What, may I ask, is your name?' 'Dee', she answered. 'Are you derived from Latin *dea*, 'goddess'?' 'Yes.' 'But that is only a generic term, hardly suited to the kind of intimacy I had in mind. What is your *Welsh* name?' The river answered: '*Dyfrdwy* is my modern shortened form. It means 'Water of the Goddess''

Then she came to a rocky stretch where her rapids spoke so fast, in a jabber of consonants and vowels, that he gave up trying to understand her language. Instead, he watched in silence as this she-river slid around the next bend and then looked calmly at her reflection in a deep, glassy reach. From there she called out to him over her peerless shoulder: 'As for my real name, discover it, if you can.'

Her laughter was lost in the tumult created by a small *ceffyl-dwr*, one of many fabulous 'water horses' that haunt Welsh streams.[7] After inviting a man for a ride, these animals then plunge below and drown the foolhardy jockey. This particular stallion had swum from the neighbouring parish of Llandderfel and was revered in the area as the mount of the hero and protector, Derfel the Mighty.

He is one of only seven men to have escaped from the battle of Camlan. Until 1538, Derfel and his horse attracted hundreds of pilgrims on April the fifth each year. Devotees brought offerings of cattle, oxen, horses and money. It was said that those who worshipped the hero's steed might be pulled out of Hell by that beast, even after the wooden image of the hero had been ripped from the saddle during the Reformation, dragged to London, and burnt.[8]

Remarkably, Derfel's worm-eaten wooden horse, which the iconoclasts failed to recognise as the true source of his supernatural strength, survives. The four feet-long *ceffyl-dwr* is stabled on a bench in Llandderfel's church porch. An underwater emanation from this relic had so frightened Gwion that for a while he forgot to listen out for the sound of the greyhound, his real adversary, snuffling along the bank, as dusk fell.

Then, filtering down to his muddy bed, Gwion Bach heard an intermittent rapping, made by the hand of Marie Trevelyan, a Welsh folklore collector, as she knocked on farmhouse doors along the Dee valley. He sensed that the people who answered her questions were talking about *him.*

'Vividly to my mind comes the memory of autumn evenings spent in farmhouses, where… old farmers sat in ancient arm chairs and aged dames knitted stockings in the fireside corners of the settles. When I asked for the 'old stories', the candle was 'douted' – that is blown out, and the only light allowed was the fire-glow made by a huge log, placed on the burning coals. Reverently, almost with apologies, the old women would answer questions or relate their grandfathers' or grandmothers' experiences. The old men were bolder, and would plunge into the subject with considerable energy.'[9]

'Keep talking! Don't forget me!' Gwion mouthed from far below. His disguised human part craved the notoriety he had already earned, in the belief that he might eventually convert his meddling into positive fame. He was half-inclined to abandon the river's safety, in order to launch a campaign of self-promotion on dry land. Just at that moment, he sensed Ceridwen approach. She was swimming his way as a sharp-toothed 'otter' – a Welsh *dwrgi*, or 'water-dog', which forced him to quit the stream. In a fountain of spray he broke the surface and on new-grown wings flew off as a bird.

Bird's eye view

Air; he was held in air. It pummelled his feathers and was a thicker substance than he had imagined when he was on the ground. Yet he had drawn this same air into his lungs with each breath from the moment of his birth, without pausing once to consider its viscosity. Was he now embarked belatedly on an elemental foundation course? 'Fire of cauldron, badgers' earth, fish-eyed water, ghost of air ', he chanted aloud.

His sky-high viewpoint now overlooked innumerable *Calan Gaeaf* bonfires.[10] They seemed like orange stars, plotted to the remotest corners of Antiquity's crinkled map. From around each dying fire, faint human voices floated up to him. They were singing of Ceridwen in her many winter guises:

> 'A tail-less black sow, And a White Lady without a head.
> May the tail-less black sow Snatch the hindmost' [11]

Then, with much shrieking, they scattered in dread. Gwion detected her shadow, as it glided across frosty water meadows, way beneath him; yet the silhouette was neither that of a white lady nor a pig. Rather, it was *gwrach-y-rhibyn* shaped.[12] This fearsome creature was well-known and loathed throughout Wales. A single glance upwards was enough for Gwion to pick out her thin, pigeon-breasted shape, draped in trailing black rags, from which dangled skinny arms and claw- talons. Her bat-like wings laboured heavily, as if operated by primitive cables. Whether the screeching came from them or from her throat Gwion was unable to decide.

On carrying out evasive manoeuvres, he began to see multitudes of Ceridwen shadows – her *gwrach* or 'hag' extensions. She was the *gwrachen,* a withered female dwarf, hobbling down muddy lanes, the *gwrachastell,* 'off-board' of every plough, the *gwrach-y-coed,* 'wood-louse', a *gwrach-y-simnai,* 'furze brush', and the *gwrachod mewn ty,* 'bundles of bracken, forming the skirts of thatched roofs.' No

Top left: *Llywarch Hen's ruined* pabell *at Llanfor.*

Top right: *The Winter goddess from the Roman mosaic at Bignor, Sussex.*

Bottom left: *The underworld Gwrach; megalithic effigy, Neolithic chambered tomb, Maes y Felin, Glamorgan.*

Bottom right: *'Gwion Bach', hooded in winter; mosaic of the Seasons, Caerwent, Gwent, AD fourth century.*

landing place seemed immune from her presence. Useless to think of hiding in a sheltered 'hollow', for he could count ten, each named *Pant y Wrach*.

Was there no limit to his adversary's forms? On one occasion, disguised as a 'maiden' riding on a yellow mule, 'she' had dared to enter Arthur's Caer Llion Court. Her 'hanging, baggy-fleshed face… and one eye mottled green, most piercing, and the other black, like jet, deep sunk in her head', left a deep impression. Many recalled her 'long yellow teeth, yellower than the flowers of the broom, and her belly swelling from her breast bone higher than her chin…[and that] her feet and knees were clumped.'[13]

Because Gwion was still at the earliest stage of his apprenticeship within bardism, he was unaware of Emerson's opinion that poets 'use defects and deformities with sacred purpose… For the poet re-attaches things to Nature and the Whole, grafting even artificial things and violations of nature *to* nature.' Lacking Emerson's blithe outlook, Gwion could only view with horror, far to the north, the sight of 'the Black Witch, daughter of the White Witch, at the head of the Valley of Grief, in the uplands of Hell', as described in *Culhwch and Olwen*.[14] There, Arthur was seeking her blood. At the entrance to her cave 'he took aim at the hag with *Carnwennan* his knife, and struck her across the middle until she was as two tubs.' Cadw, or Caw, then ran off with the blood[15] (Welsh *cadw* is 'to keep, save'). Cadw was Lord of Ederion and the upper Dee, over which Gwion was now flying.

The witch Ceridwen is daughter and mother of both extremes, inextricably compounded, as seen in the dead-white mace-head with a dark central hole, found at Maes Mawr, nine miles downstream from Bala. Made *circa* 2,000 BC of exceptionally hard chalcedony, the entire surface of this object is nevertheless chiselled with an exquisite network of lozenge-shaped panels.[16] 'Am I another of the four thousand disposable wooden shafts, which have been trapped in her implacable net, before being tossed aside?' Gwion asked of the clouds.

His question echoed that of countless Welsh people on the verge of death. At country funerals up until the late the eighteenth century, it was the custom to make a pattern of diamond shapes from laurel twigs, pinned onto a white sheet and hung against a wall next to the sheet-draped corpse. A single gillyflower was then poked into the middle of each lozenge.[17]

Gwion suspected that the six inch-long Neolithic stone axe, found at Llyn Tegid, below Cerrigllwydion,[18] and stained brown by the lake's peaty water, was made at Ceridwen's command and aimed at his destruction. Likewise what J. Williams calls 'the concentration of Neolithic axes in the upper part of the Dee valley'[19] clearly showed that, as a hawk 'bomber', she could release a full load of axe-heads at him, if she chose.

In a flash, Gwion saw moonlight flicker along a sparrow hawk's rounded wings, gliding through a thin band of cloud. 'How beautiful she is!' was his reaction to the sight of her barred, grey and white, outstretched markings, resembling plough-land, dusted by a flurry of snow. 'Kek-kek-kek' rasped the hawk. 'Or perhaps more like a

Roman winged Victory, carved in low relief from Carrara marble, with her drapery stained by the passage of centuries,' Gwion thought.

The hawk was Ceridwen, playing the Celtic war goddess Andraste, alias Andarte, who Queen Boudicca had worshipped in a grove, by making human sacrifices. This Andraste, who features on the Iceni tribe's first century AD coinage, 'lives with us to this day' reported Richard Thomas in 1753. 'The vulgar inhabitants of Wales make frequent reference to her in their conversation and call her ... *Mam y Drug*, 'The Mother of Wickedness.'[20]

Sacrifice

Guest translates Ceridwen's capture of Gwion Bach as follows:

> '*She, as a hawk, followed him and gave him no rest in the sky. And just as she was about to stoop upon him, and he was in fear of death, he espied a heap of winnowed wheat on the floor of a barn, and he dropped among the wheat, and turned himself into one of the grains. Then she transformed herself into a high-crested black hen, and went to the wheat, and scratched it with her feet, and found him out, and swallowed him.*' [21]

Llywelyn Sion has:

> '*... She took the shape of a hawk, and thus left him not a moment of peace in the sky. And so when he was greatly fatigued and fearing death, he noticed a pile of winnowed wheat on the floor of a barn in the river valley. What he did was alight and take the shape of one of the grains of wheat. And she turned herself into a black, short-tailed hen, saw him amidst the wheat, and swallowed him.*' [22]

When descending into her craw Gwion screamed: 'Am I to be sacrificed? What is the meaning of this?' In reply, the hen's digestive juices squirted copiously. Churned and pulped, he was all but asphyxiated. His unregulated flight was finished. His attempt to improvise a world without rules had failed. Now he was to be destroyed by 'The Sacred' in the shape of a hen, a bird that he had supposed incapable of flying above the mundane.

The act of sacrifice may be prompted by several motives. On a simple level, it satisfies physical hunger. Intentionally or otherwise, it might also involve transferring the life forces believed contained in the victim into the killer. 'So this is how Ceridwen retrieves her precious drops', Gwion thought. 'She takes them in wheat-grain tablet form.'

Within a society prone to, yet wishing to avoid *general* violence, the dispatch of a single victim such as Gwion might provide catharsis and the hope of peace. 'Am I to be killed and eaten in atonement for a broken inter-tribal treaty, lost over some trivial instance of secular bickering? I would much prefer a *supernatural* motivation on

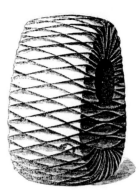

Gwion Bach recalls:

A hen received me.
The cherisher with ruddy claws.
I rested nine nights
In her womb, a child,
Of what she gave me
Scarcely can be recounted,
Greatly will it be praised.

Book of Taliesin, vii, 251–2

Top left, centre left and bottom left: *A hawk, solar flag and goddess. Bronze figurines from Woodeaton Romano-British temple, Oxfordshire.*

Top centre: *A hen on a plate, from Buckley, Clwyd; seventeenth century.*

Top right: *A white stone mace-head from Maes Mawr, near Corwen; Neolithic.*

Above: *Chicken, boy, and sun discs; slate fire back from Bethesda, Carnaervon, 1835.*

Ceridwen's part. Then I could see my death as enhancing the health of the Universe,' he reasoned.

If he had to die, he should at least be seen as a gift, sent from his yeoman father's earth world towards the realm of the gods, to which he presumed Ceridwen belonged. Then his death could link common humanity to demi-gods like himself, while feeding the hunger of full deities for worldly nourishment.

Although the Reverend Charles of Bala. Charles had preached that 'the possibility of imagining God with organs of digestion and secretion… is not entertained in the Jewish religion,' Gwion Bach felt that a body, even a chicken's body, *was* 'capable of furnishing a supernatural system of symbols.' Unlike Judaism, 'many other religions worship divinities that are incarnate in every sense.'

While Ceridwen was making the quiet, introspective music typical of a hen's more contemplative moods, Gwion was examining graffiti desperately scratched onto the inside of her stomach walls by previous victims. One anonymous message read: 'I am nothing, I see all.' Another, in a smaller hand, stated: 'Witches are Animals.' A third ran: 'Everything that can happen to a man by way of disaster should be catalogued according to the active principles involved in the universe of his particular culture.' Signed Douglas, M.P. [23]

Across a bare patch Gwion scrawled *Tachwedd.* Welsh *Tachwedd* means 'slaughter, annihilation, stench, small amount, and November.' His incarceration within Ceridwen was timed to precede the pastoralists' annual slaughter of pigs and cattle, due to an anticipated lack of winter fodder. Gwion's 'small' death would initiate and justify the farming massacre that was to follow his sacrifice.

Wheat

Gwion derived some aesthetic satisfaction from being eaten as a grain of wheat. Because Wales is a wet country, with mainly thin acidic soils, wheat is rarely grown, except in a few favoured areas. Partly for that reason, it has acquired superlative connotations; for example, a head bard is customarily called 'The Wheat of Song.' So, as a wheat grain, Gwion-the-novice could be said to have reached the summit of his poetic calling. Welsh *gwenith,* 'wheat', is also 'fine person', and a 'symbol of burial and resurrection.'

Opposite top left:	Y Wrach, *the hag as corn dolly, or idol; medieval engraved slate from Trewern, Montgomeryshire; 15 cm.*
top right:	*Romano-British goddess holding fertility emblems; from Caerwent, Gwent.*
bottom left:	*Plan of Ty Isaf Neolithic long barrow, Powys; the underworld goddess as tomb shape.*
bottom right:	Y Caseg Fedi, *or 'Harvest Mare'; corn dolly, twentieth century; Carmarthen museum.*

Secondly, Gwion appreciated the symmetry of what had happened to him, following his arrival at Llyn Tegid. Thereabouts, Ceridwen had gathered wild weeds and stewed them for a year and a day. Then he had stolen their refined juice, only for her to recover it, now encapsulated within the most sophisticated of grains, developed by New Stone Age farmers. He was the unwitting means through which Ceridwen had re-united Old Stone Age gathering with New Stone Age agriculture. By combining wilderness soup with wheat grain, he was completing the vegetable round that she, as goddess of Nature *and* of Culture, had generated.

Moreover, in Wheat, supreme among all types of seed, he shared a sacrificial destiny with her. When plaited as *Y Wrach*, 'The Hag', or as *Y Caseg Fedi*, 'The Harvest Mare'[24] (interchangeable Welsh terms for the 'Last Sheaf' of an annual harvest) Ceridwen's own fate was to be broken to bits when the next season's ploughing buried her underground. Therefore she and Gwion Bach were, and still are 'twinned' partners-in-sacrifice. As grain spirits, they mirror each other's repeated destiny. So while he had fled *from* her, Welsh farmers, including his father, were chasing *after* her, during their customary 'Last Sheaf' rite:

> *Farmer:* 'Early in the morning I got on her track. Late in the evening I followed her. I have her! I have her! I have her!'
>
> *All:* 'What do you have?'
>
> *Farmer:* 'Gwrach! Gwrach! Gwrach!' [25]

Of the limited wheat-growing opportunities in Wales, the Plain of Gwent gave the best. According to the medieval *Triad,* known as '26w', a mythic white pig named Henwen, 'Old White', had landed there from the sea and given birth to the very first grain of wheat ever seen in the country.[26] Since her *Calan Gaeaf* counterpart was the tail-less *black* sow, alias Ceridwen, who annually devoured the hind-most person to escape the bonfire sites, Gwion speculated as follows: 'Eaten by Ceridwen, reborn by Henwen.' As his wheaten body disintegrated, cell by dissolving cell, he chanted this mantra to keep his hopes of renewal alive.

Accepting his role in the rituals of pagan wheat sacrifice, Gwion Bach saw that Christianity had adopted some of the same features. Christ's death, predicted and enacted at his Last Supper through the medium of wheaten bread, was comparable. Many religions share the grain of wheat nucleus and for both Gwion and Christ the humanoid-to-wheat transformation was a reversible process. Thus Jesus' transubstantiation into bread during his 'Last' (often repeated) Supper symbolised both his immanent self-sacrifice and his return, body and soul, during the Mass.

Gwion Bach might therefore regard Christ as a brother-deity-in-suffering, whose 'foreignness' is dispelled when taking root in the wheat field's common ground. But for Gwion, the Christian *Ecclesia*, 'Mother Church', can be the magic sow, Henwen. Henwen is a maternal version of *Y Wrach*, The Hag-as-corn idol. Gwion had he been swallowed into the 'black hen' mode of that pig goddess, where the last grain of one year becomes the seed-corn and flour of the next.

Gwion and Bacchus

Talk of bread made Gwion thirsty. 'Who will bring wine to Ceridwen's feast?' he wondered. Then it dawned on him that he had brought his own bottle to the party. His name was probably on the label, for 'Gwion' probably derives from the Welsh *gwin,* 'wine.' *Gwin,* in turn, comes from Latin *vinum,* 'wine, fermented grape juice, the grape.' So Gwion Bach was to provide the sacrificed bread-grain *and* the votive wine. As Welsh *gwin,* he is 'fermented juice of any fruits', such as native 'apples, elderberries, rhubarb and gooseberries.' The word also means 'passion causing intoxication.'

'To drink wine', Welsh *gwino,* is Gwion's purpose. His head spins from Ceridwen's fermented brew of native plants and their implied fruits. Its quintessence has entered and *become* his bloodstream. In addition, his predecessor had been 'splashed' by (and made drunk on) almost four hundred years of Roman occupation, when vineyards flourished in Britain and wine was also imported in bulk from the Mediterranean. Thus for post-Roman Britons the Welsh Gwion Bach continued the role of the juvenile Roman wine god, Bacchus and *his* Greek equivalent, Dionysus.

It is hard to overestimate the importance of Bacchus in late Roman Britain. His monumental carved image was set up at the city of Uriconium, (Wroxeter, Shropshire), that for three centuries after AD 410 remained in British rather than English hands.[27] Similarly, Bacchus' story is carved into the gigantic Corinthian capital which caps the Jupiter column set up at Corinium (modern Cirencester), the administrative center of late-Roman west Britain, which included the future Wales. During the fourth century AD the Bacchic cult in rural areas grew ever stronger, until 'Britain's primeval past was merged with the pagan Roman world's love of bucolic settings, prophecy and charms.'[28]

The Welsh word *bach* in Gwion Bach derives from the Celtic word *bakkos,* 'small.'[29] This makes it possible to hear, quite by chance, the *sound* of Roman Bacchus' name reiterated twice over in Gwion Bach, who was the carrier of both pre-Roman and Romano-British traditions.

Among the Welsh, Gwion was by no means alone in regarding himself as the rightful perpetuator of Roman culture in Britain. 'The magic of the Roman name had a curious power of insinuation… In the fifth and sixth centuries the interests of native Wales were at one with those of the Empire.'[30] In AD 800 the Welshman Nennius still refers to his countrymen as Roman *cives,* 'citizens.' This attachment was enhanced by the belief that Wales was the only part of the Western Roman Empire unconquered by outsiders.[31]

When drunk, Gwion would sometimes boast: 'I am Bacchus.' If challenged, he would add: 'I am as Roman as Caer Gai fort. If you want to see my picture, go to Caerwent, the Roman Venta Silurum in Gwent There you will find me in the middle of the floor.'

Complementing the centrally displayed mosaic portraits of Bacchus found in twelve British villas, the fourth century mosaic at Pound Lane, Caerwent, depicts him as a

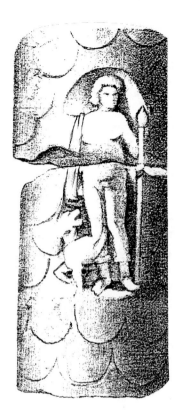

Gwion Bach as Bacchus

Top left: *Bacchus at the centre of the Pitney mosaic, Somerset, surrounded by images of deities.*

Top right: *Bacchus, seen with his thyrsus staff and a wild beast; pillar sculpture, Wroxeter, Shropshire.*

Bottom left: *Mosaic with cantharus drinking cup, symbol of Bacchus, and mosaic with cantharus and dolphins, both from Caerwent, Gwent.*

Bottom right: *A Roman flagon from the Caer Gai fort, Llyn Tegid.*

two-handled *cantharus*, a wine-mixing urn or cup accepted as 'the standard Bacchic emblem of bodily and spiritual refreshment.'[32] Just as Ceridwen is almost synonymous with her cauldron, so in Roman Britain Bacchus was closely identified with his *cantharus* and frequently depicted in this form.

As well as evoking earthly carousal, it stood for the mystic communion between the wine god and those initiated into his cult. Thanks to Bacchus, they would go on to enjoy their soul's refreshment in a post-mortem underworld, under his guardianship. On the Caerwent floor, the accompanying dolphins give a submarine emphasis to the journey.

Nearby, at Caerleon, the legionary fortress taken over by 'King Arthur', Bacchus has left his *thyrsus* or ceremonial rod behind in the Backhall Street mosaic. With flowing ribbons tied to its head, the *thyrsus* was a symbol of poetic inspiration, which eventually passed to Gwion Bach.[33] At Caerleon, according to *The Triads*, as one of 'The Three Skilful Bards', he would sing for Arthur.[34]

Gwion also adopts a Bacchic ability to change into animal form, though he cannot match the tiger or panther that appears at Bacchus' side as that god's double in statuettes from London and Wroxeter. What further serves to intertwine Gwion and Bacchus is their intense relationship with a mother goddess figure. In ancient Rome, under his former Latin name of Liber, Bacchus formed a trinity with Ceres, the Harvest goddess, and her daughter Proserpine.[35] The parallel with the Gwion-Ceridwen-Creirwy trio is plain.

As for the inherited importance of alcohol to Welshmen, J. Craddock wrote in 1770: 'We may conclude that Bacchus does more execution in this country than Mars does in Germany. Here the men estimate their strength not by feats of activity, but by the quantity of ale they can drink.'[36]

Black hen

Suffocating inside the black hen, and fearing that he was about to have a fit, Gwion begged Ceridwen to visit St Tegla's Well in Llandegla Parish. From the southern end of the Clwydian Mountains, that *Ffynnon* overlooks the Dee valley. To his surprise, Ceridwen agreed.

They arrived to find numerous pilgrims carrying black chickens in baskets. Boys brought cocks and girls hens. All these children suffered from epilepsy. As custom dictated, they came after sunset, paid 4d, and walked around the well three times saying the Lord's Prayer. Then each pricked his or her fowl with a pin before immersing it in the one foot-deep stone floored well of Ffynnon Degla, beneath which dozens of egg-shaped white quartz pebbles, of a type considered since the Bronze Age to contain magic potency, have recently been found.[37]

Next, the young pilgrims hurried into a small chamber beneath the church altar, where, accompanied by the chickens, they 'incubated', sleeping there for the night. The following morning, every child put the bird's beak into its own mouth and exhaled a breath, before letting the bird go, whereupon it was hoped that the affliction would immediately leave the child and pass into the bird, turning its flesh black. In 1885 an old man recalled seeing the birds staggering about, having accepted the ailment. These rites continued till 1813.[38]

'So stop complaining!' Ceridwen squawked to Gwion as he wriggled inside her. 'You are my malady, you stupid boy, and I will soon suffer much more for your sake.'

On Shrove Tuesdays, in many Welsh parishes, a ceremony called 'Thrashing the Hen' took place. 'A hen that did not lay an egg before noon was taken to the centre of a green meadow, where a turf was cut and a hole made, wherein the hen was buried, her head alone being out. Then any person who wished to strike her with a stick might try, his eyes first being bandaged. This process was repeated till someone hit her. She then became his property. The hen was kept till the following day, when it was killed and eaten with considerable ceremony.'[39]

In a 1744 version of the same February rite, practiced on both sides of the Welsh-English border, 'the hen is hung at a fellow's back, who has also some horse bells about him. The rest of the men are blindfolded by the girls' aprons.' As the hen and bells man shifts about, the others, with boughs in their hands, try to hit him. 'Afterwards the hen is boiled with bacon and a store of pancakes and fritters is made. She that is noted for lying abed long has the first pancake presented to her.'[40] The pancake was her sun.

The date of this ceremony had probably drifted under Christian influence to Shrovetide from the 1st February Quarter-day known as *Gwyl Fair*, which was celebrated exactly three months after *Calan Gaeaf*. Thus the black, short-tailed hen who had swallowed Gwion Bach and was the dominant force of that midwinter quarter, was herself dispatched in February.

So, in the endless chain of reciprocated life-death encounters, Ceridwen-as-fowl now became the victim. Yet after *Calan Mai* she reappeared as *Iar fach yr haf,* 'the little hen of summer', in other words a butterfly, or as *Iar og,* a 'hen salmon.' Thus was Nature's common sense morality emphasised, and presumed sustained, by well-balanced rituals.

They operated on both social and supernatural levels throughout the folk year, until re-defined by advancing Calvinism as instances of cruel, pointless, pagan superstition, that had to be prohibited. 'Great efforts were made to stamp out our 'Thrashing the Hen' custom' said David Davies of Llansanffraid yn Mechain in 1871, adding: 'It has now ceased. I could name the people taking part but I refrain from doing so out of consideration for their families, who are yet living.'[41]

By then, the divine ecology, nurtured for ages, which Gwion Bach helped demonstrate in action, had become a subject of unmentionable shame. Yet even today the forgotten wisdom of transformations can still be found, sheltering in any Welsh dictionary and – since creatures continue to feed on one another – openly confirmed in the real world.

CHAPTER FIVE

IN THE BAG

Three translators

'Guest's translation of Gwion Bach's tale continues:

> 'And, as the story says, she bore him nine months, and when she was
> delivered of him, she could not find it in her heart to kill him, by
> reason of his beauty. So she wrapped him in a leathern bag, and cast
> him into the sea to the mercy of God, on the twenty-ninth day of
> April.' [1]

Sion's account says that she

> '… stitched him into a leather bag and cast him adrift in the sea into
> the will of God, on the twentieth day of the month of April.' [2]

Elis Gruffydd has:

> 'she carried him there [in her belly] for nine months, at which time
> she got deliverance of him. But when she gazed upon him after he
> had come into the world, she could not in her heart do him any
> physical harm herself, nor could she bear to see anyone else do it. In
> the end, she had the prince put into a coracle, or hide-covered
> basket, which she had fitted snugly all around him; then she caused
> it to be cast into a lake, according to some books, but some say he
> was put into a river, others that she had him put into the sea… ' [3]

Since Gruffydd's text of 1548 is the earliest of the three, one might expect it to reflect
most authentically the ancient folk tradition, but as Ford points out, the opposite is
the case. 'Gruffydd is not content to simply copy out the story, or record a version he
knew, [since] … he is at a distance from the tradition.' (He was the steward of Sir
Robert Wingfield's London house and attended the meeting between Henry eighth
and Francis 1st of France, known as The Field of the Cloth of Gold.) 'As a man of
letters and a somewhat cosmopolitan figure who knew French and English… and
who had travelled extensively, he sometimes objects to the [Christian] impiety of the
story, or to its irrationality.'[4]

Gwion Bach Reborn

Top left: *Medieval stone sculpture in Chirk graveyard, Denbighshire, 70cm long. Ceridwen's eating and re-birthing of Gwion has parallels in the Catholic Mass.*

Top right: *Lead brooch from Dinas Powys, Glamorgan, AD seventh century with terracotta boy's head from Roman Holt, Denbighshire.*

Bottom left: *The Carreg Leidr prehistoric megalith, Llandyfrydog, Anglesey, 1.2 metres tall. Folklore describes it as a figure carrying a bag.*

Bottom right: *Effigy from Gnoll Castle, Glamorgan, 50 cm tall, AD fifth century.*

Gruffydd confesses: 'Indeed in my opinion it is very difficult for anyone to believe that this tale is true.'[5] So he 'upgrades' the story to suit Christianised upper class taste. Thus Gwion is called a 'prince', and the bag becomes a Moses-style upholstered basket. As Gruffydd's doubts over *Chwedl Taliesin's* plausibility increase, so his preference for a *historical* reworking of the folk material displaces its mythic essence. He had, we should recall, set the tale into his *Chronicle of the World; From Creation to the Present Day*, conceived as a linear, not a cyclical enterprise.

By contrast, Sion and Guest preserve the mythic ethos, not least because (as scholars have convincingly shown), they were both translating accurately from medieval scribes, predating Gruffydd's somewhat rationalising Renaissance account. It transpires that Llewellyn Sion, a conscientious copyist, reproduced a fifteenth century Welsh manuscript,[6] while Guest, in collaboration with Thomas Price, worked from a Welsh text written in AD 1370.[7] Sion and Guest were therefore fully engrossed in a magic milieu, where text and native oral tradition were in harmony. This is the spirit that they faithfully convey.

Gwion and the Mother Goddesses

Chwedl Taliesin does not specify the actual place where Ceridwen gives birth to Gwion and then throws him into the sea. Left open, it gives all Welsh seaside dwellers an equal view of, and share in the act. Yet it is hard to avoid the claims of the Dee estuary as a prime location.

The River Dee has always been regarded as divine. Afon Dyfrdwy, her current Welsh name, derives from Welsh *dwfr* 'ater', plus *dwy*, 'divine'. Thanks to this waterway, Gwion's story is carried from Llyn Tegid to the fortress and city of Roman *Deva*, a name derived from Latin *dea*, 'goddess', in recognition of the stream's divinity.[8] Deva underlies modern Chester and Chester, where the river becomes an arm of the sea, offers an excellent stage for Gwion's rebirth, echoing the 'second coming' of Roman Bacchus.

At Chester, moreover, Ceridwen might associate with the still-visible figure of Minerva, goddess of wisdom, carved by the Romans into the red sandstone quarry face, overlooking the Dee. With an owl perched on her shoulder, she gazes at the sacred stream. Minerva was above all a goddess of handicrafts, learning and the arts. Poets venerated her; and according to the twelfth century *Vita Merlini*, a certain poet and prophet named Taliesin worked 'under the guidance of Minerva, his associate.'[9]

After AD 613, when the English captured the east bank of the river, including the Wirral peninsula, the estuarine Dee's frequent changes of channel through the banks of silt which she herself deposited, were regarded as divinely given omens. Gerald of Wales noted in 1189: 'The local inhabitants maintain that the Dee moves its fords every month and that, as it inclines more towards England or Wales in this change of channel, so they can prognosticate which nation will beat the other in any particular year.'[10]

Left: Map of North Wales by H. Hughes, 1845, showing Mam Cymru, 'Mother Wales' alias Ceridwen, alias Don. She heads seawards with a sack containing the divine child Gwion Bach.

Below: The weir on the Dee at Chester coincides with the bursting of Ceridwen's birth waters.

Opposite top: *The goddess Minerva carved into a rock at Chester; first century AD. Minerva was worshipped by poets.*

left: *A Minerva altar found in Roman Segontium (modern Carnarvon).*

right: *A River Dee coracle man, at Llangollen in 1933.*

bottom: *The crowned goddess of the Dee at Chester, in Drayton's Polyolbion, 1617.*

Superstitious awe regarding the Dee persisted, even among clerics trained to reject pantheism's spirit. In 1875 the Dean of Chester, J.S. Howson mused: 'Whether it be from some reminiscence of the Druids, or whatever cause, the 'holiness' of this 'wizard stream [Milton's phrase], meets us at every turn, so that a sacred mystery seems to brood over its waters.'[11]

In a seminal essay W.J. Gruffydd establishes that the deity concealed within the generalised river names Dee and Dyfrdwy was neither Minerva nor Ceridwen, but Don. Hence the original name of the river, still used in the Middle Ages, was Dyfrdonwy, 'the waters of the goddess Don.'[12]

J. Rhys has convincingly shown that Don was the goddess mother of the entire pantheon of Welsh deities,[13] including Ceridwen, Gwydion the wizard and Amaethon the prototypical husbandman, described in the *Mabinogion*. It was Don who carried and determined the fate of nations by her every watery twist and turn. On her lively steam both Gwion Bach and Ceridwen were transported to the ocean's brink.

With a last glance at Ceridwen, his new mother, Gwion Bach sees her violent *gwrach* face suffused with the 'loving kindness' implicit in the Welsh word *ceredd*, embedded in her name. He now understands her volatile moods, whether furious or affectionate, as adjectives or adverbs, emanating from a complete language of truth, synonymous with Don herself.

Throughout her course, Don is the unacknowledged (because in recent centuries unnamed) supernatural life-stream of Wales. Yet by her continuing bank-side chatter, slurp and roar, she articulates the sacred grammar that underlies and sustains a numinous Wales, while employing Ceridwen to act on her behalf. This arrangement suits them both because, as the ultimate mystery, Don is, and probably always was, both omnipresent and unknowable.

Birthdays

Gwion Bach's rebirth is a magical event. As his story makes clear, the ordinary and the divine worlds are not synonymous. Things can happen in sacred space-time inconceivable in the prosaic realm. Yet before the age of scientific rationalism few doubted that the divine took precedence, while remaining largely inaccessible to humanity. Therefore the demi-god Gwion's uncanny voyage is undertaken on our behalf. Its purpose was to re-imbue the universe with sacred energy, without which the physical fabric of the cosmos would disintegrate.

In Wales, thanks to *Chwedl Taliesin*, these cosmogonic events were re-staged in a popular narrative, and with enough links to everyday experience to appear relevant. Yet instead of an exact match between divine and secular, people relied on the habitual use of metaphor to see the slightest overlapping resemblance as a deity-led collaboration between their own needs and those of the gods. Thus when Gwion Bach was reborn from Ceridwen-as- chicken, farmyard eggs acquired a sacred sheen, and any clucking hen could bring Ceridwen to mind as an incarnation of *Mam Daear*, 'Mother Earth.'

On this earth, what is devoured, digested and excreted makes a fertile seedbed for new life. That is the farming sense to be found in Ceridwen's belly, womb, gut, and new-laid Gwion Bach. As the dark hen, she was the earth's winter goddess, and able to perform this miraculous act, since in Welsh her devouring 'belly', *croth*, doubles as her *croth*, 'womb.' Similarly, Old Irish *croth* also means 'poetry'; and poetry conveys the words of myth, the ultimate container and producer.

Afloat in the Irish Sea, Gwion hears distorted traces of Irish 'hen' legends. For example, Ferchertne, chief poet of Ulster, goes to the King of Munster 'to beg for the monarch's single eye, in payment for Boirche's hen,[14] which the poets had brought from the West.' For the sake of this hen's supernatural power, the monarch blinds himself, while at Ard Fothaid in Co. Donegal the hero Fothad sleeps for nine months at the clucking of Boirche's hen.[15]

One 'practical' difficulty embedded in the *Taliesin* texts involves the nine months spent by the foetal Gwion within Ceridwen. Whereas this is a normal prenatal period for humanity, it does not necessarily suit the pregnancy of a deity who represents the Celtic and pre-Celtic year, which was divided into winter and summer halves of *six* months, starting at *Calan Gaeaf* and *Calan Mai*.

All but three of the two dozen surviving *Taliesin* manuscript fragments stipulate April 29th for Gwion's re-birth, and May Day for his ultimate transformation. April 29th is a mere six months after *Calan Gaeaf*. October 31st, the Celtic New Year's Eve. At *Calan Gaeaf* Ceridwen reached her cauldron-boiling climax, and then hunted and swallowed Gwion. These three events signified the death of the old year and coincided with the November start of Autumn sowing, thereby synchronising agrarian needs with her appetite for divine seed-corn and her earth-womb's desire for fertilisation by Gwion's solitary grain.

In arable terms, a single seed-grain would have produced a head of golden wheat, ripe enough to be harvested precisely nine months later, at the Welsh August 1st Quarter-day, *Gwyl Awst,* the 'August Vigil', when the first fruits of the new crop were ritually cut. As a wheat grain himself, Gwion has a personal interest in being there. At *Gwyl Awst* he would be freed from imprisonment in the ground and could at last enjoy a long-delayed maturity. Hence the nine months stipulated in the texts.

But a successful harvest always depends on the infant wheat plant showing its head above ground three months earlier. It needs daylight and summer sunshine, if it is to grow up and fill out by *Gwyl Awst*. Only then can one grain-head symbolise and sanctify the entire harvest. So Gwion had first to be reborn on the eve of *Calan Mai*, the last day of the Winter Half. Moreover, through May, June and July he would be expected to act as a solar deity, bringing the necessary light and warmth. In this sense, he would be his own 'nurse.'

Equally, one might say that from *Calan Mai* until *Gwyl Awst* Gwion acted as a 'John the Baptist' precursor to his eventual August 1st Lammas or 'Loaf mass' 'Christ.' (In fact, Wace, a twelfth century writer refers to 'Teleusin, a prophet who foretold the birth of Christ.'[16]) But both these developments lay in the future, concealed from Gwion Bach by the bag into which he had been sewn.

Irish coracle, Slane Castle, Co. Meath, circa *1900. The medieval Welsh poet Ifan Fychan describes a coracle as 'a bag of black skin, a fair vat, a bullock's tunic, a swimmer, and a fond paunchy vessel.'*

The bag

In preparation for his Summer Half achievements, the tiny child was plunged into utter darkness once again, and thrown into the sea. So Myth stays true to life by working through contrasts and by emphasising the need for preliminary labour.

Gwion-in-the-bag is a classic case of incubation. Long before the Greek god of medicine Aesculapius popularised that magic art,[17] many prehistoric communities had recommended sleep in a confined sacred place. There the patient would dream a cure for ailments of body and soul, or seek knowledge of the future from a divine being. But since Gwion was already half divine, why had he been so treated?

Gruffydd chooses to interpret the bag as a basket resembling a coracle, one of those unstable bowl-shaped, skin covered craft used on the Dee till the 1920s and on Afon Teifi to this day. Lewis Morris's 1726 account has both bag *and* coracle: Gwion *'was wrapped up in a Leather Bag (or rather a Leather Boat, such as our* Cwrgwls).*[18]

A coracle was employed in a medieval Irish punishment for wrongdoers. The miscreant was put into the frail craft without an oar and cast adrift on the ocean towards probable death, or, if he was lucky, a landfall on an 'other world' isle. On this perilous journey, the prisoner may have seen other coracles, paddled by the mythic *Fir Bolg* or 'Bag Men.' They were an oppressed tribe, compelled to carry fertile valley soil in their sacks to the tops of Greek mountains. By converting these bags into coracles they eventually escaped and landed on the western coast of Ireland, where they settled.[19]

Gwion Bach had no wish to be washed up on an Irish shore, for he had heard that when Branwen had been in Ireland, a hundred warriors had hidden in a hundred bags, pretending to be flour. Before any of them could emerge, they had been crushed to death by Efnisien-the-Quarrelsome's hand.[20] Considering his own wheat grain past, Gwion dreaded death by miller's stone.

Sadly for him, none of the Mystery religions of the Ancient World could be joined without suffering. Initiates had to undergo severe trials of physical and spiritual endurance, often in three stages, just as his own ordeals and transformations were rites of passage into the community of the goddess.

The Welsh *bol,* or *bola* is a 'bag of leather or hide.' *Bola* also means 'belly, paunch, breast, middle, sensual desire and womb.' Gwion had slipped from a hen's craw, only to be confined in cow's hide, stitched into another 'womb.' Yet it was designed as a place of enlightenment, not least because it offers so many meanings sewn together. Gruffydd calls the bag a '*voelcroen*' and Welsh *croen* or *groen,* 'leather, hide, pelt', is also 'one's life, or physical well-being'.

'So this is to be my life and well-being!' snorted Gwion, unleashing a sardonic laugh that was instantly smothered by the soft leather walls. 'If I must be bagged, let it be nothing *but* a bag, tanned clean of all sticky connotations. Is there no simple word to describe where I have been put; Welsh *cod,* for example?'

He soon discovered that *cod* ,'bag, pouch', extended into 'sack, pod, a bagpiper's wind bag, husk and scrotum.' He was now shut into the cod-piece of his own testicles, while 'husk' threatened to re-impose his experience as the wheat grain from which he had so recently escaped. To complete his discomfiture, a poet on the Welsh shore of the Dee estuary was describing in abusive terms a rival English bagpiper on the eastern Wirral bank:

> 'The coarse, bursting, shrill sound of the bottom of a sack
> Of a dwarf in the guise of a shepherd;
> … A trembling sound in a bullock's skin.'[21]

Estuary waters

Whether salt or fresh, according to Mircea Eliade 'the waters symbolise the entire universe of the virtual. They are the *fons et origo,* the reservoir of all the potentialities of existence. They precede every form and sustain every creation…. Immersion in the waters symbolises regression into the pre-formal and a re-integration into the undifferentiated mode of pre-existence.' Yet such immersion is 'not a final extinction but a temporary re-entry into the indistinct, followed by a new creation.'[22]

Gwion was not listening. These ideas sounded too abstract for him. Instead, he contented himself with thinking: 'In water there is a quality endowed with blessing',[23] a line that he would later deliver on dry land.

'But where am I drifting? What is my present position in degrees of longitude and latitude; or if they have not yet been invented, how do I lie relative to the coastal bays and headlands of Wales?' In fact, Gwion was travelling on no ordinary sea. He was rolling instead through a different kind of space, in which normal navigation did not apply. To his frustration, he was cut off from the sights and sounds that ordinary people took for granted. He would have traded his entire divine half for a glimpse of the desolate beauty of the north-facing Dee estuary and its quick sands, notorious for sucking travellers under:

'A wild waste of tidal sands, with here and there a line of stake nets fluttering in the wind, with a grey shroud of rain sweeping in from westward, through which low cliffs glowed dimly in the rays of the setting sun… A train of horses and cattle splashing slowly through shallow desolate pools and creeks, their wet red and black hides glittering.'[24]

Instead, Gwion had to be content with the sound of the vast flocks of ducks and birds feeding there. The estuary has served as a crossroads for bird migrations since the Ice Age. 20,000 little knots annually rest here before heading to Greenland, while 24,000 wildfowl feed on the banks exposed at low tide, as do 82,000 waders in the winter months.[25] There is also space for a single short-tailed black hen, should she choose to explore the fertile slime with them, and conduct Nature's 'Parliament of Fowls' of which she is Prime Minister.

Mrs Noah

Deprived of sight, Gwion's hearing became increasingly acute, to a degree that he could catch phrases from the previous year's *Noah Mystery Play*,[26] performed annually on Chester's Watergate Street by the city's Watermen. He envied the ark for its size and because the range of creatures on board expressed a sociable eco-sanity, unlike the solitary introspection of his confinement.

He gathered that Chester's 'Mrs Noye' was reluctant to join her husband on board, and was inciting her women friends to join her alcoholic rebellion:

> 'Good gossippes, let us draw nere
> And let us drinke or we departe,
> For ofte tymes we have done soe;
> For att a draughte thou drinkes a quarte'
> 'And soe will I do ere I goe
> Heare is a pottill full of Malmsine, good and stronge
> It will rejoyce bouth harte and tonge' [27]

In the surviving play texts Noah's wife has 103 alternative names, connecting her to magical practises. These titles include several deities from Classical Antiquity, such as Cybele, Rhea, Terra and Mater Deorum.[28] Together with native British variants, they form an all-time chorus that could easily assimilate Ceridwen and Don. 'No wonder 'Mrs Noye' is unwilling to embark with patriarchal Judaism. *Cerydd* Noye! Save some drink for me!' Gwion cried, in the direction of the invisible quay, before turning round to concentrate on his own trip.

Down the swilling estuary channels he then shot, one after another: Flint Deep, Bug Swash, Dawpool Deep, Wild Road, and Welchman's Gut. So he passed the twin Cold-Arse hills and rounded the Point of Ayr into the open sea.

Men of the north

'I should be well on my way towards those Scottish lands, formerly ruled by *Gwyr Gogledd*, our Welsh forefathers, the 'Men of the North'', Gwion muttered. 'A poet called Taliesin was employed in several royal Courts up there, although, like me, he was a native of Powys.'[29]

Under a Roman plan to defend Britannia against the Irish, some 'Men of the North' had migrated to Cambria in the fourth century, led by the legendary Cunedda (Welsh *couno* plus *dogos*, 'good lord'), whose son Meirion subsequently gave his name to Merionethshire.[30] Others, who fled Scotland for Wales in the fifth and sixth centuries, had been forced south by invading Angles.

'Manaw, The Isle of Man must be out there. Perhaps Manannan mac Lir, its resident god, will lend me his crane bag, made from the skin of the girl Aoife. It contains all the treasures of the *Tuatha de Danaan*, 'Children of the goddess Dana', including, they say, the letters of a secret alphabet, known only to oracles and poets.[31] Proponents of the oral tradition, such as me, should not necessarily be condemned to life-long illiteracy. I am a quick learner.'

'Whether I reach the Old North or not, I *can* claim to have floated on the waters that link Wales to Cumbria, The Solway Firth, and the former 'Welsh' kingdoms of Scotland's Central Valley', groaned the increasingly sea-sick Gwion between gasps.

He retched again, and then tried to concentrate on ancestral matters, an important aspect of his bardic training, as set down in the thirteenth century *Descent of the Men of the North*, or *Bonedd Gwyr y Goggledd*.[32] It outlines the genealogy of former legendary heroes, including the poet Llywarch Hen, King Gwendoleu, (Merlin's patron), King Ryderch (Merlin's enemy), and someone called Elffin, son of Gwyddno, a name which filled Gwion with a strange sense of anticipation.

Gwion's next assignment was to recite the location of graves belonging to other fabled heroes and gods, such as Lleu Silverhand's, which is 'under the cover of the sea.' He then listed 'The grave which the rain wets', 'the grave which the thicket covers', 'the grave of a man extolled in song' and -his personal favourite, 'the grave of Rhufawn Bebr (Welsh *bebr*, 'radiant', plus *Rhufeiniad*, 'a Roman citizen'), of princely mien, buried very young' where 'a white foaming wave wets the grave mound'[33] Rhufawn, like Elffin, was also 'a son of Gwyddno', says *Triad 61*.[34] Had Gwyddno's steeds, poisoned at Llyn Tegid, gone submarine?

Of Rhufawn's grave Stanza 42 states: There 'Elffin took me to test my bardic lore for the first time above a leader.' Whenever he spoke that particular line, a premonition crept up Gwion's spine, since he felt sure that *he* was the trainee bard in question, told to deliver a funeral oration.

Stanza 73 troubled him for a different reason. It concerned Einion Yrth, son of Cunedda, and founder of Gwion's home village of Caereinion. Yet 73 claims that Einion was killed in Scotland, and had never set foot in Wales:

> 'Each mournful person asks
> Whose is the sepulchre that is here;
> The grave of Einion, son of Cunedda,
> Whose slaughter in the North was an outrage.'[35]

No Einion, no home! Gwion's childhood parish could not exist without the founding-hero, after which it had been erroneously named. Gwion had accordingly been thrown away, never to return, because there was now nothing for him to return *to,* except a genealogical and geographical void. Therefore he had been tossed into the sea, a landless wraith, condemned to eternal 'wandering', Welsh *crwydr,* which also means 'misfortune, confusion, straying, and aberration.'

Mor grwydr, 'tossed by the waves', his tiny quanta of spirit sank into the same oceanic depth where Afagddu regularly fished in high spirits. By contrast, oblivion and perpetual homelessness was Gwion-the-thief's fate and punishment therein. Such was the price of his knowledge, whether stolen or acquired through study.[36] Overwhelmed by despair, he longed for death.

Dark

On both sides of the Irish Sea where Gwion Bach now drifted, young bards were trained in darkness. Their seminaries were underground cells, 'with no windows to let in the day.' The subject and metre to be employed was given out at night. Then each student worked on it apart, 'the whole next day in the dark, till at a certain hour in the night, Lights were brought in, and they committed it to writing.'[37] Similarly in the Scottish Isles, scholars lay in the dark for days on end 'with a stone on their bellies and Plaids about their heads.'[38] Spiritual illumination and the removal of optical distraction were thought to go together. Hence many of those who squatted, like Morda, by the cauldron of poetry were completely blind, as were many Welsh musicians.

Tossed and whirled on the sea's waves, Gwion had time to reconsider Ceridwen's behaviour after she had 'bagged' him into her hen's crop. In the natural course of events, having eaten him, she would have digested him as the wheat grain containing the stolen Three Drops back into her metabolism and then excreted its (his) residue as common chicken shit.

In doing so she would have reclaimed her poetic gift. But instead she had returned it to circulation in her child. 'She must *want* to give her inspiration away. Therefore she converted digestion into procreation and released me back into the world as a second 'Gwion'.'

He paused for breath before adding: ' Maybe I am now Welsh *eirin Gwion,* 'plums of Gwion', alias the 'mandrake' that witches uproot, also called bryony in English. It screams if cut, and enables women to conceive.[39] Did I conjure up my own rebirth from its deep whitish-yellow roots, weighing up to fifty pounds – as much as a year-old child? People complain that my 'plums' have a filthy smell when over-ripe; and my rebirth from the black hen certainly had a strange odour.'

From the black hen, Gwion's thoughts reverted to dark Afagddu. Afagddu is the cormorant sea-diver, the bird whose long beak plumbs the abyss. Had Ceridwen carried Gwion-the–usurper seawards to help Afagddu complete his nadir job? A four feet high prehistoric megalith standing at Llandyfrydog in Anglesey may depict her in the act. The effigy is now called *Carreg Leidr,* 'Thief Stone', because more than two thousand years later, Christians misleadingly redefined this natural 'sculpt' as a man running off with a sack full of Bibles.[40]

Hide

From inside his bag Gwion could not be sure whether he was sinking or floating. Sometimes the smell of wet leather took him straight back to the cow byres of his infancy. 'Father!' he shouted, beating on the 'barn' wall. 'Let me out! I'm shut in! It's *bol buwch ddu,* 'dark as a black cow's belly' in here!'

Wales was (and is) a largely pastoral country, where cattle were very important. They provided meat, milk and pulling power, and played a big part in Welsh legendary lore, since economic prosperity depended on divine prototypes. In the medieval Welsh *Triads,* kings are identified with bulls.

Gwion's father had often recited the *Triads'* bovine triplets from memory, in lieu of bed–time stories for the boy. For example, he listed the *Three Bull Protectors* of Britain, the *Three Prominent Oxen,* the *Three Prominent Cows,* and the *Three Bull Spectres,* or spirits. He had also mentioned the *Three Bull Chieftains,* who were perhaps blessed with a musical bellowing power, since all three, including one Afaon son of Taliesin, 'were sons of bards'; so *Triad 7* claimed.[41]

'Afaon, son of Taliesin', Gwion Bach repeated aloud, thinking that there might be a hidden family purpose behind his enforced incarceration in a cow's skin, if he could only look into the future far enough. Ox hide and prophecy go together in Wales. Thus after the *Mabinogion* hero Rhonabwy enters a decrepit hall, presided over by a filthy old crone, he falls asleep on a yellow ox skin. 'And the moment sleep came upon his eyes he was granted a vision… '

Dozing inside his leather purse on the Irish Sea, Gwion dreamed that Eriu, the goddess who is Ireland, had been protected in her infancy by the mysterious Codal of the Withered Breast. Codal had wrapped the little deity in his own hide. 'And every vigour that he bestowed upon her used to raise the earth under them' until it became a stupendous mountain. Eriu then begged him to feed her no more of his fish, game and venison, for fear that the sun, being now so near, would scorch them both.[42]

Irish *codal,* 'skin, hide', appears again as Irish *curach codail,* 'hide coracle.' Codal the fosterer was probably a fabulous 'boat-beast', who had sacrificed his own skin to ensure Ireland's survival at sea as an incarnate deity, and subsequently fed her till she swelled above sea level into the present island shape, named Eire, after Eriu.

'Shall I survive to re-create Wales and become be my country's saviour' Gwion asked his bag-boat? He was now bobbing up and down in the swell like a shipping lane marker buoy, flashing intermittent thoughts from the top of his head. He was glad that his hide wrapper was so soft; and a perfect fit, almost as if he had grown the material himself. 'I am turning into a beast' he declared and then burst into song, without knowing where the words or music came from:

> *'I have fled as a grain of pure wheat.*
> *On the skirts of a hempen sheet entangled*
> *That seemed the size of a mare's foal,*
> *'That is filling like a ship on the waters.'* [43]

With the categories so muddled, his mind returned to cows. Early Welsh Christianity adopted the pagan reverence for cattle by establishing a supernatural rapport between St Beuno, named from Welsh *beu,* 'cow', and pastoralists' herds. Beuno was the patron saint of Llanycil parish on Lake Bala, where Ceridwen's cauldron had split apart. At Clynnog, Caernarvonshire, some archaic cult practices, honouring this saint, were kept up well into the nineteenth century. They involved offering him calves, especially those born with a notch in one ear.[44] 'Am I another such yearling? Will I be pushed through a slot in St Beuno's oak chest, after exchanging my life for a single gold coin; or be flung over a sea cliff for the sake of the old gods?' Gwion wondered aloud.

Gwener–Venus–Ceridwen

Another way to view Ceridwen's 'bag throwing' is to see it as the reunion of her Gwion-filled womb with that of the sea goddess. One female marine deity is well known in Wales. Her name, Gwener, is derived from Latin Venus. She lives on, every week, as *Dydd Gwener,* 'Friday.'

Ceridwen and Gwener-Venus are both divine versions of the Welsh 'White Lady', *Y Ladi Wen,* who inherits their conjoined persona, developed during and after the Romano-British centuries. While Ceridwen, as a 'lake lady' is connected to the sea by river, Gwener-Venus serves as an amniotic sea, protecting a pre-natal Wales, prior to its rebirth. The 'Fountain of Venus', *Ffynnon Wenestre,* is a Welsh name for 'sea.'

Equally, Welsh *mor-gerwin,* 'the deep', derives from Welsh *cerwyn,* 'brewing vat, wine press', and so allows Gwion-Bacchus to drink from Ceridwen's bounty when at sea. In his Bacchus guise, he can readily come to Venus' side, since the Classical Bacchus frequently devolves into her Cupid, while Cupid personifies the Welsh *ceredd,* 'love', lodged in the heart of Ceridwen's name.

A stone Roman tabletop, more than two feet in diameter, found at Caerleon in 1775, is engraved with a seated figure of Venus, surrounded by myrtle sprays and holding in one hand a tiny dolphin. A vertical hole in this table, close to her other hand, served as a libation tube for pouring funeral drinks to the departed spirit of the female lying in the grave beneath.[45]

The 'dolphin', which Boon translates as Latin *dolphis,* 'womb fish', often served as an image of the soul's journey to the Fortunate Isles, and symbolised 'after-life rebirth', as did Gwener's shell-motif.[46] It held similar connotations as the 'womb of the sea' from which Venus herself sprang. Shell-born, she will rise again, accompanied by pods of leaping dolphins, as they break from beneath and draw a gleam of sunlight to their arching backs, before disappearing below.

Two six feet-long dolphins are depicted on a Roman mosaic floor discovered at Chester in 1909. Their black-striped sinuous bodies wind like river estuaries or sea serpents across a white ground, in static imitation of the Dee's tidal wave, the Bore.[47] With a rumbling sound, this moving wall of sea-water, capped by foam,

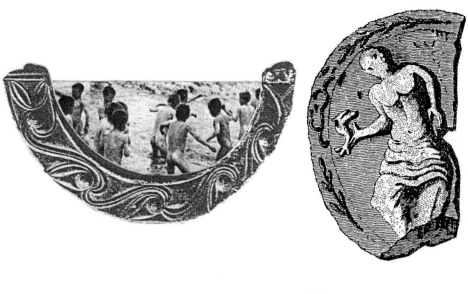

Top left: *Boys in the sea at Rhyl, Denbighshire,* circa *1900; and part of a bronze collar from Llandysul, Ceredigion, first century BC.*

Top right: *Stone table with low relief of Venus and dolphin; from Roman Caerleon, Gwent.*

Bottom left: *Terracotta antefix, showing Cupid, dolphins and myrtle of Venus; from Caerleon, Gwent.*

Bottom right: *Venus on a shell; Hemsworth moaic, Dorset; AD fourth century.*

periodically runs up the estuary at nine miles an hour, while a weird voice, coming from somewhere cries:

> *'Let the billow cover over the shingle, That the land becomes ocean*
> *So that it leaves not the cliffs, Nor hill nor dale...* ' [48]

On that drowned 'shore', Welsh *mordai*, Gwion senses blind Morda, the Llyn Tegid fire-tender, sitting contentedly, as if he had at last found himself a cauldron of the correct oceanic size. Through his leather bag, Gwion then hears the future Taliesin chant:

> *'God preserve the heavens*
> *From a flood wide-spreading.*
> *The first surging billow*
> *Has rolled across the sea bench.'* [49]

Here he is apparently calling on the God of the Cistercians from Basingwerk Abbey. It has overlooked the Dee estuary since 1132. For centuries they claimed all the fish from Llyn Tegid.[50] Yet Taliesin also disparages monks for their lack of elemental understanding. He complains:

> *'Monks congregate like dogs in a kennel...*
> *They know not when the deep night and dawn divide,*
> *Nor what is the course of the wind, or who agitates it.*
> *In what place it dies away, on what land it rears.'* [51]

By contrast, Gwion's enforced salt-water excursion can be seen as an extension of the pagan Gwener-dolphin partnership, as displayed on the Caerleon table. He was in that deity's hands and in her oceanic uterus. When finally pulled ashore, he is mistaken for a fish. The Welsh word *croth*, 'womb, uterus', has a diminutive, *crothel*, 'any small freshwater fish', which strengthens the link.

When at sea, Gwion shares the vast space with the immortal female sea serpent whom the coastal Tegid had encountered, and who was identified as a marine form of Llyn Tegid's Ceridwen. Therefore when she flings Gwion into the ocean, she is returning a version of her own foetus-filled womb to her alternative 'Gwener' self. Gwion has exchanged the chicken womb of a lake-land goddess for that of the ocean's queen. Together, Ceridwen and Gwener ensure that he receives an all-round Welsh education, even if *he* would rather come ashore, in order to enjoy Gwener in her 'morning and evening star' shapes, and to hear her *Gwenen Awst*, 'Lammas bees.'

Play time

In fact Gwion's dark daydreams were a sign of his progress towards a different state of consciousness. Like a submarine that has gone too low, his skin began to leak. Outside and inside merged. Empirical fact, along with simple notions of cause and effect, vanished, with the eclipse of his ego. A world that called for action, or even for self–absorption had gone, and in its place came wakefulness at rest within itself; a state without desire, fear or hope. In this way, his loss became enlargement. He was now bound only by boundlessness. Through sheer drift and self-abandonment, the inclusive indivisibility of the world of play now possessed him.

> 'Then the sea
> And Heaven rolled as one, and from the two
> Came fresh transfigurations of freshest blue.'[52]

Gwion had been thrown where subject and object combine, all at sea. There everything and nothing are stirred into a comprehensive Ceridwen-type stew, seasoned by his particular essence. Thanks to this marine cookery he sailed into an unpredicted paradise, an eternally blissful Present, a prenatal and post-mortem solution to a non-problem. Gwion Bach was at true North's absent iron needle, in the sea of endless beginning, where voyage, voyager, water, sky, stars, light and dark, idea and rock-strewn materiality, cast off their separate labels and arrive at an All's Well together, on the lip of Calan Mai's joy.

Now content to drift, Gwion discovered another self, permeated by the amplitude of Welsh *mor,* 'sea, plenty, abundance' and was intoxicated by unfamiliar powers. From the invisibly far side of the great ocean words came to him, which he sang in return:

> 'The sea of spuming thought foists up again
> The radiant bubble that she was. And then
> A deep up-pouring from a saltier well
> Within me bursts its watery syllable.'[53]

Like Noah and his wife, or Tegid and Ceridwen beneath the waves, Gwion Bach was regenerated by immersion. So he inhaled a big breath and prepared to come ashore.

Cantre'r Gwaelod

'How should I land? What is the correct procedure?' Gwion wondered. Then, by pounding the leather skin, he hit on an international signalling code and transmitted the following messages:

'My position is doubtful. Will you give me my position? I am in dangerous situation. I am drifting. I have sprung a leak. I need a doctor. I am in shallow water. I do not see any light. I wish to anchor at once. My ship is named Gwion Bach. I am abandoning my vessel. Mayday Mayday.'[54]

In response, instead of a life-boat, he heard Manannan, the Manx sea-god, riding past in a chariot, assuring all mariners that from his perspective they were already wind surfing over dry land!

> 'The sea-light where you float, The glint from lifting oars
> Is also solid earth, Moulded yellow and blue…

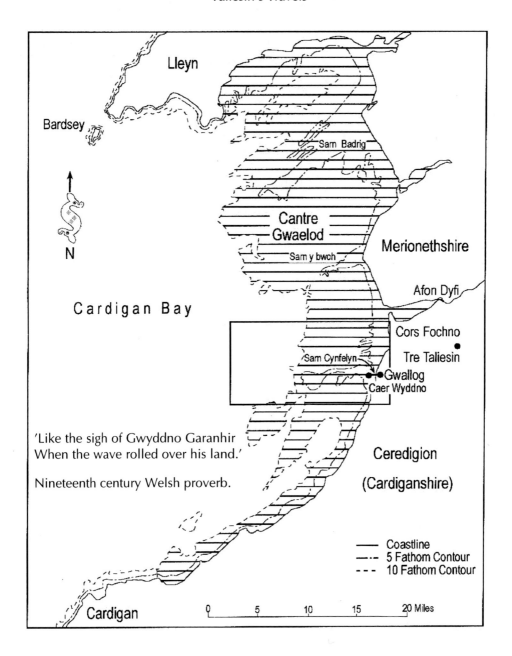

Labels on map: Lleyn, Bardsey, N, Cardigan Bay, Sarn Badrig, Cantre Gwaelod, Merionethshire, Sarn y bwch, Afon Dyfi, Cors Fochno, Sarn Cynfelyn, Tre Taliesin, Gwallog, Caer Wyddno, Ceredigion (Cardiganshire), Cardigan

'Like the sigh of Gwyddno Garanhir
When the wave rolled over his land.'

Nineteenth century Welsh proverb.

Legend:
——— Coastline
—··— 5 Fathom Contour
- - - 10 Fathom Contour

0   5   10   15   20 Miles

Above: *Map of Cantre'r Gwaelod, the drowned lands under Cardigan Bay.*

Opposite left: *Maps of Sarn Cynfelyn, with Caer Wyddno, 1800–5.*

Opposite right: *Ordnance Survey map of 1830,
showing 'Patches' over Gwyddno's Caer.*

76

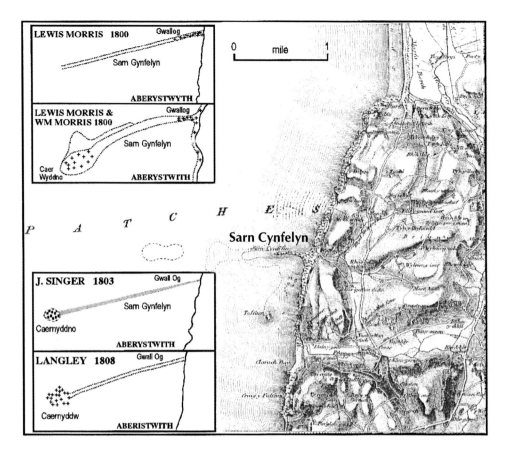

Salmon are calves, fleecy lambs.
Across ridges, the crest of a wood, your curragh sails.
A forest, heavy with mast, sleeps under your keel.'[55]

At first Gwion dismissed these words as raving of an old god, drunk on salt water; but then he recalled that *The Mabinogion* describes how Branwen's brother, Bendigeidfran, wades from Wales to Ireland to rescue her. While doing so, his nose is mistaken for 'a lofty ridge' and his eye sockets for two lakes.[56]

Geologists go further. They state that until 15,000 years ago the Irish Sea was dry land. Britain and Ireland were joined to each other and (even more recently) to continental Europe. The submergence that followed continued into the Neolithic era, from fifth to third millennia BC.[57] Ancestral memory of these former lands probably became the basis for the legends transmitted by remnants of the Neolithic race to later immigrants settling on Welsh shores. Consequently everyone knew about the drowned 'land' across which Gwion was now bobbing.[58]

Whether by chance or pre-ordained destiny, he found himself floating over shallow waters of Cardigan Bay, the sixty mile-wide gulf which lies between the Lleyn and the Pembroke headlands of Wales. This extension of the Irish Sea swamped an extensive clay plain, formerly part of Wales' landmass. In Welsh folklore this lost territory is named *Cantref Gwaelod,* 'Bottom Hundred.' There, 'Lands the most fertile, and habitations the most beautiful in all Wales' were inundated, together with 'sixteen cities and towns', according to Sir S.R. Meyrick.[59]

Gwion greeted those early Neolithic farmers, his father's ancestors, by floating over them. White foam, trailing freehand behind his bag, signed a treaty of reconnection, from which he hoped to absorb a trace of Stone Age sagacity, and put it into words.

Physical evidence of *Cantre'r Gwaelod* is visible today in the mysterious *sarnau,* or under-water 'roads', five in number, that wind for miles from near the present shoreline and run towards Ireland. They appear at low tide as 'highways' of white water, breaking over clay and stone 'embankments.' Geomorphologists are puzzled by these features. As wave-eroded ridges between former river basins they are hardly convincing, for as Steers concedes: 'It is difficult to see why they should be so narrow in relation to their length.'[60]

Seventeenth century writers believed that one such ridge, *Sarn Padrig*, which starts near Harlech, was 'a great stone wall, made as a fence against the sea' when *Gwaelod* was inhabited.[61] At lowest tides the exposed sections are over twenty yards wide and composed of rounded pebbles up to a foot in diameter. Although he was still miles out, Gwion felt an uncomfortable turbulence as his leather vessel rolled over the foaming ridge, along which St Patrick had reputedly walked to Ireland.

After a calm interlude, the bagged sprite was then tossed over the seething tip of *Sarn y Buwch*, 'Buck's Road', projecting westwards from Towyn beach. 'Enough of this! Enough!' Gwion begged. Mistakenly blaming the sudden bucketing on a wind squall, he yelled:

> '*Great God! How the sea whitens when it comes from the beginning!*
> *Great are its gusts when it comes from the South;*'[62]

With this cry he unintentionally began the great task allotted, unbeknown to him, of re-integrating air, water, fire and earth. Upon his success the summer world depended.

Seithennin and Mererid

Having come from Bala, Gwion sensed an ominous familiarity about Cardigan Bay's drowning. 'Is Gwawr's well-head negligence at Llyn Tegid repeated here, but on a far grander scale? Am I more or less back where I started?'

One popular version of *Cantre'r Gwaelod's* story blames the inundation on a King Seithennin, whose lowlands had extended fifty miles from Bardsey Island to Afon Teifi's mouth. His plain was protected by a sea wall, with sluice gates at intervals, allowing rivers to enter the sea at low tide. The gates had to be closed at high tide, but on one 'night of feasting and mirth, when the inhabitants were buried in sleep and wine, and the king among the rest, they were left open.'[63] The *Triads* denounce

Seithennin as one of the 'Three arrant Drunkards of the Isle of Britain', while a fourteenth century poem instructs the 'weak-minded' king to inspect the damage that he has caused:

> 'Seithenhin, stand thou forth,
> And behold the billowy rows'[64]

On hearing of Seithennin through his leather skin, Gwion was reminded of Silenus, the old, wine-loving and often intoxicated companion of his own 'Bacchic' self. As a son of Hermes and Gaia, Silenus was full of wisdom and prophetic knowledge. In his lonely craving for congenial companionship, Gwion hoped that Seithennin was equally well endowed with wisdom and drink.

Had he been able to poke his head out of his bag, he could readily have confirmed the drunken king's positive value. By flooding *Cantre'r Gwaelod* Seithennin had created a gigantic mirror, in which The Pleiades were reflected, like *Calan Mai* pearls on the breast of Spring. Throughout Europe, the arrival of these 'Seven Sister' stars in the constellation Taurus was greeted as a vital sign of Summer's approach. The leading star of the group is called May, and in Wales the entire cluster is known as *Saith Seren Seriol*, the 'Seven Joy-bringing Stars.'

From the sky's unfathomable height Seithennin's *Gwaelod* 'mirror' brings The Pleiades down to Wales, and into a bay across which Gwion is destined to sail. He thereby takes on their efficacy. They will pilot him from the winter to the summer half of the year. As a local guarantee of intent, the King's name incorporates the plan, for Seithennin combines Welsh *seith*, 'seven', with Welsh *ennyn,* 'bright, sparkling, being alight'.

A piercing female cry then cut into Gwion's head. It came from Mererid, another *Cantre'r Gwaelod* character. She dominates the fourteenth century Seithennin poem; and it was she who was really caused the *Gwaelod* flood. She was the female power behind the king's throne. Rowlands' translation calls her 'the server of the wild sea.'[65] Skene's version goes:

> 'Accursed be the damsel, Who, after the wailing,
> Let loose the Fountain of Venus, the raging deep.'[66]

Rhys prefers:

> 'Accursed be the maid who released it after the feast;
> The fountain cup-bearer of the raging sea... [or]
> Accursed be the maiden
> Who after supping let it loose –
> The well-servant of the high sea.'[67]

The following five stanzas name the maiden as Mererid. Welsh *mererid* means 'pearl' and she is a reminder of the maidens who are said to have breathed on the pearl-studded rim of an Otherworld vessel, described by Taliesin in his *Spoils of Annwn* poem:

> *'From the breath of nine maidens it was gently warmed,*
> *Is it not the cauldron of the chief of Annwfn?*
> *A ridge about its neck and pearls'* [68]

On account of its singular origin within a shell (itself a symbol of Venus-Gwener's genitalia), the pearl has long been regarded in many countries as both a sacred child and an emblem of maternal power, the epitome of regeneration. No wonder that Gwion felt Otherworld warmth, beginning to suffuse his cold and clammy bag. He was being reborn by and from the maternal sea. Her salty bloodstream coursed through his veins like the Welsh *gwin,* red 'wine' that gave him his Gwion name. Only now, so close to a landfall, did he recognise his oceanic mother.

Stanza 7 of the *Seithennin* poem starts with the words:

> 'Mererid's cry over strong wines.'[70]

(Welsh *gwineu,* 'wines', plural of *gwin.*)

As the living embodiment of Welsh 'wine', *gwin,* Gwion was now floating immediately above a party where he could rightfully claim a place of honour. Indeed, the hostess Mererid, while presiding over the punch bowl, was beckoning to him. Yet wishing above all to be born ashore, he reluctantly declined to drop into her intoxicating depths, and instead faced the roaring surf.

CHAPTER SIX

MAY DAY CHANGES

Caer Gwyddno

Landing is often the most dangerous part of a voyage. Elements are prone to clash when forced to meet. Sailors are often shipwrecked and drowned within sight of harbour. Aware of this, Gwion sang to keep up his spirits:

> *'In a dark leathern bag I was thrown,*
>
> *And on a boundless sea I was set adrift*
>
> *Which was to me an omen of being tenderly nursed.'* [1]

Was he drawn to this particular shore because it fringed the lost lands, he wondered? Perhaps he would be expected to help in their recovery. As he speculated on a wave that intermingled geological fact, tribal legend, on-shore breeze, and the warmth of a burgeoning Spring, the sound of rolling pebbles told him that his maritime adventure was all-but complete.

In many myths of origins, a New World is said to emerge, whole and entire from the waters of rebirth, as a small island, manifesting above the waves.[2] Caer Gwyddno, a legendary islet in Cardigan Bay, presents just such a microcosm as the germ of a renewed cosmos. The 'isle' is situated eight miles offshore at the seaward end of Sarn Cynfelyn, an underwater 'road', revealed at very low tides. This *sarn* joins the mainland three miles north of Aberystwyth.

'Caer Wyddno is a spot of foul land which comes dry on spring tides', wrote Lewis Morris in 1765.[3] He marked it on his chart of *Y Mor Wyddern*, alias 'The Irish Sea', published in 1800. Owen Pughe claimed to have sailed over the *caer* or fort on a calm day in 1770 and seen a ruined 'city': 'Many stones, large slabs, lying in a heap.'[4] Recent Admiralty charts rename this elusive place 'Outer Patch', and record 'three large stones'.

Fish weir

According to most of the *Chwedl Taliesin* manuscripts, Gwion Bach did not come ashore at Caer Wyddno, but nearby, at the landwards end of the adjoining Sarn Cynfelyn. Guest has:

Sarn Cynfelyn, a natural mud, stone and shingle spit, where Gwion Bach's bag was caught in Elphin's salmon weir on May Eve. Sarn Cynfelyn leads to Gwyddno Garanhir's submerged castle.

'I have been a wave on the extended shore.' Book of Taliesin, *xxviii*, *ll. 63*.

'I was truly in the enchantment with Dylan son of Wave.' Book of Taliesin, *viii*, *181–2*.

'And at that time the weir of Gwyddno was on the strand between Dyfi and Aberystwyth, near to his own castle, and the value of an hundred pounds was taken in that weir every May eve.

And in those days Gwyddno had only one son, named Elphin, the most hapless of youths, and the most needy. And it grieved his father sore, for he thought that he was born in an evil hour. And by the advice of his council, his father had granted him the drawing of the weir that year, to see if good luck would ever befall him, and to give him something therewith to begin [in] the world.[5]

Sion says that it was at Gwyddno's 'wife's request' that he assigned the catch to Elphin, while Gruffydd elaborates in a worldly-wise manner on Elphin's habits:

'He was an incorrigible spendthrift – as are the majority of courtiers. As long as Gwyddno's health lasted, Elphin did not lack for money to

Flotsam washed up on Sarn Cynfelyn, May Eve, 2003.

spend among his friends. But as Gwyddno's riches began to dwindle, he stopped lavishing money on his son.[6]

Guest goes on:

> 'And the next day when Elphin went to look, there was nothing in the weir. But as he turned back he perceived the leathern bag upon a pole in the weir. Then said one of the weir wards [who Sion refers to as a 'lad'] unto Elphin: 'Thou wast never unlucky until tonight, and now thou hast destroyed the virtues of the weir, which always yielded the value of an hundred pounds every May Eve, and tonight there is nothing but this leathern skin within it.[7]

Gruffydd prefers:

> 'When Elphin and his people came within the arms of the weir, they saw there neither head nor tail of a single young salmon... nothing but some dark hulk within the enclosure.' But on a second look, Elphin 'immediately found a coracle or hide-covered basket, wrapped from above as well as from below. Without delay, he took out his knife and cut a slit in the hide, revealing a human forehead. As soon as Elphin saw the forehead, he said, 'behold the radiant

83

forehead!' [i.e. *tal iesin*] To *those words the child replied from the coracle, 'Tal-iesin he is!' People suppose that this was the spirit of Gwion Bach, who had been in the womb of Ceridwen*[8]

Here Guest gives less detail:

"How now', said Elphin, 'there may be therein the value of an hundred pounds.' Well, they took up the leathern bag, and he who opened it saw the forehead of the boy, and said to Elphin, 'Behold a radiant brow!' [Sion has: 'There is a 'beautiful', *jesin*, 'forehead', *tal*.'] *'Taliesin be he called,' said Elphin. And he lifted the boy in his arms, and lamenting his mischance, he placed him sorrowfully behind him. And he made his horse amble gently, that before had been trotting, and he carried him as softly as if he had been sitting in the easiest chair in the world.'*[9]

By contrast with Guest, Sion makes Taliesin responsible for the horse's change of pace:

'And then Taliesin caused the horse, which had been trotting, to amble smoothly,[10] while Gruffydd simply says: *'Elphin took the bundle and placed it in a basket upon one of the horses.*[11]

Though the prince treated Taliesin kindly, he remained bitterly disappointed over the lack of fish.

Taliesin's response is contained in the first translation of his words into English. In 1764 the Reverend Evan Evans of Lledrod, Cardiganshire published *Some Specimens of the Poetry of the Ancient Welsh Bards*. In two of these, Taliesin addresses Elphin 'to comfort him upon his ill-success at the Wear':

'Fair Elphin, cease to weep, let no man be discontented with his fortune...There never was in Gwyddno's wear such good luck as tonight. Fair Elphin, wipe the tears from thy face!... Though I am but little, I am endowed with great gifts.... Though I am but small and slender on the beach of the foaming main, I shall do thee more good in the day of distress than three hundred salmon.[12]

So begins a string of boastful claims made by Taliesin, including:. *'I have been a blue salmon.'*[13] Like the accretion of tree rings around its heartwood, Taliesin seems to identify completely with each event and thing that he encounters. Through this power of empathy he literally becomes the 'other'. While his assertive tone implies that this power is unique to him, it also hints at the same innate capacity, lying unused in others, such as Elphin or humanity in general.

Taliesin's language of interconnections comes straight from the nature goddesses. For example, 'the surf', Welsh *y don*, which washes him ashore, can be the body and voice of Don, whose 'pudenda', Welsh *gwarthle*, protects every 'beach', Welsh *gwarth*, in Wales. A divine superhuman anatomy operates around the entire country, while an alternative term for 'surf', *ewyn,* also brings 'whiteness, purity'.

Fish Weirs

Top left: *Catching the Gwion-Taliesin 'double creature'. Bronze plaque from Tal y llyn, 'Head of the lake', Merioneth, circa 200 BC.*

Centre left: *A salmon weir at Awre, Severn estuary, 1964.*

Bottom left: *A coastal gored or fish trap, Aberarth, Cardiganshire, 1924.*

Right: *Boy with his salmon catch, at Llangynog, Montgomeryshire, 1954.*

'I have been a blue salmon', Book of Taliesin, *vii, 221.*

'And no one knows what my flesh is, whether meat or fish' *(Ford 1977 p173).*

Likewise, Welsh *traeth*, 'beach', is also a 'spoken declaration, or account', heard in the language of breaking waves. Taliesin arrives to voice this unity, saying:

'I have been a wave on the extended shore.[14]

Welsh dictionaries confirm this sense of total unity with Nature, orally transmitted from antiquity and spoken afresh by Taliesin. The rich connotations of Welsh words reflect this pagan legacy. And because common speech is enlivened and amplified by Taliesin, people continue to love and identify with him.

When Gwion Bach emerges reborn as Taliesin from 'the bag of a net', Welsh *llawes*, he is simultaneously delivered from the sea goddess' 'vulva', Welsh *llawes*. Whether envisaged as Gwener-Venus, Don, Ceridwen, or as the fishy-tailed mermaid Muirgen who is said to swim in Cardigan Bay, the poetic truth thereby expressed makes ecological sense. By contrast, the analytical urge to dissect such composite images is at odds with Taliesin's wisdom and risks cutting his cohesive understanding into lifeless categorical bits.

The 'shore', Welsh *glan*, where Taliesin is born as a poet, by the same *glan* word's definition is 'clean, good, virtuous, honest, beautiful, and handsome'. This is because a nation that lives by his vision regards the collaboration of sea and land as a fundamental need. Similarly, the light on his brow is understood to usher in the summer sun's fire, necessary for the splendour of seasonal renewal.

Throughout the ages, mystics from many traditions have plummeted into different versions of 'Cantre'r Gwaelod', and come up with harmony. For example, the philosopher William James writes of 'a manyness-in-oneness… Our consciousness arises out of the whole earth-consciousness, which we forget to thank…Our full self is the whole field, with all those indefinitely radiating subconscious possibilities of increase that we can only feel without conceiving and can hardly begin to analyse.'[15]

Pulled from the fish weir, Taliesin invites Elphin (and us) to that synthesis, where thing, thought and feeling, matured in one bag, can emerge, survive, and grow together, on exposure to the light of day.

Cored and salmon

Until twentieth century industrialised fishing depleted the stocks, the waters around the British Isles teamed with fish. Along the Welsh coasts numerous *goredau*, 'fish weirs' were constructed to catch the passing shoals. Such trapping is one of the oldest known methods of fishing. Mesolithic pebbles, engraved circa 10,000 BC with fish trap designs have been found at Rhuddlan, North Wales.[16] Similar cone-shaped baskets of plaited withy, set up in tiers at right angles to the shore were still in use along the Severn estuary fifty years ago.

On the boulder-strewn west coast of Wales it was the custom to pile up two banks, running seawards like a pair of giant lobster claws from the beach, enclosing a stretch of tide water, oval in plan. Its narrow seaward entry was spanned by a

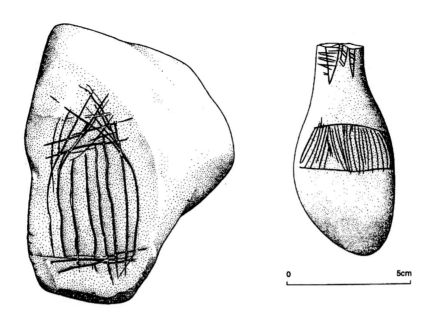

Left: *Incised pebble from Afon Clwyd at Rhuddlan, Denbighshire; Mesolithic, 10,000 BC. The design is presumed to represent a fish trap.*

Right: *Womb of the sea goddess as source of fish.*

bridging stone, from which a wattle gate could be lowered as the tide ebbed, so trapping salmon, whiting and grey mullet. In 1864, Cardiganshire, the county of Gwyddno's weir, had a douzen *coredau* in working order, but by 1924 of these only two had survived and they have now disappeared.[17] As with Gwyddno and Elphin, nineteenth century *gored* ownership passed from father to son, and there was a strong conviction in Cardiganshire that the technique had been inherited from the 'Ancient Britons'.

Sarn Cynfelyn would have made an obvious (perhaps god-given?) ridge to use, as one arm of a *cored* (Welsh *gored*, 'dam'). At low water, more than a hundred yards of its fifty-yard width is exposed, and lies under Gwyddno's eye in his adjacent '*Caer*'. Where the *sarn* joins the mainland at Gwallog, Elphin had the means and the temporary authority to fish. To his surprise, he caught a Welsh *cor*, 'dwarf, pigmy, little urchin'. From the future poet Taliesin's perspective, such half-hidden wordplay is more than coincidental.

That Gwyddno's weir had supernatural quality is suggested by the medieval Welsh list of the *Thirteen Treasures of the Isle of Britain*. They include the *mwys* or 'hamper' of Gwyddno Longshank. 'If food for one man would be put in it, when opened, food for a hundred men would be found in it.' Of the same *mwys*, the *Culhwch and Olwen* text states: 'If the whole world should come around it, thrice nine men at a time, the meat that everyone wished for he would find therein to his liking.'[18]

Made of withes, like many fish traps, *mwys* means 'some kind of fishing basket' or 'a measure of three score herrings'. The word derives from Latin *mensa*, 'a table for sacred vessels and offerings to the gods'. If it is admissible to think of Gwyddno's fish-weir as his *mwys*, then Gwion's transformation takes place inside one of the magic '*Treasures of Britain*'. It thereby captures some of Taliesin's character, since *mwys* is also 'ambiguous, clever, skilful, melodious and eloquent'. So each new Taliesin emerges from the basket of old enchantment.

For him to have been found in a salmon weir was no disgrace. On the contrary, the salmon was regarded with awe on both sides of the Irish Sea. The demi-god Finn acquired his uncanny knowledge from that fish. In the *Culhwch* story the salmon knows more than the 'oldest creature in the world', the eagle, and carries the hero up the Severn to rescue the demi-god Mabon, son of the goddess Modron, from imprisonment.[19] (Mabon has that, and much else, in common with Taliesin.)

The salmon owes its mythic importance partly to the fact that, like Gwion Bach, its life cycle runs from salt to sweet water, and from the deep ocean to estuaries and the upper reaches of rivers.

Salmon migrate from sea to river in early summer, in order to spawn. Therefore, since *Calan Mai* marked the start of summer in Wales, the supernatural 'first fruits ' of the annual salmon harvest were notionally attached to that date. If roasted over the specially charged May Eve 'need-fire', the fish could pass divine secrets to those who ate its flesh. Taliesin's shining brow *was* that golden fire, combined with the lunar silver of an entire May Eve salmon haul.

Taliesin's changes

From the fish weir at Sarn Cynfelyn Taliesin did not need to look back, because his previous experiences were integrated within his current understanding. Yet when, according to Guest's source, Gwyddno (perhaps in a scribal error for 'Elphin'), asks the strange boy '*what he was, whether man or spirit*', Taliesin replies by alluding to his 'imprisonment':

> '*First, I have been formed a comely person,*
> *In the court of Ceridwen I have done penance.*'[20]

An obscure couplet then refers either to Ceridwen's stomach, or his bag, or to the depths of Annwn; or perhaps to all three. He has been drawn into the *Annwn*, the Otherworld, by Ceridwen, his muse of poetic inspiration:

> '*Though little I was seen, placidly received,*
> *I was great on the floor of the place to where I was led.*
> *I have been a prized defence, the sweet muse the cause.*'[21]

It was Ceridwen who, having captured him, eventually grants his release:

> '*And by law, without speech, I have been liberated*
> *By a smiling, black old hag. When irritated*
> *Dreadful her claim when pursued*'[22]

Taliesin then recalls the guises in which he attempted to escape her clutches:

> *'I have fled with vigour, I have fled as a frog*
> *... a crow, scarcely finding rest;*
> *... I have fled as a chain.*
> *I have fled as a roe into an entangled thicket;*
> *... as a wolf cub as a wolf in a wilderness;*
> *I have fled as a thrush of portending language;*
> *... as a fox;... as a martin, which did not avail;*
> *... as a squirrel, that vainly hides, as a stag's antler of ruddy course.*[23]

With the reluctance of a non-martial spirit, in desperation he turns himself into iron, the metal most likely to scare himself and his pre-Iron Age adversary; but the spear proves useless against her.

> *I have fled as an iron in a glowing fire;*
> *I have fled as a spear-head, of woe to such as has a wish for it*[24]

He then adopts Nature's horns and tusks:

> *'I have fled as a fierce bull bitterly fighting,*
> *I have fled as a bristly boar seen in a ravine*[25]

Finally, he becomes the kernel of *Cantre'r Gwaelod's* drowned Neolithic agriculture achievement.

> *'I have fled as a white grain of pure wheat...*
> *A hen received me,*
> *With ruddy claws,*[and] *parting comb.*
> I rested nine nights.
> *In her womb a child,*
> *I have been matured,*
> *I have been an offering...*[26]
>
> *I have been dead, I have been alive.*[27]

His understanding is founded on more than objective scrutiny. Rather, he *is* what he describes. He inhabits Nature so intimately that the subject-object gap vanishes, even in the abyss:

> *'I know what base there is beneath the sea.'*[28]

He has plummeted to the bottom of himself and of the world.

Taliesin and Gwyddo Garanhir

From that submarine rift arose Gwyddno's 'castle',[29] as a primary bank of solid matter in shallow water, ready to surface above the waves. Even when Gwyddno's *caer* was submerged, Taliesin surely recognised that king's important role in the poetics of creation. Indeed, *Cantre'r Gwaelod* is often named *Maes Gwyddno*, 'Field

of Gwyddno',[30] for the king was submergence *and* emergence personified. Therefore his name includes Welsh *gwydd,* 'poetry', which is the art of effectively harnessing opposites.

Both Elphin and Taliesin are inescapably connected to Gwyddno Garanhir's 'long legs' (Welsh *garan hir)* by mythic events. It was the same king whose horses were poisoned when Ceridwen's cauldron split apart at Llyn Tegid, after Gwion had stolen the magic drops. Six months later, at *Maes Gwyddno,* 'Gwion-Taliesin' encounters Gwyddno again.

This suggests that the king's steeds should be linked to a solar chariot. Their power is weakened in winter, causing them and the sun they pull, to lie low, often beneath the horizons of lake and sea. By May Eve, however, steered by Gwyddno, they are ready to gallop forth again, cured of the poison's debilitating effect. So, from his submarine *Caer,* the King conveys 'summer half' sunlight to shine on Taliesin's brow, and then lends the horse on which he and Elphin ride away.

An equally potent symbol of winter's end, recognised across Europe, is the arrival of migrating cranes. Here again, Seithennin and Gwyddno collaborate, with King Garanhir offering shelter inside his second name to Welsh *garan,* the 'crane', or 'heron'. Since cranes and horses frequently feature together in Celtic art, their joint presence within Gwyddno can be described as orthodox.[31]

In Wales great importance is ascribed to the crane's long-shanked near relative, the heron. To this day, the owners of some Welsh heronries truly believe that their family will die out if their nests are ever deserted.[32] Reverence for the bird leads us straight back to the magic 'Crane Bag' of Irish Sea myth, which, according to Graves, contained the runic alphabet of the god Ogma Sun-face.[33]

When the sea was in flood, poets could make sense of these otherwise incomprehensible symbols. Therefore Welsh *gwydd,* 'poetry, knowledge', and the *garan*-bag, combine in Gwyddno Garanhir's full name. Taliesin's landing place, one

Opposite : *Gwyddno Garanhir, with horse and crane*

Gwyddno's garan, *Welsh 'long leg', matches both horse and crane.*

top row, left to right: *Submarine horse, re-emerging as solar steed, with swastica, crane and goose; Greek vase images from Heraeum, Corinth, seventh century BC; A solar horse on a gold coin of the British Iceni tribe; first century AD.*

centre: *Gold-bronze horse figurine, engraved with solar discs, from Roman Silchester, AD 100.*

bottom: *'Gwyddno' and his horses, seen rising from the sea; Glamorgan County Hall, Cardiff; 1910*

may infer, was selected so that he could benefit from that poet-king's proximity and influence. In fact, Taliesin himself identifies with the crane when claiming:

'I have been a crane well filled, a sight to behold.'[34]

Cynfelyn and Cymbeline

Like an umbilical cord in its amniotic sea, Sarn Cynfelin snakes seven miles from Caer Gwyddno to the shore at Gwallog. The personal name Cynfelyn, scholars agree, is a Welsh derivative of Cymbeline; and Cymbeline's original name was Cunobelinus. From AD 10 to 40 he ruled the Catuvellauni and Trinovantes tribes who occupied modern Hertfordshire and Essex. His silver money is stamped *Rex Britannorum*, 'King of the Britons'.[35]

Three years after his death, the Roman invasion and conquest of Britain began. To the Welsh, Cymbeline therefore represented the last pre-imperial British monarch, and became an ancestor around whom dreams of island-wide freedom could be woven. As a remnant of the pre-Roman population, driven from Eastern Britain and its coasts by the Anglo-Saxons, the Welsh honoured Cunobelinus-Cymbeline under the name Cynfelyn.

But having lost their eastern coast, where the sun always rises, they were obliged to commemorate him on Britain's west or sunset side. By naming the drowned Sarn Cynfelyn after him, they marked both his loss and hope of recovery, since all westerly off-shore 'islands', such as *Caer Gwyddno* were regarded as Otherworlds of the Immortals. By pointing in that direction, Sarn Cynfelyn becomes the perpetually extended (though rarely seen) phallus of a truly British (Welsh) kingship. At the fish-weir, set on its root, the Welsh druids could stage the symbolic recovery of a regal, island-wide, 'summer half' dawn, incorporating Cymbeline and Gwyddno's combined essences, reincarnated as Taliesin.

During his reign it is estimated that Cunobelinus had struck one million gold staters. They display a solar horse, often shown leaping a 'sun wheel', and an ear of corn on the obverse side.[36] Memories of this archetypal design were used by the Welsh legend-coiners, when they minted the Gwyddno-Taliesin story. In this way, they spun summer's energy from pre-Roman times onto the emergent Gwion Bach's head.

As a result, 'Gwion Transfigured' became Taliesin, who would show an uncanny knowledge of horses, and receive poetry's annual equivalent of the British 'crown'. Moreover, he claims capital connections:

'I have been on the White Hill, in the Court of Cynfelyn.'[37] This 'White Hill' is generally recognised to be Tower Hill, London, with London standing in for Cunobelinus' former stronghold at nearby Camulodunum.

To complete the annual cycle, and to form a bridge between religions, the Welsh also honoured a *Saint* Cynfelin. His festival was held on November 1st, the start of the Celtic year and of its 'winter half'.[38] A chapel dedicated to him stood on the cliffs a mile south of Sarn Cynfelyn.[39] So myth remoulds various histories into one resilient alloy, which remains acceptable (if not legal) tender, for ages.

Taliesin and Gwallawg

When Gwion Bach is pulled from the fish weir at Gwallog and re-named Taliesin, he is acclaimed as Welsh *iesin*, 'fine, fair, beautiful, handsome, radiant, sparkling, shimmering, bright and gleaming'. But there is a human price to pay, in the form of Welsh *tal*, 'fee, tax', on his new *tal*, 'forehead', as the double meaning of the word implies. At Gwallog, where *sarn* and mainland meet, the man who bears the cost is the heroic Gwallawg, after whom that tiny hamlet is named. His one-eyed ghost wanders between its shoreline farm, an abandoned lime kiln, and a large Victorian house.

Gwallawg was a sixth century Welsh warrior. From his little kingdom of Elmet (now part of West Yorkshire) he fought with conspicuous gallantry against the English. He was the perfect Welsh hero, and is described in the *Triads* as 'One of the Three Pillars of Battle' of the Island of Britain', with Cynfelyn is listed as another.[40] Elsewhere Gwallawg is called a 'son of a privileged dynasty, the affliction of England'.[41] Poets assert that 'They cannot reckon the battles fought by Gwallawg. He sees not a hero who saw not him.'[42]

Gwallawg's memory was kept alive for many centuries after his death and carried south by Welsh migrants from Northern Britain to Cardigan Bay. There, says the *Book of Taliesin*, a goose plucked out one of his eyes. The hero sacrificed half his sight in order to equip Taliesin with earthly courage.

At the Gwallog salmon weir, Gwallawg therefore became Welsh *gwallog*, 'faulty, defective'. The poem rages: 'May the 'goose' [Welsh *gwydd*], be cursed which pulled out his [Gwallawg's] eye from his face.'[43] It goes on to curse black, white and grey geese for doing likewise. However, the anonymous speaker, probably Taliesin, also believes that 'because the one-eyed man is so generous... I myself will be wealthy.'[44]

One effect of this sacrifice is to re-unite the two versions of Taliesin. The mortal sixth century bard of that name, who composed praise poems for several North British martial princes, is resurrected on the *Calan Mai* beach through the gift of Gwallawg's eye. 'Reset' into the head of the supernatural Taliesin, it enables him to understand the violent Welsh court to which he is heading, by reminding him of the equally turbulent royal households known to Gwallawg. Thanks to him, Taliesin is endowed with worldly valour and cunning, essential for his survival among Welsh kings.

As for the goose, whatever its colour, it may have flown in from *Caer Gwyddno*, less than seven miles away. There, Gwyddno's name encloses a goose sanctuary, since Welsh *gwydd*, means 'knowledge' *and* 'goose'. In medieval Wales the goose was regarded as a sacred bird.[45] By its divine agency, an eye transplant could be performed between the human donor, Gwallawg, and the demi-god recipient, Taliesin, so completing a charitable exchange between worlds.

Calan Mai, May Day

On 1st May 2002, the following flowers, yellow and gold, were in bloom on the Gwallog cliffs: primrose, gorse, aconite, dandelion, and the yellow-centered daisy. While delighting in these, Taliesin, being famished, plucked a big handful of fat hen leaves, growing on Gwallog's storm beach. As he chewed this 'poor man's spinach', a short-tailed black hen clucked in his head. 'Be quiet. It's my turn now', he said aloud, between mouthfuls.

From Gwallog, Taliesin rode with Elphin under arching hawthorn trees and between banks of bluebells and drifts of star-white wood garlic, which in that month fringe the track leading inland. Soon they came within earshot of May Day celebrations and saw a group of young people gathered around the silver trunk of a birch tree, about to bud into new leaf.[46]

The prettiest girl had been chosen as 'Queen of the May' and was crowned with a hollow ceramic ring, on which the potter had raised three small beakers. These were filled with malt liquor called *bragawd*. Between the cups and a phallic-looking pottery handle were set several lighted candles. Young men were taking it in turns to drink from the cups, while trying to avoid both burning their hair and spilling hot wax onto the girl's head; hence the hilarity.[47]

Similar 'crowns' have been excavated from Romano-British sites,[48] while a surviving example from Rhyl, Denbighshire, was still in use in the nineteenth century. Regarding this ceremony, Taliesin's pleasure was mixed with the realisation that his own newly acquired 'golden head', like the sun, had to be shared with, the female line, as the Mabinogion's *Dream of Macsen Wledig* confirms. In that tale, Elen, later to become Empress of Rome, is described sitting on a chair of red gold at Caernarvon:

'No more than it would be easy to look on the sun when it is brightest, no easier would it be than to look on her, by reason of her excelling beauty,'[49] the storyteller relates. This was the Elen who was credited with building all the old roads that criss-cross Wales, along which Taliesin travelled. Similarly, one maiden, chosen annually by each of a thousand meagre settlements, scattered across the country, reflected Elen's sun-derived gilding. Queen for a day, these girls acted as a royal intermediary between parish and pagan deities. They were Taliesin's female counterparts.

Opposite: *Gwallog and Gwallawg*

top: *Taliesin rides with Elphin up this Gwallog lane each May Day, exchanging black bag for green bliss.*

left: *Gold coins of King Cunobelinus [alias Cymbeline or Cynfelyn], AD 10–40, with sun horse and barley.*

bottom right: *Sarn Cynfelin meets the shore at the hamlet of Gwallog, named after the legendary hero, Gwallawg.*

Top left: *Winged figure with raised firebrand, accompanying the head of 'Summer'; Seasons mosaic, Caerwent.*

Top right: *Pottery crown, from Rhyl, Denbighshire, worn by the May Queen. Similar vessels have been found on Roman sites, such as Wilderspool, Lancs.*

Above: *Flower-crowned Calan Mai Queen, Pwllheli, Caernarvon,1930.*

Every house and cow shed that he and Elphin passed had crosses of mountain ash pinned to the door as a 'Keep Out' sign addressed to the *Gwrach*.[50] People were determined to stop her leaping from winter into summer's domain. Yet some poets remembered to thank that hag's cauldron, a symbol of the underworld, for making Summer possible:

> You're the cauldron, wondrous tale,
> Of *Annwn*, life's renewal
> You are the source of singing
> The home of each sprouting shoot,
> Balm of growth, burgeoning throng,
> And chrism of crossed branches.
> 'My fate it is, mighty feat,'
> Sang the sunshine
> 'To come three months to nourish
> Foodstuff for the multitude.' [51]

On Mayday, throughout the country, harper and fiddler ascended the *twmpath* or 'play mound',[52] to start the first of the summer season's open-air dances. The pudding-shaped *twmpath* was often, as at Llangower, located within a churchyard and symbolised the pregnant swelling of *Mam Daear*, 'Mother Earth'. By her Welsh *chwys yr haul*, 'sweat of the sun', or 'sun dew', she would deliver her harvest child three months later, having already produced her *Croesor Gwanwy*, 'Welcome to Spring', alias the 'daffodil', Cymru's national yellow-gold floral emblem.

In Wales, as in most of Europe, May Day rites are an international amalgam of elements grafted onto a common celebratory impulse. For instance, the *Cangen Haf* Fool and his accompanying musicians, who led the *Calan Mai* antics and parades in Wales, have English affinities.[53] Yet the blackened faces of these participants, merging with those of the chimney sweeps, who played an important part in England's May Day events,[54] also matched the cormorant Afagddu's dive to *Annwn*, from where, though still sooty from the journey, they brought back the sun.

Considering his own dark voyage in a bag, Taliesin had no difficulty in identifying with these musicians, especially since on May Day, they carried Venus-Gwener's pubic triangle, in the form of a Y-shaped branch, tightly covered with a white sheet, and hung with silver trinkets.[55]

Taliesin and Elphin tagged on to the tail of a *Cangen Haf* or 'Summer Branch' procession, as it wound from farm to farm, thereby combining Welsh *cerdd*, 'a walk', with *cerdd*, 'minstrelsy', an itinerant art, formerly common throughout Wales. 'To walk', *cerdded*, as a homeless 'vagrant', *cerddaf*, was recognised as a likely way to arrive at *cerdd*, 'song, poem'. Taliesin could pick up his craft on the road, thanks to folk ritual.

Taliesin believed that folk ceremonies encapsulated the universal mystery of being. After taking one sip from a May Queen's cup, he exclaimed: 'All art is mythological', because it restores unity to the divided consciousness, by re-uniting everything in the

Absolute; not by proliferating images of reality, but by rendering a 'primary image' of the Absolute.'[56] He was quoting from Schelling. 'Absolutely!' replied Elphin with a sardonic laugh, and jumped back onto the horse, since talk of 'Absolutes' sounded like fanaticism to him.

Sensing his companion's unease, Taliesin went on: 'Our folk rites celebrate an elusive truth that undermines all sectarian divisions. Such folk play is a whole-hearted surrender to Fate, personified in whatever costumes come to hand. At root, farmers everywhere mime the same drama, yet evade dogma while remaining true to the core of general experience. And like me, these people are content with their mongrelish 'lack of breeding'. That is why *I* have lasted so long. Gods come and go. As a born scavenger I feed on them all, and so help to keep the people's broadminded show on the road.'

Elphin said nothing, but he shot his 'catch' a disdainful glance and thought: 'No salmon, no pedigree.'

Taliesin, divine hybrid

'Who am I? Will someone please tell me?' At times Taliesin asked himself these rhetorical questions. He knew the answers, or thought he did, but as a composite figure, he was not sure that he had traced all the ingredients. When listing them, he often began with Maponos.

'*Maponos*, 'Divine Youth' and part of me!' he cried, while flicking through his catalogue of mental images. 'As Maponos-Apollo, a young sun god, I was introduced into North Britain from Roman Gaul. By that double-barrelled name I became popular around the Solway Firth, and occur in at least five inscriptions up there. Four of these equate me with Apollo.'[57] Glowing with animation, he shouted:

'I am the head carved on the whetstone found beneath Lochar Moss, near Annan, close to that great boulder, the *Clochmabenstane,* which is named after me. As Maponos-Apollo my skills are in poetry and music. At Ribchester, in Lancashire, I, that is *we* -Apollo, the Greek sun god and Maponos, are carved side by side.[58] I mention this to remind myself that although very *fond* of Wales, I am not parochially confined to its territory. It would be more accurate to think of me as a near-universal deity, with many Classical connections, including of course those that survive within Wales.'

'Such as?' It was Elphin's voice. He was willing to play the Socratic stooge, in order to encourage Super-boy's flow. 'Such as the terracotta roof tile *antefix*, depicting me, grinning like a 'Gorgon', with a sun ray hair style and sun wheel, found at the Caerleon fort. There, as an indigenous solar deity, I was expected to protect an entire Roman legion'! 'And don't forget, with each sunset I had to endure a ducking in the sea. No wonder I smiled to be on the eaves by day.'[59]

'Of course, I never really split from Mabon.' Taliesin was rambling. 'Part of me *is* him; and *he* is the youth in the *Culhwch* story who is imprisoned under the tidal

Taliesin as Maponos

Left: *Maponos as a radiant 'North British' god; AD 100; found in Armagh.*

Centre: *'Mabon's head', as the Clachmabenstane, 2.2 metres high; Solway Firth, Dumfries-shire.*

Right: *Mabon's church at Llanfabon, Glamorgan.*

Severn at Gloucester. By the same ebb and flow, it is partly me, as Mabon-Maponos, who underlies the *Mabinogion's* title.'[60]

The horse's hooves padded quietly on the turf. Occasionally the riders passed a large fire, of which Taliesin said: 'The return of my dazzling head is acknowledged through such bonfires, lit on the May Eve 'spirit night' by each community.' As you surely know, these *coel certhau,* literally 'right belief or omen fires' contain sticks of nine different trees, placed crosswise. After the 'first flame' has been kindled, by rubbing two bits of oak together, round oatmeal cakes are cooked, quartered and put into a flour bag. Those who pull out a brown segment have then to jump the flames and run three times between two fires, thereby ensuring a good harvest. See! There they go! These fires are my summer eyes', Taliesin said. The smoke made them water.[61]

'Oh yes?' replied Elphin; 'but what of your claim that as 'Gwion' you are another Bacchus? How does that fit with your sun-god pretensions?' 'My dear Prince' replied Taliesin, excitedly, 'Macrobius stated in AD 400 that Apollo and Bacchus-alias-Liber, who, like the sun and I, have the 'freedom', Latin *liber,* to roam, are one and the same god. That is why I share their shrines at Delphi and Parnassus. Hence the Greek Bacchus, known as Dionysus, also has a speedy solar name, derived from the

Top: *Sheet gold eyes, 6cm across; from Romano-British Wroxeter, Shropshire (formerly in Powys).*

Above: *The 'Summer Half' sun comes to Wales at Hafod y llyn, Llenfair, Merioneth, where the Blessed Virgin Mary bathed with her maidens.*

Greek word for 'whirling, circling.' Furthermore, just as my main Gwion-Bacchus journey occurs in the dark, so Macrobius allocates the night-time solar arc to Bacchus-Dionysus and the day-time arc to Apollo, while recognising their essential one-ness.'[62]

Taliesin was now galloping: 'As regards my demi-god status, which I need to preserve in order to retain a humanoid aspect, I remind you of the importance of Mithraism in late Roman Britain. For example there is a notable Mithraic temple in Segontium-Caernarfon,[63] and I often feel Mithras' warmth within me. He is one of the divine mediators between the supreme god Sol and humanity,[64] and I am another. I have undertaken to perform that role for as long as the sun circles the earth.'

'In pre-Copernican terms, I suppose you mean', said Elphin, a remark that made Taliesin frown.

On their left they were passing the golden sand dunes of Mochras. To the right rose the cloud-topped Rhinog Mountains. '*Through the language of Taliesin It was a bright day*' sang Elphin. 'Who taught you those words?' asked Taliesin, taken aback, for they were from one of his own poems.

'Oh, I must have remembered you muttering them during the many times that I've carried you this way before' replied the prince, casually.

Elphin's wife

Lulled by the horse's rhythm, the companions then fell into a deep silence. It was broken miles later, when the thought broke over Elphin that he had no fish. He burst into unmanly sobs. Then, as Llewelyn Sion relates, '*Taliesin made a song of praise to cheer Elffin and to prophecy dignity for him, which is called* Elffin's Consolation, *and he began like this in the englyn metre:*

> '*Fair Elffin stop your weeping!*
> *Let no one revile what is his;*
> *Despair brings no profit;*
> *Man sees not what nourishes him;*
> *The prayer of Cynllo is not in vain;*
> *God breaks not what he promises;*
> *No catch in Gwyddno's weir*
> *Has ever been as good as tonight.*
> *Elffin of pleasant qualities...*
> *On the appointed day, I shall make*
> *You riches better than three hundred!...*
> *Grieve not for your catch;*
> *Though I am weak in my leather pouch*
> *There are wonders on my tongue...*
> *By remembering the name of the Trinity*
> *No-one can overcome you.*' [65]

Sion concludes: '*Taliesin sang it.*' [66]

Elphin stopped snuffling. 'Which Trinity', he asked himself? 'Is my passenger referring to the Triple Mothers, celebrated on the mountain *Moel Fammau* in Clwyd, who are known in Britain from dozens of Latin inscriptions as the *Deae Matres*, or 'Mother Goddesses'?[67] And who is this un-named god with a capital G? Could it be the deity favoured by the Emperor Constantine, and rumoured to replace all other divinities known to humanity? If so, why is the broad-minded Taliesin invoking such an intolerant deity? Does my friend think he can absorb that jealous god into his own polytheism? That would be unlikely to work. I must warn him of the danger.' But he did not.

Instead Elphin confined himself to thanking Taliesin for mentioning Cynllo, 'Wolf-calf', an obscure Cardiganshire culture hero, descended from the founder of that territory and later canonised. He was invoked for rich harvests. The word *cynllo* means 'pregnant cow, prior to calving at *Gwyl Awst'* and St Cynllo's feast is held on August 8th.[68] Thus holy man, word, and event form a united trilogy.

As the two riders approached the coastal parish of Llanfair, they prepared themselves to meet the most far-fetched arrival from abroad, namely Mary, the mother of Christ. Legend says that she landed here with her maidens. She then walked two miles inland, past the spot where a church would later be named after her, to a small, exquisitely beautiful lake, *Hafod y Llyn,* where she and her maidens bathed, which caused splendid water lilies to float on that water to this day.[69]

So the Welsh landscape acquires its sanctity by an incorrigible process of addition, and in this task no one has worked with less embarrassment than Taliesin. But even a demi-god needs rest, and he was relieved at last to arrive at the house of Elphin's wife.

'*Elphin turned over his 'catch'*[namely Taliesin] *to his wife'*, writes Elis Gruffydd, and '*She raised him lovingly and dearly.'* [70] '*She nursed him tenderly and lovingly'* is Guest's translation, which continues: '*Thenceforward Elphin increased in riches more and more, day after day, and in love and favour with the king* [Gwyddno], *and there abode Taliesin until he was thirteen years old…* [71]

CHAPTER SEVEN

KING MAELGWN

Elphin and Maelgwn

When Taliesin was thirteen years old, *'Elphin son of Gwyddno went on a Christmas invitation to his uncle, Maelgwn Gwynedd, who... held open court at Christmas-tide in the castle of Deganwy, for all the number of his lords of both degrees, both spiritual and temporal, with a vast and thronged host of knights and squires. And among them there arose a discourse and a discussion. And thus it was said:*

'Is there any in the whole world so great as Maelgwn, or one on whom Heaven has bestowed so many spiritual gifts as upon him?' [1]

After lavishing praise on the King's form, beauty, meekness, strength, and the quality of his soul, the courtiers asked: *'Who had more skilful or wiser bards than Maelgwn?'* Then they turned to shower compliments on his Queen, proclaiming that her *'comliness, grace, wisdom and modesty... surpassed those of all the ladies and noble maidens throughout the whole kingdom.'*

Then Elphin spoke: *'Of a truth, none but a king may vie with a king; but were he not a king, I would say that my wife was as virtuous as any lady in the kingdom, and also that I have a bard who is more skilful than all the King's bards.'* [2]

In making these counterclaims, Elphin's dislike of court flattery was coupled with the self-confidence of a prince, whose father, Gwyddno Garanhir, ruled in realms, both marine and solar, superior to any ordinary kingdom such as Maelgwn's. Moreover, Elphin had kept Taliesin as a long-term guest and was aware that *his* extraordinary bardic powers probably surpassed those of Maelgwn's bards. The story continues:

> *'In a short space some of his fellows showed the king all the boastings of Elphin: and the king ordered him to be thrown into a strong prison, until he might know the truth of the virtues of his [Elphin's] wife, and the wisdom of his bard.'* [3]

King Maelgwn's Deganwy Castle was sited on two steep hillocks, overlooking Conwy Bay in Carnarvonshire. The deep quarry, cut into the west summit and marked 'Dungeon' on some maps, is popularly believed to have been Elphin's *'secure prison'*, stipulated by Gruffydd.

Top: *Deganwy, Carnarvonshire, site of Maelgwn's sixth century castle. His kingdom, Gwynedd, was the strongest in Wales. He lived on her breast.*

Top right and above left: *Two aspects of a thirteenth century king's sculpted head, found at Deganwy.*

Above: *The west or 'dungeon' summit of Deganwy, with an 'Elphin in chains' carving from Llanrhidian, Gower.*

> 'Now when Elphin had been put in a tower of the castle [according to Guest], *with a thick chain about his feet* [it was said that it was a silver chain, because he was of royal blood], *the king, as the story relates, sent his son Rhun to enquire into the demeanour of Elphin's wife. Now Rhun was the most graceless man in the world, and there was neither wife nor maiden with whom he held converse, but was evil spoken of'* [4] for he was *'one of the lustiest men in the world.'* [5] He would ruin any woman's reputation.

> 'While Rhun went in haste towards Elphin's dwelling, being fully minded to bring disgrace upon his wife, Taliesin told his mistress how that the king had placed his master in prison, and how that Rhun was coming in haste to strive to bring disgrace upon her. Wherefore he caused his mistress to array one of the maids of her kitchen in her

apparel; which the noble lady gladly did; and she loaded the maid's hands with the best rings that she and her husband possessed.' [6]

Finger and ring

'In this guise Taliesin caused his mistress to put the maiden to sit at the board in her room at supper, and he made her to seem as her mistress... ' (and vice-versa). When *'Rhun suddenly arrived... [and was invited to supper with the disguised maid] he... began jesting with the maid, who still kept the semblance of her mistress.'* During the meal *'the maiden became so intoxicated that she fell asleep. It was a powder that Rhun put into her drink that made her sleep so soundly, that she never felt it when he cut from off her hand her little finger, whereupon was the signet ring of Elphin, which he had sent to his wife as a token, a short time before.'* [7]

Rhun then returned to the king with the ring on the severed finger as proof that he had seduced Elphin's wife. *'The king rejoiced greatly at these tidings... and caused Elphin to be brought out of his prison.'* After telling the prince that *'it is but folly for a man to trust in the virtues of his wife further than he can see her,'* he added *'thou mayest be certain of thy wife's vileness, behold her finger with thy signet ring upon it... '* [8]

This story echoes another, in which Maelgwn tells his own wife, the queen, to accompany him on a cliff-top walk, during which her wedding ring accidentally drops from her finger into the sea. On noticing the ring's absence, the monarch accuses her of infidelity. However, thanks to the prayers of St Asaph, a fish is caught, in whose belly the missing ring is found. [9]

The tale also overlaps with Gwion's sea-dunking, where he traces the submarine half of the sun's circular course, enabling him, on landing, to complete the round golden outline of his Taliesin face.

For Elphin's uncanny wife, the sacred wedding ring that bound two willing people together in love, was now grimly parodied by the prison chains that her husband bore. When Rhun displayed the ring at court, Elphin accepted that it was his, but denied that the severed finger was from his wife's hand. It was far too fat, the fingernail *'had not been pared for a month'*, and was encrusted with traces of rye bread from dough kneading, a task that his wife never performed. [10]

Annoyed by this irrefutable evidence, the king returned Elphin to prison, until such time as his boast concerning Taliesin was either demolished or shown to be true. Hearing of this, Taliesin felt obliged to go to Maelgwn's Court to free his master, just as Elphin had once freed him.

'A journey will I perform, and to the gate I will come;
The hall I will enter, and my song I will sing;
My speech I will pronounce to silence royal bards.

> *In the presence of their chief, I will greet to deride,*
> *Upon them I will break and Elphin I will free. ...*
> *'I Taliesin, chief of bards, with a sapient Druid's words'*
> *Will set kind Elphin free from haughty tyrant's bonds.'* [11]

After directing a long-distance curse at Rhun and Maelgwn, Taliesin travelled towards Deganwy, set at the base of the Creuthyn or Great Orme peninsula. Yet the nearer he approached, the less enthusiasm he felt for his mission. Having suffered so much to become a supernatural entity, human Court life held little appeal for him.

Further, Maelgwn's reputation, as disseminated by his sixth century contemporary Gildas, was dire. Gildas vilified the king as 'the first in mischief, exceeding many in power and also in malice; licentious in sinning [and] drenched in the wine of Sodom.' Gildas writes that after reneging on a brief Christian conversion, Maelgwn had 'returned like a sick dog to his vomit, revelling in the song of his own praises, spat out by his crew of Bacchanalian revellers, full of lies and foaming phlegm.' Maelgwn was also rumoured to have murdered both his wife and his nephew, whose wife he had then married.[12]

Though alarmed by these reports, Taliesin made due allowance for clerical exaggeration and, as a 'Bacchus' figure himself, was cheered by the prospect of good wine. Recent archaeological finds of amphorae sherds of Mediterranean type at Deganwy provide a solid basis for his hope.[13]

Equally appealing were this ruler's well-known delight in poetry and his generous patronage of bards, for which, apart from King Arthur, no legendary Welsh monarch has earned more renown. Yet for Taliesin this largess also stirred embarrassing memories of the eulogies that his mortal 'double' and namesake Taliesin had composed, when employed in the sixth century Welsh Courts of North Britain. For example, he cringed to recall his flattering lines, addressed to King Urien Rheged:

> *'My heart is set on thee of all men of renown;*
> *... The bravest prince... thou art the best that is,*
> *That has been and will be, Thou hast no peer.*
> *When men gaze on him, widespread is the awe;*
> *... Golden prince of the North, chief of princes.'* [14]

Despite many misgivings, including the possibility of encountering his mortal ghost, Taliesin pressed on, being determined to rescue his friend Elphin from Maelgwn's capricious injustice.

Taliesin's revelation

As soon as he entered the hall, Taliesin placed himself in a quiet corner, near where the bards and minstrels normally entered. As they passed the spot in which he was crouching, he played '*Blerwm, blerwm*', with his finger upon his lips.

The bards took little notice of him as they moved forward to the king and '*made obeisance with their bodies.*' But when they tried to sing his praises in their usual unctious manner, not a word could they utter. Instead, they pouted, made mouths at Maelgwn, and played *'Blerwm, blerwm'* on their lips with their fingers, as they had seen the boy do.[15]

The king assumed that they were all drunk and sent one of his lords to tell them to behave properly, but to no effect, for the bards had been spellbound by Taliesin. Then the king twice commanded all twenty-four bards to leave the hall, but they did not go. So he ordered a squire to hit Heinin Vardd, the chief bard. Struck on the head with a broom, Heinin fell back into his seat.

When he came to his senses he begged forgiveness of Maelgwn and blamed his dumbness and that of his fellow bards on 'the influence of a spirit that sits in the corner yonder, in the form of a child.' The 'child' was then brought before the monarch, who asked what he was and where he came from.

> *'Primary chief bard I am to Elphin,*
> *And my original country is the region of the summer stars;* [The Pleiades?]
> *Iddno* [Idno, abbot of Belly Moor, Herefordshire?] *and Heinin called me Merddin* [alias Merlin],
> *At length every king will call me Taliesin.'* [16]

He then describes the realms he has explored. These include Old and New Testament venues, and at least one from Classical Antiquity, in addition to many 'Welsh' mythological locations. In total, he announces himself as an omnipresent divine life force that has permeated the universe from its inception. Continuing in verse, he claims:

> *'I was with my Lord in the highest sphere,*
> *On the fall of Lucifer into the depth of hell;* [Welsh *Annwn* can mean 'Hell', a case of syncretism.]
> *I have born a banner before Alexander;*
> *I know the names of the stars from north to south;*
> *I have been on the galaxy at the throne of the distributor;*
> *I was in Canaan when Absolom was slain;*
> *I conveyed the Divine Spirit to the level of the vale of Hebron;*
> *I was in the court of Don before the birth of Gwidion.* [Don, mother of the pantheon and her wizard.]
> *I was instructor to Eli and Enoc;'* [Eli = Elijah, and Enoch, after whom the 'first city' was named.]
> *I have been loquatious prior to being gifted with speech;*
> *I was at the place of crucifixion of the merciful Son of God.'* [17]

The *Genesis* hunter, Nimrod (here attached to the Tower of Babel), employs the wandering bard to construct a building for the world's many languages, as their imagined initial unity is shattered, enabling Taliesin to state:

> *'I have been the chief director of the work of the tower of Nimrod.'* At the same time, he declares that his own beginnings are a mystery: *'I am a*

wonder whose origin is not known.' Yet he *is* sure about the source of his poetic inspiration:

'I have obtained the muse from the cauldron of Ceridwen.' [18]

As for music, he claims *'I have been bard of the harp to Lleon of Lochlin.'* Since Lochlin is a term for 'Scandinavia' in early Welsh texts, Taliesin brings Nordic influence to Wales, centuries before the Vikings arrived. The sacred arts of poetry, music and song may be said to form the basis of most 'primitive' knowledge systems. Having mastered these arts, Taliesin regards himself as a universal guru. He concludes:

'I have been teacher to all intelligences,
I am able to instruct the whole universe.' [19]

Whatever Maelgwn made of it, such bragging is unlikely to appeal to a modern audience, though it might provide extra material for a midwinter pantomime buffoon. Our difficulty may be that he speaks for a mythic, pre-Socratic world, that we have largely abandoned in favour of a belief in linear, unrepeatable time, whose eras are confined in separateness. But as Aristotle reminds us, poetry is more important than such history because poetry speaks for All-Time, to every generation.[20] So Taliesin's nonsense becomes intelligible again if received as the reclamation of concentrated patterns that are hidden within, yet take precedence over, apparent divisions. These unifying 'ideas' are displayed in his actions and in the radiating connotations of his words.

Two big difficulties faced Taliesin at Maelgwn's Deganwy. First, the immanent spirit within all matter was being increasingly denied by Christian influence. Secondly, the bardic tradition was being undermined by sycophantic insincerity. The Court 'poetry' practised at Deganwy was a sham, degraded to a degree where what had been lost could no longer be imagined. Taliesin revealed, challenged, and offered to cure this dismal state of affairs with the words of folk experience, honed on hardship and blessed by Nature's intrinsic divinity, revealed to him by Ceridwen.

Opposite top: *Taliesin arrives at Deganwy with the midwinter sun.*

centre left: *'Taliesin in a winter cloak', as seen on mosaic of the Seasons; from Caerwent.*

centre: *A Bronze Age gold ring from Milton, Hampshire; 1800 BC. Elphin's wife wears the repeatable cycle and gold wren, 1.3 cm wide; Garryduff, Co. Cork; AD eighth century. The wren, Troglodytes, is an underworld midwinter bird, considered sacred.*

centre right: *'Rhun' disputes with Taliesin; stone carving from Llanrhidian, Gower.*

bottom: *A midwinter wren house from Marloes, Pembrokeshire; wood and rags, 1869. A live wren was placed within on 26th December.*

After displaying the mythic range of his prospectus, Taliesin attacks the Court bards for neglecting the two-way route between poetry and the divine. In a set of verses, *The Reproof of the Bards*,[21] he mocks their ignorance of the firmament, the elements, and of Language's power to comprehend phenomena by the act of naming. He follows up this onslaught with *The Spite of the Bards*,[22] in which he accuses them of greed, sloth, impiety, lechery, drunkenness and lying, while condemning the triviality of their compositions. His critique attempts to re-engender in them a measure of *his* belief in the poetry's central role – provision of a goddess-inspired template for harmony on earth.

Extricating Elphin

Just as Elphin had pulled Taliesin from the sea and cut him from the bag at *Calan Mai*, so, given the reciprocating balance on which Myth operates, it was essential for Taliesin to rescue Elphin from midwinter incarceration. Failure might put the sun's ascent from solstitial hibernation at risk. As Taliesin explains to the assembled bards, he will try to achieve Elphin's release through poetry, rather than force:

> *'By a gentle prophetic strain ... Strengthened by my muse I am powerful.*
> *For three hundred songs and more Are combined in the spell I sing.*
> *There ought not to stand where I am Neither stone, neither ring;*
> *... Elphin the son of Gwyddno Is in the land of Artro,*
> *Secured by thirteen locks, For praising his instructor;*
> *And then I Taliesin, Chief of the bards of the west,*
> *Shall loosen Elphin out of a golden fetter.'* [23]

He then challenges the audience to solve an extended riddle:

> *'Discover thou what is the strong creature from before the flood,*
> *Without flesh, without bone, Without vein, without blood*
> *Without head, without feet; It will neither be older nor younger than at the beginning...*
> *It is without an equal, It is four-sided; It is not confined, It is incomparable;*
> *It comes from four quarters... It is sonorous, it is dumb, it is mild, It is strong, it is bold,*
> *When it glances over the land.'* [24]

Thus by word of mouth, Taliesin invokes his invisible agent, a divinely inspired gust, 'The Wind', to come to his aid. Timeless as his own spirit, he calls up the 'Great Spirit' of the world's air currents, as extensions of his own small breathings. The resulting alliance succeeds '*By a tremendous blast.'*[25]

'And while he was thus singing his verse near the door, there arose a mighty storm of wind, so that the king and all his nobles thought that the castle would fall on their heads. And the king caused them to fetch Elphin in haste from his dungeon, and placed him before Taliesin. And it is said that *immediately he* [Taliesin], *sang a verse... the chains opened about his* [Elphin's] *feet.'* [26]

Then, in a song of thanksgiving, Taliesin praises an unspecified *'Supreme Lord of all animation'*, and wishes an *'abundance of mead'* on Maelgwn. After that he recites an 'ode,' *The Interrogation of the Bards*, containing questions about Nature that they cannot answer. Unlike him, they have not been literally immersed in Nature, and have yet to know her from the inside out.

> *'Taliesin, having set his master free from prison, and having protected the innocence of his [Elphin's] wife, and silenced the bards, so that not one of them dared to say a word, now brought Elphin's wife before them, and showed that she had not one finger wanting. Right glad was Elphin. Right glad was Taliesin.'* [27]

The horse race

> *'Who had fairer or swifter horses?'* than Maelgwn, Heinin's bards had asked. *'Then Taliesin bade Elphin wager the king, that he had a horse both better and swifter than the king's horses. And this Elphin did; and the day, time and place were fixed. And the place was that which to this day is called Morfa Rhianedd.'* [28]

This 'Sea marsh of the Queen or Maiden' runs across the neck of the Great Orme headland from Deganwy to Llandudno Bay, through the eastern suburbs of modern Llandudno.

> *'Thither the king went with all his people and twentyfour of the swiftest horses he possessed. And after a long process, the course was marked and the horses were placed for running. Then came Taliesin with four-and-twenty twigs of holly, which he had burnt black.'*

> *'He caused the youth who was to ride his master's horse to place them in his belt; and he gave orders to let all the king's horses get before him, and as he should overtake one horse after another, to take one of the twigs and strike the horse with it over the crupper, and then let the twig fall; and ... do in the like manner to every one of the [king's] horses, as he should overtake them... [Then Taliesin] enjoined his horseman strictly to watch where his own horse should stumble, and to throw down his cap on the spot.*

> *'All these things the youth did fulfil, giving a blow to every one of the king's horses, and throwing down his cap where his own horse stumbled. And to this spot Taliesin brought his master after his horse had won the race. And he caused Elphin to dig a hole there; and when they had dug the ground deep enough, they found a large cauldron full of gold.*

> *'And then said Taliesin: 'Elphin, behold a payment and reward unto thee, for having taken me out of the weir, and for having reared me from that time until now.' 'And on this spot stands a pool of water,*

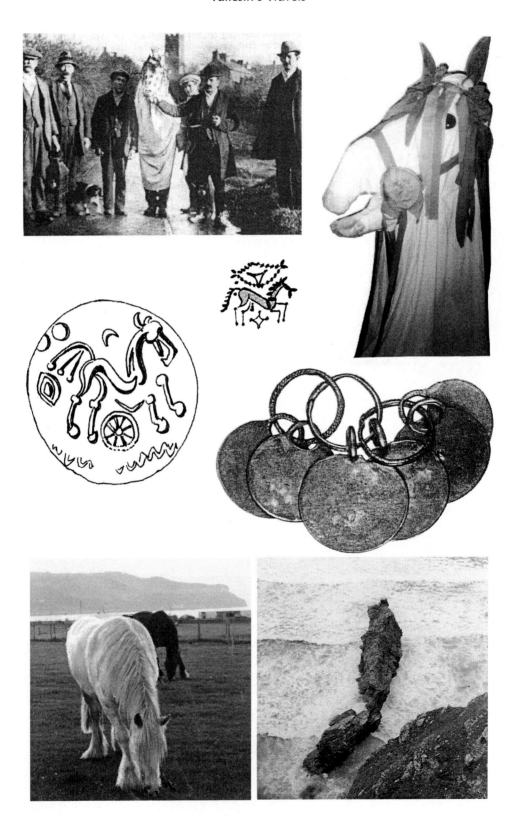

which is to this time called Pwllbair[30] [a corruption of *pwll y pair,* 'cauldron's pool'].

Winnings

Today, '*Pwllbair*' playfully reappears as Llandudno's *Pwll Plant*, her Childrens' Paddling Pool. Likewise, the simple story of a mid-sixth century horse race sends beneficial ripples far beyond one particular winter's day. Rather than history's 'shallow end', we are plunged into myth's copious deeps, as a glance at Elphin's cauldron-full of winnings makes clear.

Elphin, son of Gwyddno Garanhir, whose horses were poisoned when Ceridwen's cauldron split, is rewarded with the gift of a restored pot, filled to the brim with gold. Moreover, it is the boy Gwion, who was indirectly responsible for the original poisoning, who, as the gold-headed Taliesin, leads Elphin's horse to the spot where the reimbursement or 'fine payment', (Welsh *tal-iesin*) is made.

Gold, the incorruptible 'sunshine' dug from the rocky underworld, has been a potent symbol of many mythic claims to eternal value. A hoard of gold objects discovered on The Orme's Head, overlooking Morfa Rhianedd, contained a woman's double cone-shaped ear rings, made from Irish gold more than three thousand years ago.[31] At the eastern end of the same beach, 'several finely wrought Druidical ornaments of gold' were found in the nineteenth century on the summit of Little Orme.[32] In addition, two hoards of Roman coins identifying the Emperor with the sun god, Sol Invicta, carrying a horse whip and orb, were found at nearby Penrhyn Manor.[33]

To recompense Elphin for rescuing Gwion from the weir, the hidden gold of Pwyllbair may also represent the nocturnal passage of the sun, just as Cunobelinus' gold coinage figured the sun's passage in a horse and sun-wheel design. Heads or tails, the gold-filled cauldron reconnects the spendthrift Elphin to his estranged solar

Opposite: *Magic Horses*

'I have been a stallion over a stud.' *Taliesin*, Book of Taliesin, *vii. 230.*

top left:	*The Mari Lwyd 'horse'; paraded at midwinter in Glamorgan,* circa *1900.*
top right:	*Close-up of a Mari Lwyd horse, St Fagan's, Glamorgan.*
centre left:	*Coin of the British Iceni, AD first century.*
middle centre:	*Gold stater of the west British Dobunnic tribe; first century BC.*
centre right:	*Gold-bronze harness jingle from Parch y meirch, Denbighshire;* circa *900 BC.*
bottom left:	*Horses grazing on Morfa Rhianedd, Llandudno.*
bottom right:	*Horse Rock, near Newquay, Cornwall.*

'horse-father', Gwyddno Garanhir. The father-son breach is demonstrably healed, when the annual Pwyllbair fortune is lavished yet again on the prince.

Gwyddno's generosity finds echoes in the beneficence of solar deities towards humanity's royal intermediaries, including Maelgwn. Though Maelgwn's twenty-four royal steeds (two per month, covering both day and night journeys) took second place to the divine horse from which they were originally bred, in losing they effectively reminded the king of his dependence on sacred bloodstock from Gwyddno's stable.

In the contest, both Taliesin and Elphin, as trainer and owner, held a supernatural advantage. No wonder they won. Yet the racetrack itself was fair to both sides. Morfa Rhianedd was Maelgwn's 'home ground', named after a 'queen', Welsh *rhian*. At the same time, the place-name all-but whinnies with the Welsh horse goddess, Rhiannon. She features in the *Mabinogion's Pwyll* legend.[34] Able to assume both equine and human shapes, she gives birth to a colt *and* a boy-child. From Ireland to India, ritual coition between humans and horses is a well-documented feature of Indo-European sacred weddings between royalty and their gods.[35]

Morfa Rhianedd's location suggests that Elphin's race may have involved mares and fillies, galloping with the Welsh *mor gaseg*, literally 'mare of the sea', the wave that perpetually runs around Llandudno Bay's sandy shore. If so, Taliesin's advice that Maelgwn's horses should be struck across the rump with burnt holly twigs brings connotations of impregnation. Holly, the red-berried emblem of renewal-at-midwinter, scorched by solar fire, renders the king's fillies pregnant, and thereby slows them down. Welsh 'holly', *celyn*, also means 'penis'. Here men, animals and vegetables evidently collaborate in an annual rite, designed to enhance the fertility of the King's realm. That is Maelgwn's runner-up prize.

Taliesin's son, Afaon

Following from his need to repay Elphin and to facilitate a new solar cycle, Taliesin may have gained a son from the horse race that he had organised. Afaon, son of Taliesin, is said to have lived at Bodafon, named after him.[36] Bodafon Hall farm still stands on a slope overlooking the Morfa Rhianedd racetrack. From *Tan'r Allt*, 'Fire Hill', adjoining Bodafon, a tiny stream named Nant y Gamar, perhaps a corruption of Welsh *gamaur*, 'golden and be-gemmed', ran straight to the sea, along the line of what is now Nant y Gamar Road. It enters the bay a few yards from the twentieth century paddling pool.

Opposite top: *Pwll Plant, The childrens' paddling pool at Llandudno.*

centre left: *Romano-British coins from Little Orme, Llandudno, showing Emperor as sun god.*

centre right: *Goldsmiths Minute Book frontispiece; Chester,* circa *1550.*

bottom: *Bodavon Hill Farm, Llandudno, named after Taliesin's son, Afaon.*

Two views of the Craig y Don cadair or 'chair' of limestone boulders; on Bryn Gader, overlooking Llandudno.

Taliesin Street, Llandudno, built circa *1840. Taliesin permeates the modern resort.*

Therefore when Taliesin's solar beam emanated from the fiery Tan y'r Allt 'grandstand' at midwinter, it could have 'entered' a mare as she raced to the winning post, before retiring to the Bodafon stable, where she eventually give birth to a colt named Afaoan. No one knows the name of Afaon's mother. She might have been a horse.

Afaon grew up to be 'the most accomplished and wise young man in the kingdom.'[37] His name is sometimes spelt Addaon, derived from Welsh *addon*, 'special, noble.' A series of religious verses in the *Book of Talgarth*, collectively called *The Advice of Adaon*, are attributed to him, while in *The Triads* he is celebrated as one of Britain's Bull Chieftains and Battle Leaders.

Craig y Don and the horse-head promontory

Bodafon lies in a district named Craig y Don, after the mother of the entire Welsh pantheon of deities, the goddess Don. When in his 'Gwion' mode, Taliesin had encountered her in Afon Dyfrdonwy, the original name of the River Dee. By contrast, here, above Llandudno, she sits on her grey limestone *cadair* or 'chair'. Since Neolithic times, European mother goddesses are typically shown to give birth in a sitting position.

The Craig y Don *cadair* is a flat-backed boulder, with a stone seat to match, sited on *Bryn Gader*, 'Hill of the Chair', at 100 feet above sea level, with a fine view of the Great Orme headland. Here Don and her human representative can be joint mothers of all they survey – land, sky, and ocean.

Great Orme's Head as 'Horse Head'

Above: *The setting sun returns an 'eye' to the two mile-long horse-head shaped peninsula.*

Opposite left: *Ffynnon Caseg, 'Mare's Well', at the Great Orme's Head seaward end.*

Opposite top right: *Celtic sea-horse brooch from Lamberton Moor, Berwickshire; second century BC.*

Opposite centre: *Gold earing, made circa 2,200 BC, from Great Orme.*

Opposite bottom: *A horse's jaw-bone, decorated circa 8,000 BC, found buried in Kendrick's cave, Great Orme.*

The dramatic two-mile long promontory, which ninth century Viking sailors named *orme,* 'worm', appeared to them as the head and neck of a living sea monster. Seen from Bryn Gader however, their 'worm' looks much more like a stupendous horse's head. It may well have been so regarded by the Paleolithic artist who, *circa* 10,000 BC, skilfully engraved a horse' jaw bone with nine parallel rows of chevrons, and two further sets of seven zigzags, all probably denoting 'water.' This equine relic was part of a ritual deposit, associated with bones from more than four humans, carefully laid in the peninsula's Kendrick's Cave, named after its nineteenth century discoverer.[38]

If that old horse's jaw could find its tongue, it might share the Welsh description of the waves, crashing against the headland, as: 'A flock of sheep of Gwenhidwy, And nine rams along with them.' Gwenhidwy was the mermaid queen of Gwydion,

118

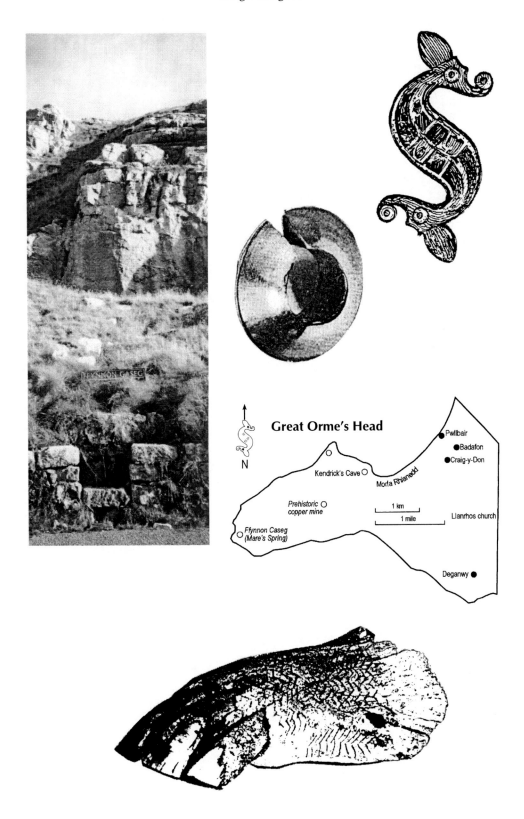

Great Orme's Head

N

Pwllbair
Badafon
Craig-y-Don

Kendrick's Cave

Morfa Rhianedd

Prehistoric
copper mine

1 km
1 mile

Llanrhos church

Ffynnon Caseg
(Mare's Spring)

Deganwy

Don's first-born son.[39] The sea was her pasture. The nine rows of chevrons cut into the bone may have described a similar flock of salty 'rams.'

Regarding shoreline beasts, several rock stacks around the coasts of Celtic Britain retain their 'Horse' or 'Mare' place-names and one may guess that prior to the Vikings' arrival, 'Great Orme's Head' was known as either *Pen Meirch Mawr,* 'Great Horse Head', or *Pen Caseg Mawr,* 'Great Mare Head.' To this day, at its seaward tip, there is a copious spring named *Ffynnon Caseg,* 'Mare's Well', which continues to grant the limestone 'grey mare' a last drink of her own fresh water, before she heads out to sea and turns again into *Mor Gaseg,* the white-maned 'Mare-Wave.'

Supervising these elemental transformations, as they thunder from beyond the Stone Age, sits Don. One may guess that each year at *Gwyl Awst,* Lammas, a heavily pregnant woman played the role of 'Mother of the Universe' on the Craig-y-Don birthing *cadair,* thereby complementing the 'May Queen' election, months before.

Although a male, Taliesin was eager to climb Bryn Gader, in order to see the world through Don's eyes. Having made the ascent, he saw the gleaming sands and water channels of the Conwy estuary, with the mountains of Snowdonia beyond. Over these, Don had conjured up a glorious sunset, clothed in tattered veils of cloud. The golden ball turned orange and then red, as, fattening, it sank into Anglesey's distant, low-slung form. Yet no sooner had the fire been extinguished than white sparks appeared in constellations, to decorate the night's dome. While breathing in this panoply Taliesin said only one word: *'teg'* ('beautiful').

Then he walked downhill to Llandudno's Taliesin Street, laid out about 1850, and named in his honour. It was filled from end to end with small terraced houses. After admiring the electric street lamps and the glow of 60-watt bulbs, visible through the half-drawn curtains of many a room, he checked the horsepower of each car, parked alongside the pavement. 'Don is so versatile', he thought. 'Such multifarious inventions; Praise be to Don!'

Eurgain and Taliesin

Next, he made his way east for two miles and climbed Bryn Euryn (Welsh *euryn,* 'little gold coin, gold jewel, darling') a fortified hill behind Penrhyn Bay, to await the next sunrise.

A Welshman, calling himself *Cilmyn,* wrote in 1853 that: 'Every Welsh disciple or noviciate of the bardic profession should approach this hill bare-footed and with due reverential awe... [since] around this Parnassian *bryn* the phantom of Taliesin has been hovering and uttering... for a period of seven hundred years.'[40]

The editor of *Archaeologia Cambrensis,* in which these remarks appeared, attached the following comment: 'We are sorry to see so many bare assertions introduced into this letter without the slightest attempt having been made to substantiate them. We do hope that our correspondent will endeavour in future to avoid all such unnecessary extravagancies.'[41]

Top and centre: *Llanrhos church, near Deganwy.*

Bottom: *The Caergwrle 'boat-cup', Flintshire; made circa 1,000 BC.*

In blackness, Taliesin settled down on a bed of Bryn Euryn's heather to await the dawn. After several hours had passed he was astonished to see a faint 'first light' spreading from the North, rather than the East. Its source was Eurgain, Maelgwn's daughter. Tradition declares that she 'set the candle to the wild birds to show her lover the way to Wales.'[42] Her name means 'golden and beautiful, gloriously radiant.' She was Taliesin's female equivalent.

Lewis Morris names her lover as the Anglian king Aethelfrith of the sunrise coast, Northumbria,[43] which implies that she lived for more than one mortal life-span, since that king was still alive in AD 617. Other sources state that her husband was Elidyr-the-Courteous, who had carried her from the far North on a horse called *Du y Moroedd*, 'The Black One of the Seas'. Seven-and-a-half people were on that steed. The half-person was Gelbeinevin, the cook, 'who swam with his two hands to [or in?] the horses crupper.'[44] Here, as so often in Wales, politics and legend merge, for Elidyr (Welsh *elydr,* 'copper, brass, bronze') journeyed to Gwynedd to claim his right to Maelgwn's kingdom, via his wife Eurgain. They landed close to the biggest prehistoric copper mine in Europe, recently recognised on Great Orme's Head.[45] Therefore Eurgain's shadow falling across Morfa Rhianedd signals Maelgwn's end.

Maelgwn's death

Of Maelgwn's death, Taliesin had predicted that:

> *'A most strange creature will come from the sea marsh of Rhianedd.*
> *As a punishment of iniquity on Maelgwn Gwynedd;*
> *His hair, his teeth, and his eyes being as gold,*
> *And this will bring destruction upon Maelgwn Gwynedd.'* [46]

'Oh dear! I think I am turning into a god', the Roman emperor Vespasian is reported to have whispered when on his deathbed. For most late Roman rulers the god in question was Sol, the divine sun. Thus in life emperors wore a solar-rayed crown. The tradition whereby an earthly monarch dies back into a deified sun may be reflected in Taliesin's description of a monster, coming over the marsh to reclaim and reunite with the body of its royal but mortal representative.

Taliesin's prophecy disguises 'Eurgain' beneath maleness and Christian notions of punishment, yet supernatural 'sun creatures' of both sexes were active in North Wales long before Eurgain came ashore in the sixth century. One such deity is probably depicted with gold leaf rays and discs, arranged above deep-set eyes, on the miniature Caergwyl 'boat.' This was carved and inlaid circa 1,000 BC, and may show a sun-deity undertaking its nightly voyage through a subterranean ocean.[47] With a new 'eye' at sunset, such 'she-boats' carried the dead to Otherworld isles, said to lie in the west.

When on *his* sea voyage, Taliesin had encountered a different marine monster. He tells the Deganwy bards about *'a noxious creature from the ramparts of Satanas, which has overcome all, between the deep and the shallow. Equally wide are his jaws as the mountains of the Alps. Him death will not subdue, nor hand nor blades. There is the load of nine hundred waggons in the hair of his two paws. Three springs arise in the nape of his neck. Sea-roughs thereon swim through it.'*

That creature could easily have consumed Maelgwn, but after considering the different appeals of Paganism and Christianity, the King plumped for the latter. He preferred to retain his posthumous individuality as an immortal soul, rather than merge with the stew of pagan all-life, or with the sun. To win back favour with the Church that he had deserted, Maelgwn therefore bequeathed the fertile lands around Deganwy to the bishopric of St Asaph's.[48]

Nevertheless, according to *Annales Cambriae,* in the year of Our Lord 547 a great pestilence broke out, known as *Y Fad Felen,* 'The Yellow Plague.'[49] In this instance, History reared its head 'either as a basilisk, or under the form of a fair woman,'[50] writes Pennant. *She* was the 'strange creature' from Morfa Rhianedd.

Fearing for his life, Maelgwn fled to St Mary's church at Llanrhos, a mile from Deganwy. In the last resort, it was the mother of Christ to whom he turned for help. There he hid, in the belief that if he did not *see* the plague monster, she could not touch him. However, curiosity led him to peer out through the keyhole in the church door, whereupon he was fatally contaminated.[51] His body was shipped nine miles west for burial to the tiny island of Ynys Seiriol, owned by St Seriol.[52]

Elidyr and Eurgain then fought her brother Rhun for the vacant throne of Gwynedd, and Elidyr was killed in the ensuing battle near Clynnog. Perhaps his ghost and that of his wife rode on, eventually plunging into Marchllyn Mawr, the 'Great Horse Lake', in Snowdonia. Over that water a huge stone pillar, Carnedd Elidyr, marks the place of his dive. It is said that below the surface, a gold crown set with pearl lies on a table of pure gold. Here Eurgain's coronation hopes are stored, though local legend adds that King Arthur now claims the submerged treasure.[53]

King Maelgwn's death brought Taliesin's time at Deganwy to an end. He was grateful to that monarch for giving him a platform on which to find his mature voice. For his part, Maelgwn had come to value Taliesin's insights. For example, Gruffydd maintains that the king asked the new bard to outline the origins of the human race. In his *Four Pillars of Song* Taliesin responded to this request at heavily Christianised length, thanks to a Late Medieval revision of his words.[54]

The Taliesin-Maelgwn alliance had served to keep pagan tradition alive in the kingdom of Gwynedd. To ensure that this heritage was retained and revitalised beyond the brief limit of his own lifetime, Maelgwn had given Taliesin lands around the shores of Llyn Geirionydd, 'Lake Language', situated in a remote tributary valley of the upper Conwy river.[55]

There, through poetry, the king hoped that the bard might give voice to the sacred universal fabric. In doing so, Taliesin would serve as a counter-balance to the incoming doctrine of Original Sin, which the monarch common ground between the two theologies. If, by magic, anyone could encourage a working collaboration between such incompatible attitudes, it would be Taliesin, for that was part of his calling. So he left Deganwy and headed towards where he imagined the distant 'Lake of Words' might lie.

CHAPTER EIGHT

TREK TO LLYN GEIRIONYDD

Conway Castle

The first obstacle set across Taliesin's path on his walk to Llyn Geirionedd was Conway castle, founded in 1283. It rises only a mile from Deganwy at the mouth of Afon Conwy, and is one of a ring of castles, built around the coast of North Wales by King Edward 1st of England, which effectively brought an end to Welsh independence. By then, Llewellyn ap Gruffydd, the last Welsh-born Prince of Wales, had been killed and Wales was due to be Anglicised.[1]

Conway's castle and the adjoining English town share a curtain wall studded with twenty-eight towers. Twin bastions, a portcullis and drawbridge protects each of its three gates. Maintained on a war footing till the mid-seventeenth century, Conway stands for foreign colonialism. Taliesin was transfixed. He foresaw that Welsh political collapse in the late thirteenth century was to be followed by the erosion of Welsh language and culture. What honourable course would be left to a humiliated Cymric seer, but suicide? So suggested Thomas Gray in his poem *The Bard*, where the last Welsh prophet throws himself over a cliff:

> 'He spoke, and headlong from the mountain's height
> Deep in the roaring tide he plunged to endless night.'[2]

Yet for the nineteenth century English poet, Matthew Arnold, the allure of what remained of Welsh culture exerted a strong pull. In 1864 he wrote to his mother: 'I long for Wales – that is a country which has always touched my imagination.'[3]

Later that year, after a stay in Llandudno, he said: 'the poetry of the Celtic race and its names of places quite over-powers me. It will be long before Tom [his invalid son] forgets the line: 'Hear from thy grave, great Taliesin, hear!' from Gray's *Bard,* of which I give him the benefit some hundred times a day on our excursions.'[4]

Taliesin shouted in reply: 'Don't worry!' Then he paraphrased Gray's next line: ''They breathe a soul to animate my clay'; so I am not dead, nor is the Welsh bardic tradition. Follow me!'

With that, he hopped across the busy roundabout where the A546 from Llandudno meets the A547 causeway to the castle. Then he jumped over the river's bank, sloshed across Afon Conwy's low-tide mudflats, and belly flopped into the water.

124

Conway Castle; built by King Edward I after his conquest of Wales in 1293.

After a struggle, his inelegant 'dog-paddle' brought him dripping to the western shore, where, arms raised, he stood shivering and defiant.

This rash plunge recalled the challenge once set by Maelgwn, that all his harpists and poets should swim across the Conwy, to see which group could then best perform. All the harps were ruined by submergence, so the poets, who had memorised their words and kept them safely dry, won the day.[5]

Ugnach and Dinas Dinlle

No sooner had Taliesin crossed the river than a poem sprang into his mind. It was the dialogue between himself and a horseman, recorded in the thirteenth century *Black Book of Carmarthen*.[6] As he spoke the first words, so the rider, whose name Taliesin had forgotten, manifested again:

'*A horseman resorts to the city, With his white hounds and his large hunting horn.*' Packs of Celtic white dogs invariably carry Otherworld connotations. Taliesin was facing a being from that realm.

'*Come with me, I may not be denied*', the huntsman commanded, but Taliesin politely replied: '*I will not go there now; Bear with the conduct of the delayer. May the blessing of heaven and earth go with you*'. As a demi-god, Taliesin belongs to both realms and was often in danger of being pulled in half.

The stranger asked: '*How long will you absent yourself? When will you come?*' Taliesin replied: '*When I return from Caer Seon , From contending with the Jews, I will come to the city of Lleu and Gwydion.*'

Lleu and Gwydion are both mythic figures. Gwydion, wizard and shape-shifter, is the most famous of Don's children. Among many fantastic deeds, he made a supernatural woman, Blodeuwedd, out of flowers. He also stole pigs from *Annwn*, and created horses and saddles with gold fittings.[7] He is often regarded as 'King' of the Welsh fairies, *Y Tylwyth Teg*.

125

Dinas Dinlle, Carnarvonshire, an Iron Age coastal fortress,
reputed home of the god Lleu, to which Ugnach invites Taliesin.

Although Gwydion's chief residence was The Milky Way, alias *Caer Gwydion*, he also shared an under-earth home with his son Lleu, at Dinas Dinlle,[8] a prehistoric coastal hillfort, five miles south-west of Carnarvon. Now half eaten by the sea, its 'underworld', a cliff of brown glacial moraine confronts strollers on the beach. On top are the remains of two ramparts, nearly twenty feet high in places. Traces of Roman pottery, circular Iron Age buildings and a Bronze Age round barrow, point to successive phases of use.[9]

Taliesin was being invited to a nether-world existence, where, the horseman promised: *'You will have mead which has matured… and pure gold on your clasp… You shall have high foaming wine.'*

As the post-Roman personification of Bacchus, who led the inhabitants of Britain's fourth century villas to their 'afterlife', how could Gwion-Taliesin resist? He *is* wine; and beneath Dinas Dinlle he could drink and be drunk among supernatural native friends. *'Fairly and sweetly you speak,'* he replied, but again declined the offer. Even when the rider, Ugnach son of Mydno, called Taliesin: *'Chief of men, Victor in the contest of song,'* and begs him to stay at least *'until Wednesday'*, (Welsh *Mercher*, Latin *Mercury*), the bard responds with further courtesies, but emphatically concludes: *'I do not deserve censure; I will not stay.'*

A wandering demi-god belongs everywhere and nowhere. Prone to give offence to gods and to men, he is a perpetual half-fit, generally perceived as an awkward, troublesome loner, whose mercurial behaviour arouses suspicion on every side. But it is his *duty* to move between rival camps, different perspectives and modes of reality. On this occasion he rejects the comfort of Dinlle because he is obliged instead to visit Caer Seion, the Welsh 'Mount Zion', *'to contend with Jews.'* [10]

Caer Seion

Caer Seion is a mountain, fortified in the Iron Age, which rises less than two miles west of Conway. The Welsh regarded Caer Seion as the 'holy hill' (Hebrew *tsiyon* 'hill') of Jerusalem, which stood for Israel's theocracy and the Kingdom of Heaven. Taliesin *had* to go there if he was to learn the language of Judaic monotheism, with its total rejection of any godhead other than Jehovah. Through their Old Testament, the Jews had indirectly been responsible for bringing theological intolerance to Wales, along with unqualified patriarchy, linear notions of Time, and a dualistic division between matter and spirit.

That these features were alien to Taliesin's paganism made it the more imperative that he should engage with them. By infiltrating Caer Seion he hoped, for example, to soften the hatred of non-Christian imagery expressed by the sixth century Welsh monk Gildas. Gildas had attacked 'those diabolical [Romano-British] idols of my country, which almost surpassed in number those of ancient Egypt, and of which we still see some, mouldering away within or without the deserted temples, with stiff and deformed features, as was customary.'[11] Another name for Caer Seion is Caer Lleion, 'Monk's Fort.'[12]

Part of Taliesin's task was to enrich Britain by incorporating the latest Judeo-Christian filament into its fabric, despite that thread's claim to exclusive value. Such was the

Overleaf: top left: *A 'bearded head', seen on the Caer Seion cliff face, overlooking Deganwy.*

top right: *Iron Age fort of Caer Seion, southern entrance; on Conway Mountain.*

bottom left: *St Luke; in the eighth century Book of Teilio, formerly held in Carmarthenshire.*

Overleaf bottom right: *Maen Chwyfan, Whitford, Flint; 11 feet high; tenth century [Welsh chwyf, 'motion.']*

Page 129: *Harvest Festival*

'I have been a bill-hook, curve, that cuts'. Book of Taliesin, *i, 7*.

top left and bottom centre: *Late September at Llangelynin church, near Conway; font and altar rail.*

top right: *English corn dolly and child, Reading, Berks.*

bottom left and right: *Basalt sickle sharpner, incised with solar swastica; from Llandudno Junction.*

paradox he faced. He could no more deny that a type of Judaism had arrived in Britain than that Stonehenge continues to exist here. To understand both, he had to learn their languages, whether through architectural iconography, or god-given words. He recognized in this jumble of material the disparate ingredients in his own comprehensive make-up, and was willing to sing:

> '*I was with my Lord in the heavens when Lucifer fell into the depths*
> *of hell;*
> *I was in the ark with Noah and Alpha; I upheld Moses through the*
> *water of Jordan*
> *And was with my Lord in the manger of oxes and asses;*
> *I was atop the cross of the merciful Son of God.'* [13]

Sir I. Williams sees the introduction of Biblical themes into the pagan body of Taliesin's original sayings as a gradual process that took place between the tenth and fourteenth centuries.[14]

When near the summit of the 'New Jerusalem' at Caer Seion, Taliesin saw how imagination can move mountains across time and space in searching for the divine, which is modified in transit. For example, *this* mountain's north cliff, dropping almost sheer to the sea, ignores the Judaic ban on graven images by displaying the natural rocky profile of a bearded Old Testament prophet, or even of 'God the Father.' 'He' measures at least 100 feet from beard tip to the crown of his head.

First occupied in 200 BC, the highest Caer Seion enclosure has unmortared walls, sixteen feet thick. They remain up to four feet tall and are presumed to belong to a pre-Christian temple or sacred *temenos*. Nearby, the circular outlines of nearly fifty dwellings are discernible, in which spindle whorls, stone pot-boilers and grain-crushing saddle querns have been found.[15]

On Caer Seion Taliesin discovered a Biblical Heaven mixed with common Earth; and he planned to re-heat them into a true Heaven-on-Earth compound, where the word 'halo' would once again become synonymous with 'threshing floor', as in Ancient Greek.

Another name for Conway's Caer Seion is *Mynydd Dref*, 'Mountain of Twenty-four Sheaves' (Welsh *drefa*). When harvesting, Gwynydd farmers normally arranged their sheaves in two stooks of twelve, so making the twenty-four horses of Maelgwyn's race. Each 'steed-stook' was a potential *Caseg Fedi*, or 'Harvest Mare', as the ritual end-of-harvest corn dolly was often named in Wales. On Mynydd Dref, Taliesin's burnt holly twigs had evidently sired golden offspring, every one a winner, on God's holy mountain overlooking Morfa Rhianedd.

As one who had himself been 'a white grain of pure wheat', Taliesin felt doubly happy. He could extol '*The wheat pure and white... Every man to feed*' [16] as a divine gift, old as the Neolithic, while simultaneously regarding the wheaten wafer as '*Christ's pure body.*' [17] '*I have been winged by the genius of the splendid crosier*', [18] he admitted.

Possessed by the exultant mood found in G.M. Hopkins' *Hurrahing in Harvest* (a poem written in North Wales), Taliesin then leapt and tumbled downhill among bracken and boulders, sheep and lambs. He was at one with the implausible Wales, described in 1864 by Matthew Arnold: 'where the past still lives, where every place has its tradition, every name its poetry, and where the people, the genuine people, still know this past, this poetry, and live with it, cling to it.'[19] Taliesin chanted:

> *'A grain which grew on a hill, I was reaped and placed in an oven; I fell to the ground when I was being roasted And a hen swallowed me.'* [20]

Ten minutes later, as he paused for breath, he saw the railway, main road, and bungalows of Llansanffraid Glan Conwy, on the opposite shore of Afon Conwy. Then his joy deflated into doubt. He was aware that by 1864 old people were ashamed of their youthful pagan beliefs, while the young were largely ignorant of what had been suppressed. Moreover, the collapse of pre-Christian folk beliefs had been quickly followed by the decline of Welsh Calvinism. By AD 2000 many of Zion's chapels stood abandoned, leaving a doubly evident absence. On both sides of the pagan-Christian discourse, the divine fire had almost died, and been replaced by ashen utilitarianism. Taliesin felt a chill in his bones, threatening his annual rebirth. In desperation, he shot out an arm and snatched one syllable from the Llansanffraid Glan Conwy name. Ffraid; he picked out Ffraid. She was in his hand, and he in hers.

Ffraid and *Gwyl Fair*

There are ten parishes in Wales named Llansanffraid in honour of St Ffraid. In addition, seventeen churches and six chapels are dedicated to her. Ffraid is the Welsh form of the Irish Brigid, and her popularity, especially in north and west Wales, is partly due to Irish migration during the fifth and sixth centuries AD. They brought with them a strong devotion to a pagan goddess, Bri, or Brig, who had recently merged with the mortal St Brigid of Kildare.

This saint travelled from Ireland on a sod of turf, landing either at Holyhead, or, as some accounts say, here, right in front of Taliesin, at Llansanffraid. Arriving during a famine, she pulled up a handful of rushes and tossed them into the stream. They instantly turned into a shoal of fish akin to salmon, the sparling, Welsh *brwyniaid*, which are reputed to taste either of rushes, Welsh *brwynenu*, or of cucumber. Sparlings are said to smell of violets, while blood may be seen, racing round their transparent bodies. For centuries, the shoals continued to arrive in notable abundance during January-February, coinciding with Brigid's Quarter-day festival, on February 1st and 2nd.[21]

The fame of Ffraid's Conwy fish, confirmed by excellent catches, may have persuaded Elis Gruffydd to relocate Taliesin's fish-weir experience there, rather than on the west coast, nominated by all other versions of the story. Overlooking the Conwy, the demi-god considered slipping into the water again to satisfy Gruffydd, but decided that his account was wrong.

Nevertheless, the sprite grew increasingly captivated by the scene. Despite its superficial banality, he saw one village in the air and, inverted beneath it, *another* in water, its animated reflection, wobbling below. Here was a bifocal, double-act, in which different realities were happily conjoined. Thus at Llansanffraid the goddess of the British *Briganii* tribe of North Britain,[22] merged with her Irish equivalent[23] *and* with the sixth century *St* Brigit.[24] Also incorporated in the Welsh version of her cult was Mary [Welsh *Fair*], mother of Christ. *Gwyl Fair*, the February vigil, was Brigid *and* Mary's feast

A hymn attributed to Columcille, who worked during the sixth century as a Christian missionary on both sides of the Irish Sea, refers to Brigid as: 'flame-golden, sparkling... She, the sun fiery, radiant!... She, the branch with blossoms, the mother of Jesus!'[25] Brigid's potency is echoed in Welsh *bri*, 'honour, esteem, power', from the same root as Irish *brig*, 'genius personified, pre-eminent power'.

In Wales, Ffraid's Eve was celebrated on February 1st as *Gwyl Fair*, 'Mary's Vigil.' By this simple yet daring act, Mary and Ffraid, were conjoined, just as in Ireland Brigid is called 'the Mary of the Gael.'[26] Thanks to Ffraid, Christianity and the pre-Christian legacy were combined. Taliesin was gladdened by their merger, which was annually celebrated in Wales for twelve hundred years. Until about 1780, Fair-Ffraid's folk ceremonies performed the re-entry of her shared candle light into the *hendre,* or 'old house.' These rituals marked winter's weakening grip, and were a declaration that Spring's forth-coming renewal was a divinely led spiritual arousal, emerging from physical fact.

Candles and wassail

In purely Christian terms, *Gwyl Fair* marked the Catholic feast of the Purification of the Virgin Mary at the temple, after giving birth to Christ. In Rome, this re-enactment involved a candle-lit procession, derived from a torch light walk, held each February, to honour the mother of Mars.[27]

For Celtic Wales, *Gwyl Fair* was also a nocturnal vigil. It began with groups of young men, travelling from house to house, and singing at front doors, closed against them. In burlesque verses, they claimed to have an order, 'got between Denbigh and Bala', granting them access. They then compared the cold outside to the warm fire within, promised harvest-time help to the inmates, and pleaded that they were following their great-grandfathers' example, adding: 'We also have undertaken to do the same. We cannot obstruct their customs.' After suffering the sung taunts of the occupants, and having pledged to behave properly, they were then admitted. As so often in mythic affairs, the desired acts were conjured up by words.[28]

Once inside, the travellers found themselves gazing at a 'wassail bowl', Welsh *gwyrod.* This round-bottomed wooden vessel contained from four to six pints of sweetened ale, on which pieces of toast floated. The bowl's rim was decorated with lighted candles. A youth then stepped forward. After toasting 'The Infant Queen of the Revels', he offered to drink to the bottom of the bowl without burning his hair. This reflected the *Calan Mai* rite, between a young man and the May Queen's three-pot flaming crown, described in Chapter Six.[29]

Top left: *Infant god and holy mother, draped with offerings, Holywell chapel, Flintshire; 2003.*

Top right: *Llansanffraid Glan Conwy. Here St Bride landed from Ireland.*

Bottom left: *Hendre Waelod, a Neolithic burial chamber at Llansanffraid; fourth millennium BC.*

Bottom right: *A bronze 'wassail' bowl, with apple decoration from Glastonbury, circa 100 BC.*

But at *Gwyl Fair* we are still in the lower, or 'Winter Half' of the year, symbolised by the liquor-filled bowl of the goddess' underworld womb, from which Gwion Bach received his three fateful drops at Llyn Tegid. Yet here, the presiding female is transformed into a very young and undoubtedly virgin girl. Carefully selected for these qualities, she is seated in the middle of the floor, close to the bowl, from which she drinks first, while carrying a *living* baby in her arms.[30]

In the Irish version of the ceremony, 'Brigit' is herself regarded as 'the baby' and brought into the house as the effigy of a new born infant.[31] The Welsh *cadair*, or 'chair' placed at the centre of these rites may be related to the Craig y Don *cadair*, to the Roman *Dea Nutrix* birth-giving chair, *and* to the 'golden chair', mentioned in a Carnarvon *Gwyl Fair* carol of 1762.[32] All were occupied by the new 'sun goddess.' In February the little girl *is* Ffraid, seen with her 'offspring', on the potent threshold of the year's infancy, miming the *Gwyl Awst* harvest birth which is due six months later.

After a concluding song of thanks, all having drunk from the wassail bowl, the young men departed, and set off to the next farm, for another encounter with 'Mair-Ffraid'.

Of all Ffraid's houses at Llansanffraid-Glan-Conwy, none is older than Hendre Waelod, a fourth millennium BC burial chamber, of 'portal dolmen' type.[33] It stands on the edge of an oak wood, overlooking the river, two miles south of the village. A pair of six feet high megaliths are set outside the threshold, like young men seeking entry. With a roofing capstone estimated to weigh 25 tons, the chamber seems to wait for February sunlight to penetrate its dark interior. Similar monuments in Staffordshire and North Yorkshire are known as 'Bridestones.'

At Hendre Waelod, the discouraging initial response, addressed to visitors by *Gwyl Fair* householders, takes on extra force. There it may truly be said: 'The cellar is empty, our utensils are of slate, and we have only snails and moles instead of puddings', as the *Gwyl Fair* girls always claimed.[35] And yet, when opening to a glimmer of light on this wintry 'spirit dawn', the bleak death chamber becomes the unlikely source of the world's victuals, as they grow from putrefaction's bed.

Taliesin climbed onto the Hendre Waelod capstone. Dangling his legs over its mouth, he felt as if he had been propelled from *Annwn*, with instructions to continue his quest to find a banquet of words on earth. Then, to Ffraid and Fair he sang a carol. 'How old you are, how young,' was the first line. The second, 'You are everything, And everything is you,' he borrowed from a 1970s popular song.

'My God,' he thought, 'here I am, on Fair's knee. Someone might mistake me for Jesus!' But because, as he understood it, the main purpose of the Catholic mass and of most other religions *is* to inter-mingle human and divine attributes, and since he already *had* 50 percent of each in his make-up, he didn't worry. Instead, he called to Fair-Ffraid by her double title, and by many others: 'Matres, Minerva, Brig, Eurgain, Suil, Gwrach, Grassi, Mererid, Ceridwen, Dee and Don.'

Allor Moloch

Moloch was not on his list. However, a group from the Welsh Archaeological Society which visited the site in 1882, claimed that another name for the Gwaelod tomb *was Allor Molloch*, the 'Altar of Moloch', a designation confirmed by the *Royal Commision for Ancient Monuments [Denbighshire]*.[36]

The Welsh word, *moloch,* 'restless, uneasy, troublesome, uproar', derives from Moloch, a Biblical god of the Netherworld, beneath Ur in Mesopotamia. The Canaanites turned Moloch into a sun god. Given Taliesin's pleasure in foreign travel, he could identify with both modes of the deity. He, Taliesin of the shining brow, had found another male partner, rising from abyss to sunrise. However, on checking Moloch's Biblical credentials, Taliesin discovered an Israelite belief that this deity demanded the sacrifice of first-born children, by making them pass through fire.

On Allor Moloch, Taliesin had set himself up as Moloch's next victim. In horror he jumped from the capstone, crying: 'Please, not me! I have been swallowed alive once already. I have passed through a hen's entrails. I am impure!' In his panic he fled, forgetting that the 'Moloch' place-name was only a nineteenth century invention, devised to kill off any lingering folk loyalty towards the cromlech. Running to the river, he crossed a bridge at Tal y Gafn and repeated six times the medieval prayer: 'May St Ffraid bless us on our journey',[37] before risking a backward glance.

Martial arts

A party of Roman soldiers on a scouting foray spotted Taliesin as he skirted their camp at Caerhun, a mile south of Tal y Gafn. Thinking that he might be a native spy, they seized him. The Caerhun fort is now named after Rhun, Maelgwyn's lusty son and illegitimate heir, who took the throne of Gwynedd in AD 547 and may have organised the camp's post-Roman re-occupation.[38]

Taliesin was marched towards the north gate along a fourteen feet wide cobbled road, edged with larger boulders. This road was later became known as one of the *Sarnau Helen*, supposedly created by the legendary Welsh Empress, Helen of Segontium.[39]

Because the challenges and responses between gate guards and the incoming squad were bellowed in Latin, Taliesin realized that the square, four-acre camp, enclosed by a *fosse* and *vallum*, was still in Roman hands.[40] From beneath Dark Age Caerhun, Roman Canovium sprang into view again.

He was frog-marched along the camp's *Via Principalis*. On his left, he noted barracks for one hundred and fifty men of the five-hundred-strong garrison. The granary lay to his right. The party halted under the arched gate of the *Principia*. There, a centurion of the 20th Legion Valeria Vitrix, based at *Deva* (Chester), forced him to swear oaths of allegiance to Jupiter, Best and Greatest, to the Deity of the Emperor, to the God Mars the Preserver, and to the Genius of the standard-bearers of the 20th Legion.[42]

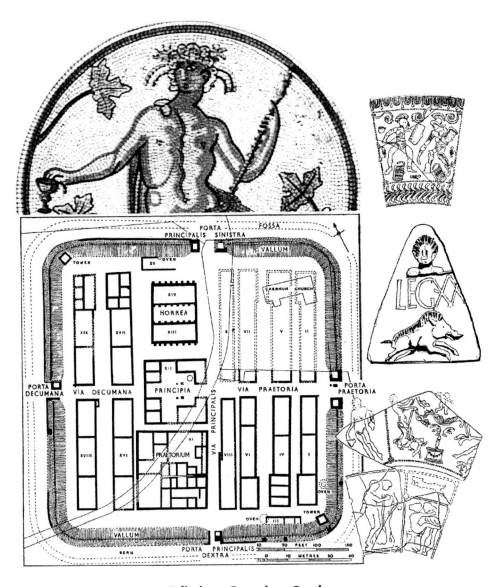

Taliesin at Canovium-Caerhun

Top left:	*Gwion Bach as Bacchus, with grapes and wine cup; from a Roman mosaic from Thruxton, Hampshire.*
Bottom left:	*Plan of the Roman fort, occupied first to fourth centuries.*
Right centre:	*'Taliesin' as a 'sun god' with boar; antefix insignia of the 20th Legion's soldiers' at Canovium.*
Right top and bottom:	*Three sherds of Samian pottery from Canovium; showing Gladiators, Bacchus with cupids, and lovers.*

Taliesin's Latin was poor. When he mispronounced words, a knobbly vine-stem was brought down across his back. 'Scourged with a rod from my own vineyard', he gasped, between the blows. 'Don't you recognise me? I am Gwion, *your* wine-god, Bacchus'. The men laughed. The thrasher said: 'If so, you must have stole that name from us, you sneaky, cup-sized godlet. We'll make a real man of you!' Thwack; the beating continued.

Afterwards, the victim was interviewed by the commandant, who asked about the disposition of Ordivician forces in the locality.[43] 'The Ordivician is a geological formation, lying between the Silurian and Cambrian series',[44] the bleeding prisoner replied, in an expressionless tone. The *Praetor* frowned and ordered an attendant to bring wine. An amphora, resting in a metal tripod, was produced, along with two Samian-ware goblets. Just such an amphora, found in pieces at Caerhun, is now in Llandudno museum.[45]

'Congratulations on your second century improvements to Agricola's earth and timber fort of AD 77', said Taliesin, in an attempt to combine ingratiation with military knowledge. 'As we came in, I couldn't help but admire the stone revetting, and the new corner towers'.[46]

'Oh? I suppose you seize every chance to register the latest developments in fort design. How many of our installations have you managed to penetrate so far', the commander asked?

'Thank you Sir', said Taliesin, accepting a top-up of wine, in which he saw his own boyish face, reflected on the trembling surface of the liquor. 'Yes, wherever there are Romans, you'll find me. The morale of your troops depends on my presence. If you had endured the over-sweet mead or flat ale of the post-Roman era, you would think yourself lucky to have Gwion-Bacchus, in your midst.'

Then, unsteadily, due to his wounds, he stood up and held out a hand, saying: '*Praetor*, allow me to thank you for your time and generous hospitality. Unfortunately I must now be off, for it is a long and arduous way to Llyn Geirionydd, where I must dredge up words from underwater powers. So, with a last toast to your military success, I request permission to depart.'

As he turned to go, two guards blocked the door, while from a shelf the *Praetor* produced a box. Inside was an *antefix*, made at Holt-on-Dee, the legionary supply base. This triangle of fired clay, soon to be fixed onto the cornice of his camp residence, featured the 20th Legion's totem, a wild boar, above which was an image of the radiant head and shoulders of a sun god.[47] 'You see, Taliesin-Bright-Brow, we have captured your image; you are obliged to stay. You have been trapped by your own claims to divinity. We depend on your golden light, *and* your equally holy blood-red wine'.

Caged alone in the camp gaol, Taliesin despaired. Then a shaft of morning sunlight shot through his tiny cell window, to create a glowing amber badge, which moved with imperceptible stealth across the west wall. It was a sign that he had joined the

Roman Army, and a reminder that his mixed ancestry included the sun god Apollo-Maponos, repeatedly inscribed near Hadrian's Wall.[48]

'I am this army's sun-god *and* I serve the ancient British and their Welsh descendants, but with no weapons except light, warmth, wine and words. So I will compose an epitaph for Rhun of Caerhun, despite his finger-chopping deceit:

> *'By the death of Rhun I mourn the fall of the court and girdle of*
> > *Cunedda.*
> *For the tide of the sea, for the salmon of the brine, for the herds and*
> > *abundance...* ' [49]

'Since sunlight and the wild boar's charge belong to everyone, I am imprisoned within human consciousness as a whole, including its fighting instinct.' Then he began to regret having ever disparaged his praise poems addressed to Urien and other warriors of the Old North.

'There is war in Nature, and between stars,' he argued. 'Conflict between elemental forces cannot be denied. That is why the four gates of this camp, are aligned with the bloody battles of the east-west sunrise and sunset, and with other fights at the north-midnight and south-noon extremes. These cardinal wars provide the battle plan for life on earth. Therefore the staccato sound of parade ground drill that punctuates my time here, should be matched by a poet's equally strict command of rhyme and metre, without which my work will amount to nothing but flaccid self-indulgence.'

He then uncoiled himself from the dank cell floor. Reaching up, he grabbed the window bars with both hands and roared: 'I swear by the red blood of Bacchus-Dionysus and by the light of Apollo-Maponus to marry spontaneity with order, and liberty to discipline, or die in the attempt.'

Having completed his basic training, Taliesin was free to go. He was carried from the camp on a Welsh buckler, a fencing shield of the Tudor period, which may have belonged to his own story-teller, Elis Gruffydd.[50] It was found in a Caerhun ditch and made of leather, reinforced with iron rings and studded with bronze nails. Such shields were often eulogised by late medieval Welsh poets in cosmic terms:

> 'A picture of the sun full of rivets... A steel moon for the old brave
> > soldier
> 'A buckler with snowflakes or with flowers of steel scattered all
> > over it.
> 'Many ribs are found from its body... Three girdles as if around
> > a maiden.
> 'Rivets are sparks from the sun, Stars thickly powdered as on
> > the Milky Way.'[51]

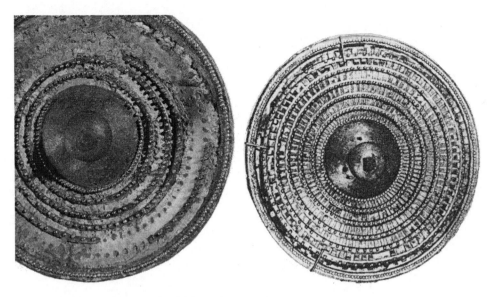

Left: *Welsh buckler or shield found at Caerhun;* circa *AD 1500.*

Right: *A late medieval buckler.*

Maen y Bardd

Taliesin was dumped two miles west of Caerhun, beside a Neolithic burial chamber called *Maen y Bardd,* 'Stone of the Bard.'[52] There he assessed the size of his task. War, sport, technology, sex, agriculture, politics and art; he had to tie them all together with sunbeams, converted into memorable words. 'King Arthur, where are you?' he shouted, 'I need your help!'

No sooner had he uttered that legendary monarch's name than he saw 'Arthur's Spear', Welsh *Picell Arthur,* a slender megalith, more than seven feet tall, standing a few yards away.[53] His namesake, Welsh *arth,* 'bear', is extinct in Wales, but the legendary Arthur often resurfaces when needed. To Taliesin, he was a solar godfather who might dispense advice.

Another name for the 'Arthur's Spear' megalith is *Fron y Cawr,* 'The Giant's Stick.' Folklore maintains that a giant threw this stone 'stick' at his dog, which retreated into the nearby chamber and would not come out; hence the cromlech's alternative name, *Cwt y Filiast,* 'Kennel of the Greyhound Bitch'.[54] 'I am to share my bardic lodgings with a dog,' sighed Taliesin, as he crawled in.

Squatting there, he recalled that several such monuments in Wales were believed to house the same mythic hound, leader of the *Annwn* pack, through whose jaws mortals passed on their way to death. In this B&B the dog breakfasted in bed on the guests. Taliesin's Roman captors had tricked him into entering an execution chamber, deceptively renamed *Maen y Bardd.* There he would be dispatched in the traditional manner, but since it was raining hard outside, he decided to stay in the dry.

As he waited for the lethal snap of canine incisors on his neck, he saw through the cromlech entrance a mountain range, beyond which he imagined Llyn Geirionydd's quiet shore. 'Goodbye, Lake Language. Forgive my failure to arrive.' I tried my best to come to you,' he said.

Welsh folklore repeatedly speaks of *three* outcomes for occasional barrow-dwellers. Either they die, go mad, or become poets. Reflecting on these outcomes while within the 'kennel', Taliesin guessed that the best poetry might be generated from *inside* the goddess-muse. Within the tomb, he could become part of the original tomb-deity, in body, spirit, and capacity for inspired speech. Ceridwen-as-tomb-bitch[55] offered him her megalithic 'lung', breath by breath, as she had to the ancestors. He longed for the courage to trust her and to deeply inhale. But on considering the madness or death that could ensue, his nerve failed and he *held* his breath. So the opportunity was lost.

He rationalised his refusal on the grounds that the cromlech's echo was composed of dry, hard-edged consonants, with insufficient vowels between them. Furthermore, as a demi-god, destined to travel *between* worlds, he could not commit himself to her underworld, any more than he could agree to the Dinas Dinlle offer of a perpetual Otherworld feast. His job was to persuade hidden powers to come to the surface, rather than for him to descend to them. Therefore he crawled out and stumbled onwards 'as far as the wind dries, as far as the rain wets.'[56]

Hag attack

Some time later, as he was passing beneath the ramparts of a British Iron Age hillfort, *Pen y Caer Helen*, he found himself in a sloping field of innumerable Welsh 'dragon's teeth.' Set on end, these stones erupted through the turf, as part of the outer defences.[57] He had halted, wondering if he should go through or around the hazard, when a loud shout rang out and man, waving his arms, came panting up from behind.

The stranger blurted: '*Gwrach y rhibin*! It's her. Run!' Grabbing atTaliesin he added: 'I saw her. The mist was thick; washing her hands in the *Gwrach* stream near Llwyn pen Ddu, she was. Her shriek froze my blood.'*Oh! Oh! Fy ngwr! Fy ngwr*', she wailed: 'My husband, my husband.' Her words burn me. Unless I can find that foul creature another mate, I am done for! I beg you, marry her. Release me from her black breath.' The man retched, lost his grip on Taliesin and collapsed on the heather.

Opposite top left: *Maen y Bardd, alias Cwt y filiast, 'an allusion to Ceridwen in her Greyhound form', writes Lowe. This fourth millennium BC chambered tomb stands in Caerhun parish, Caernarvon*

top right: *Picell Arthur, 'Arthur's Spear', a seven feet high standing stone, sited a few yards from the tomb*

bottom left: *The view from inside Cwt y filiast.*

bottom right: *The meat eater waits.*

Taliesin knelt over the prostrate figure. A report of 1882 states that people *were* killed at the local Gwrach stream-head, to placate 'false gods', *and* nearby on Penmaenmawr, for the same reason.

When the man came round he squinted and croaked at Taliesin: 'She wants *you*. Marry her, and give us all some peace'. But Taliesin said: 'I cannot. She is… ' He paused. 'She is my mother. She would eat me again. In any case, she already *has* a husband under Llyn Tegid, who is named Tegid Voel. Return home. Open your door to her. She needs someone in this area to catch her cries. You are honoured to receive them.'

This incident is based on an event reported in *The Cambrian Register* of 1831 by William Howells. The pursued man in question lived on, haunted by his *Gwrach y Rhibin*. He never married.[58]

Water bull

Taliesin continued on his pilgrimage. The mountains grew steeper as he advanced and seemed increasingly permeated by mythic characters. For example, he saw how *Penyrhelgiddu*, 'Head of the Black Hound Ridge' was about to swallow a rival, the 'brilliant' god Lleu, son of the moon deity, Arianrhod. Lleu was dropping his sunset eye into *Ffynnon Llugwy*, the fountain-head tarn and river's source named after him, set immediately below the hound's cliffs.[59]

Turning west in fading light, Taliesin lost his footing on a nearby mountain named *Pen Llithrig Y Wrach*, 'The Hag's-Head Slide' and found himself glissading unstoppably down a steep scree slope. It launched him, roaring and terrified, into the air. Opening his eyes against the onrushing wind, he saw, far below, a long lake, surrounded by precipices.

In free fall, he yelled: 'Llyn Geirionydd! At last! I'm coming!' Then, 'Splosh!' a ring of foam appeared on the dark water. A raven flew over to investigate the noise, but nothing resurfaced and the white circle of froth soon dispersed.

Hours later, beneath the horns of a rising moon, a small shuddering thing slowly clawed itself onto a shoreline boulder. It flopped there, exhausted and inert. In this manner Taliesin arrived on Llyn Cowlyd's shore, instead of the *geirionydd* 'language' lake of his desire. And although Llyn Cowlyd *is* tongue-shaped, it can utter only the bellowings of its legendary water bull.

Opposite top: *A sighting of Gwrach y rhibin, [after Sikes] on the summit of Pen Llithrig y Wrach, 'The Hag's Slide'.*

centre and bottom: *Llyn Cowlyd, with a superimposed embossed bronze figure from a pagan temple at Wood Eaton, Oxfordshire, AD second century.*

bottom right: *Bronze bull's head bucket handle clasp from Welshpool, Powys; AD second century.*

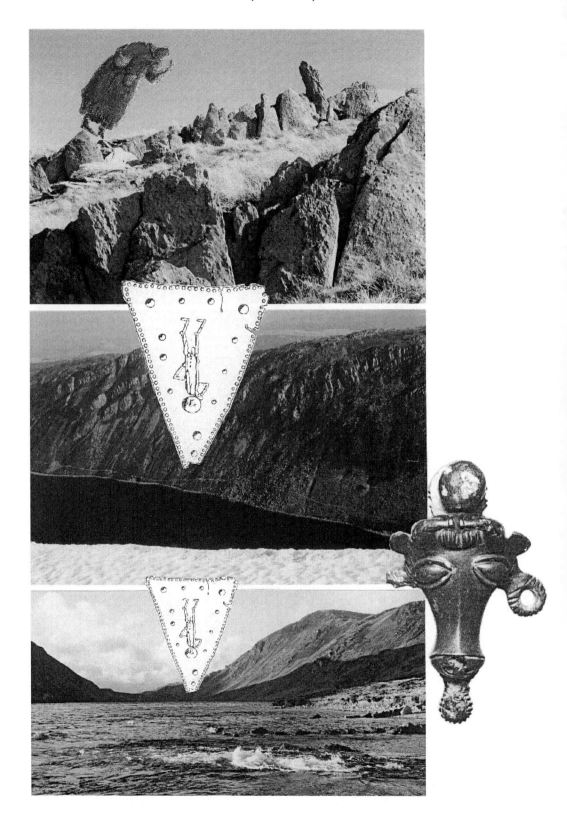

The angler Frank Ward noted in 1930: 'There is reputed to be a Water Bull residing in the depths of this lake, having fiery horns and hoofs, with flames issuing from its nostrils. It was supposed to come from the lake at night to drag the solitary wayfarer under.' He added that 'the water has been sounded to 360 feet without finding bottom.'[60]

From remote antiquity, writes Webster, the supernatural Water Bull has featured prominently in Western Europe as 'the Great God, the male element in nature, fertility and abundance.'[61] The Cowlyd water bull's 'cousins' include the pair who drew Luna's chariot into the ocean, as depicted on the Roman carving from London's temple of Mithras.[62] There, as at the Mithraic site of Segontium (modern Carnarvon), a sacrificed bull was the principal image, with the blood being drunk by a snake. (In Welsh folk belief the Hag is sometimes said to hiss like a snake.)

A bowl made from a bull's scrotum was still venerated near eighteenth century Harlech,[63] while at the bog at Dowris, Ireland, Bronze Age instruments in bull's horn shape, found under its waters, gave the bull's bellow a place of honour within ritual art.[64] Similarly, The Hag's Slide above Llyn Cowlyd implies that a Ceridwen-like figure might have required a bull's sacrifice by drowning, so echoing the goddess Cybele's *Taurobolium*, or sacred bull's slaughter in east Europe.[65]

For Taliesin, seizure by Cowlyd's Great Bull would enhance the maleness within his own make-up. His identification with the bull was complete, judging by his later claims: '*I have been a violent bull,*' and '*I have fled as a fierce bull fighting.*'[66]

Dragged below by the beast, he recalled that his only son, Afaon, is described in *The Triads* as: 'One of the Three Bull-Chieftains of the Isle of Britain.'[67] Down the generations, encounters with a divine bull, epitome of maleness, were thought essential for a would-be warrior, bard *or* seeress. Taliesin's brush with the Cowlyd fire bull made a freshwater counterpart to his sea voyage into a bull's-hide 'boat'. During that trip he came close to exchanging human skin for hide, while immersion at Llyn Cowlyd gave an opportunity to emulate some of the mythic animal's strength.

The place-name Cowlyd derives from Welsh word *cowlaid*, 'that which is embraced, an armful, foetus, lap, darling, dear one'. Moreover, the lake's alternative name, Cawlyd, suggests Welsh *caw,* 'swaddling clothes or clouts', for a new-born 'lake-child', whether bovine or humanoid, to wear. Within that lake, power and love coalesce; brute force and paternal tenderness merge beneath the mountainous shadow of the Hag's stoney 'head.'

Through his Llyn Cowlyd, experience Taliesin realised what terrific forces a would-be poet must reconcile in his work before it can ring true. Determined to start composing with fresh insight, he first jumped from the lakeside rock on which, hours before, he had landed, and shook himself dry.

With renewed determination he then set off again, and this time he sang:

> '*Sky of Geirionydd, I would go with thee,*
> *Gloomy like the evening, In the recesses of the mountain.*'[68]

Llyn Geirionydd, viewed from the north end.

Adroitly, he picked his way up and down another steep ridge, and over yet another, till, with an intake of astonished breath, he finally caught sight of his yearned-for destination. Stretched out beneath his high viewpoint, it shimmered and tantalised beneath a dispersing veil of mist. At his feet and beyond doubt lay King Maelgwn's gift to him; unwrapped at last, gilded Llyn Geirionydd.

CHAPTER NINE

'LAKE LANGUAGE'

Arrival

A folk tradition which assigns land around Llyn Geirionydd to Taliesin was recorded by Lewis Morris in 1726, but he confessed: 'Where this Llyn Geirionydd is, I cannot tell.'[1] In fact it fits snugly in a trench between two Snowdonian mountains, twelve miles south of Deganwy.

Llyn Geirionydd is small, only twelve hundred yards long, by three hundred across at its widest, and not particularly deep. However, it holds a value far in excess of its size, due to the 'language' of its *geirionydd* name. That word combines *geirio*, 'to enunciate, to phrase', with *nyddu,* 'to spin.'

Throughout pre-modern times, languages were believed to have come from the utterances of deities, as they spoke the universe into existence. When St John writes: 'In the beginning was the Word', he is expressing a belief, shared by most pre-Christian religions.

Thus in pagan Wales each cosmos-engendering divine syllable was held to have passed from a supernatural mouth, via demi-gods, shamans, prophets and poets, to the Welsh people in general, so forming the basis of their tongue. One of the best places for them to receive it afresh was at Llyn Geirionydd. Designated as the physical embodiment of Language's ineffable source, the lake was a reservoir of sacred narrative, and filled to the brim with mythic truths.

Between tree trunks, which rise like temple forecourt columns from the steep slope overlooking the lake, Taliesin saw dancing balls of light, at play on each wavelet, signalling him forward. 'Here I am!' he thought, and hurried to the shore.

There he discovered [like Scott, finding Amundsen's flag at the South Pole], that the sixth century mortal Taliesin had beaten him to it, as a thirteenth century poem fragment, *Anrec Urien, 'Urien's Present',* makes clear. Composed *circa* AD 570 by the mortal Taliesin who served Urien Reged, this poem ends: *'And I, Talyessin, from the bank of Llyn Geirionydd';* or *'I am Taliesin, whose habitation is by the pool Geirionydd'* in Evan Evans'rendering, while Ifor Williams' prefers: *'I, Talyessin, of the true lineage of Geirionydd.'* [2]

Llyn Geirionydd, Carnarvonshire; the west shore.

A sixth century *Dialogue* between Taliesin and his 'brother', the wizard Merlin, includes Merlin's words to Taliesin: 'Thou art experienced and the possessor of Llyn Geirionydd at the edge of Blawdd Wood'.[3] Having retired to, and died at the lake, the ghost of this thoroughly human Taliesin may emerge to greet the arriving demi-god. The historical bard might then coalesce with his supernatural namesake, the Taliesin who is also Gwion Bach. By drawing inspiration from the same 'language' water, the two Taliesins could come to speak with one voice.

Silence

Whenever the demi-god Taliesin arrives at Llyn Geirionydd, he sits by the shore and listens to what the *llyn* has to say. On windless occasions, when not the faintest lapping sounds come to his ears, he is puzzled by the lake's silence, thinking: 'Have I come all this way, and endured so much, for no response? Lake Disappointment, you are cruel!' Sulkily he stares at the glass-smooth surface and sees his image, floating there. His inverted self lies captured by the lake in a companionable quiescence. *Geirionydd* is sharing a pause, as she mimes the positive value of absolute stillness and calm. So, at the core of his febrile travels Taliesin discovers a sublime repose lying beyond words.

After that, the faintest ripples appear on the lake, as if from a submerged oracle, whispering the coalescence of every possible sound, making the chord that may underlie all languages, but audible only to itself. Putting an ear to the water, Taliesin hopes to catch something of that proto-Esperanto, but hears nothing.

He then recalls Tegid Voel, the taciturn lord of Llyn Tegid, whose name is from Latin *tacitus,* 'passed over in silence, not spoken of, kept secret.' As Ceridwen's husband, silent Tegid shared her mysteries. In doing so, he aligns with a world-wide tradition that regards silence as 'one of the essential elements in all religions' and understands divine silence as 'a fullness beyond words', with 'pure silence as the highest form of religious expression.' 'We learn silence from the gods,' Plutarch says.[4]

Thus in Wales the legendary fifth century Welsh law-maker, Dyfnwal Moelmud was mute, as his name implies (Welsh *mud,* 'dumb'). His wisdom came from a wordless, supernatural, 'deep', Welsh *dyfn.* Only after that immersion did Moelmud prove useful to humanity; for example, by organising the re-opening of lost roads to temples, and by drawing up an entire legal code.[5]

At times, the loquacious Taliesin also required silence. Because his work involved mythic (and therefore cyclical) restatement, a period of quiescence between each circuit was essential for him. He had arrived at Llyn Geirionydd entirely drained and literally speechless. Rather than *geirionydd,* he craved a rest from volleys of words, however inspired. Accordingly, his stay at the lake always began with a Holy-Day-in-silence, a wakeful, curative incubation, similar to 'the pledge of sweet slumber'[6] offered by sixth century Gildas, to those who recline on the banks of Wales's transparent rivers.

During this mute interlude, Taliesin's reflection in the water ensured that his 'I' and its 'Thou' were combined. His face *turned into* the lake and vice-versa. They shared the same skin. Then Taliesin saw that the 'normal' boundaries of self-hood were a delusion. His 'me' had evaporated. By extension, his self-hood was lost, surrendered to and annihilated in everything. It was a free for all. Constellations entered his eyeballs without permission. His ego and self esteem collapsed. He had lost control. The silence he had sought had turned into his 'absence'. Similarly, on a historical level, 'because of some falling out, [King] Maelgwn took Taliesin's [Geirionydd] lands away', as Lewis Morris reported.[7] So Taliesin lost his tongue. The gift of inspired speech deserted him. It was tossed as a dissolving ingredient into a universal stew, such as Ceridwen made in her cosmic kitchen.

Since he could find no words to extricate himself from this entanglement with his enemy Ceridwen, who had come to epitomise 'The Other', he decided at least to obliterate the lake's portrait of their dreadful union. He seized a dead birch bough. After raising it above his head, he smashed it into and through his own reflected 'water face', and that of Ceridwen's haunting presence, thereby shattering the double image into a thousand quivering bits.

As he stood over the disintegration, ready to strike a second blow when it re-assembled, he noticed three small drops of water. They hung suspended from the silver birch bough that he still grasped. Filled with gold sunshine and miniature rainbows, all three globules grew in size, till one by one, they dropped back into the lake. In doing so, they dissolved the tongue-tied spell that had gripped him since his arrival at Llyn Geirionydd.

First words

Toes in the water, squatting on his haunches, a single sob convulsed his chest. Then Taliesin-Gwion Bach grunted: 'Forgive me, grand mother. It was *I* who stole your drops of wisdom'. Gasping for breath and croaking like a cormorant he added: 'A poet has no identity, but continually fills other bodies. My job, I now see, is to give voice to their disregarded sayings'.

> 'A cry from the sea, a cry from the mountain…
> Wood, field, dale and hill.
> Every speech without anyone attending… ' [8]

Then he saw a flotilla of pink, tongue-shaped, fibreglass canoes, passing in front of him. Each craft contained a laughing child, dressed in helmet and lifejacket. Engrossed in serious enjoyment, this zigzagging squadron stirred the lake with their double-ended paddles. Waving to him, one of the canoeists almost capsized, much to the amusement of the others.

Taliesin returned the wave and thought to himself: 'Play! Gwarw! You again![9] You stir things about and from old materials make a fresh start. Thanks to you, these children can spoon me some *Geirionydd* words.' As if at an infant school, he then repeated in a sing-song chant the vocabulary doled out by their black paddle blades. The words included: '*geirio* 'to word', *geirwd* 'a murmur', *geirw* 'waves', *geirswn* 'the charm of words', *geirwir* 'truth-speaking', *geirber* 'sweet-spoken', *geirwfais* 'rippling water', *pwll padio* 'paddling pool', and *geirwgain* 'a lake ruffled by foamy waves'.

Welsh is a relatively new language,[10] splashed up by chance from the Indo-European reservoir of tongues. When the human Taliesin arrived at Llyn Geirionydd in the sixth century, the Brittonic, spoken alongside Latin during the years of Roman occupation, was in decay.[11] It eventually mutated into a primitive form of Welsh, now known as neo-Brittonic, or Old Welsh.[12]

The mortal Taliesin's arrival at Llyn Geirionydd coincided with the birth of Old Welsh. His poetry helped to bring that new tongue into the world as an entirely oral language, which did not take written form until the ninth century.[13] Likewise the words and poems attributed to the 'demi-god' Taliesin, were initially delivered and passed on by word of mouth.

The ability to talk comes naturally to humanity. Language is a gift from nature, rooted in the biological structure of the human mind. A 'language gene', FOX P2, which evolved 50,000 years ago in humans, has recently been identified.[14] As flowers produce nectar and songbirds sing, so people instinctively speak.

For Taliesin, Nature was synonymous with Ceridwen, and the ability to speak involved voicing her divine words, though she invested some of her vocabulary in

Left: *Boy paddling; a new generation takes to the water. He may soon swim towards an eloquence that will remake the world.*

Right: *Childrens' canoe lesson on Llyn Geirionydd, the reservoir of inherited speech.*

other creatures. *'I have fled as a thrush of portending language,'* Taliesin says.[15] Welsh folk-lore often reports trans-species dialogues and claims that the languages of birds, beasts, reptiles and fish can be understood by those who eat the flesh of white snakes – an intuited image of the DNA helix, common to all life.[16]

Until modern times, languages were thought of as the divine revelations of deities. After inventing a new tongue, they passed it, via demi-gods and inspired individuals, to the general populace. However, when conveyed down the human generations, words were seen, little by little, to lose their divine strength, turning into worn-out clichés. When this happened, renewed *direct* engagement with the sacred source was deemed essential. This was the dangerous task allocated to demi-gods, shamans and poets. They worked tirelessly to restore a fresh verbal connection between godhead and people. The two Taliesins, mortal and immortal, 'retired' to Llyn Geirionydd for that purpose.

Awen

Other means of access to the supernatural voice believed to underlie ordinary speech, are recorded by Geraldus Cambrensis in his twelfth century *Description of Wales*. 'Among the Welsh there are certain individuals called *awenyddion*.... When you consult them about some problem, they immediately go into a trance and lose control of their senses, as if they are possessed... Words stream from their mouths, incoherently and apparently meaninglessly, without any sense at all, but all the same well expressed; and if you listen carefully you will receive the solution to your problem.' Gerald continues: These *awenyddion* 'seem to get this gift of divination through visions which they see in their dreams. Some of them have the impression that honey or sugared milk is being smeared on their mouths.'[17]

When 'speaking in tongues', these fortune-telling *awenyddion* were held to be in touch, however slightly, with Welsh *awen*, the inspiration of a divine 'muse'. *Awen* was synonymous with 'poetic inspiration'. Without *awen*, Taliesin would be lost. '*God supreme, be mine the Awen! Amen; fiat!*' [18], sang a ninth century bard, Cuhelyn, forgetting that in Wales *awen* usually comes from a female deity, who supervised human destinies. Taliesin was in no doubt that he '*obtained the muse from the cauldron of Ceridwen* , which enabled him to chant:

> '*The Awen when it flows,*
> *Concerning skilful payments,*
> *Concerning happy days,*
> *Concerning a tranquil life*
> *Concerning the protection of ages,*
> *Concerning what beseems kings*' [19]

As in Graeco-Roman myths, the Welsh and Cornish *Awenau,* or 'Muses' sometimes gather in parties of nine, as at Cornwall's prehistoric *Nine Maidens* megalithic ring. Equally, the nine rows of chevrons incised on the Palaeolithic horse's jaw from Kendrick's Cave suggests that the muses could speak directly from a horse deity's mouth. (One accepted derivation of the word *awen* is from Latin *habena,* meaning 'bridle rein, mandible, jaw bone'.) The Welsh notion of *awen* stems from a widespread archaic tradition.

Taliesin's creativity depended on inhaling *awen*, found in the water droplets of Ceridwen's steaming cauldron, her sacred 'breath.' He inhales and then broadcasts this *awen* through his literally *inspired* verse:

> '*The Awen I sing, From the deep I bring it...* ' [20]

In one instance he attributes the sacred fountain of *geirionydd* to magical *submarine* outpourings, reminiscent of the Irish 'Well of Sacred Knowledge', called *Segais,* sited in the Atlantic beyond the Shannon estuary.[21] So Taliesin sings:

> '*The ebullition of the sea, How is it not seen?*
> *There are three fountains in the mountain of roses,*
> *Under the ocean's wave.*' [22]

Yet from this depth, he can soar to embrace the firmament:

> '*A bard with the breast of an astrologer,*
> *When he recites the* Awen, *at the setting in of the evening,*
> *On the fine night of a fine day.*' [23]

When sunset comes to Llyn Geirionydd Taliesin's head may drop beneath the water, enabling him to replenish his supply of deity-granted words from the lake, before retiring to his on-shore house to sleep.

Opinions vary as to the precise position of his supposed lakeside home. In 1808 Hyde-Hall was shown 'a low heap of rubbish near the [south-west] head of the

lake... as being the place of his abode.'[24] However, in 1837 G.J. Bennett noted that 'At the *eastern* side of the lake is a mound, upon the summit of which there is a kind of hollow. In it are the remains of an ancient edifice, which was probably the residence of Taliesin.'[25] By contrast, a writer, known as H.L.T, puts *Bod Taliesin* at the *northern*, or outflow, end of the *llyn*, 'among traces of banks and early buildings.'[26]

Ceridwen's cauldron

Inside his hut, set *somewhere* near the lake's brink, Taliesin often sat on a three-legged stool, as he stirred the pot containing his evening meal. Occasionally a bubble of jealousy would burst from the broth's surface and he would think:

> *'Shall not my chair be defended from the cauldron of Ceridwen?'* [27]

Then his simple stool became the bardic chair or throne of honour, awarded annually to the chief poet of Wales. Taliesin would resist any attempt by Ceridwen to reclaim the poetic power that she had invested in him, as symbolised by the chair.

> *'With me is the splendid chair, The inspiration of fluent and urgent song.'* [28]

It may represent a later form of the Neolithic goddess' stool on which she was so often modelled in the act of giving birth.[29] Determined never to surrender 'the chair' at the year's end, though custom decreed that he should, Taliesin wanted to cling to it in perpetuity, rather than let it drop back into the cauldron of inspiration, or vacate it for a rival poet to claim.

Yet a poem named *The Chair of Ceridwen*, copied into the fourteenth century *Book of Taliesin*, makes it clear that it belonged to Ceridwen, rather than to him, or to any other poet. She states:

> *'When are judged the chairs,*
> *Excelling them all will be mine,*
> *'My chair, my cauldron, and my laws,*
> *And my pervading eloquence, meet for the chair.'* [30]

Moreover, she makes it clear that Taliesin is by no means her only divine offspring. He must learn to share her bounty, just as she allows *Yr Awenau*, the 'Nine Muses',

Taliesin's home?

Opposite top and centre: *A traditional timber and thatch Welsh long house at Strata Florida, Cardiganshire, 1888.*

bottom left: *Ty Uchaf, 'Upper house', at Llyn Gerionydd's headwater stream.*

bottom right: *Plan of a circular Iron Age hut and enclosure, Llyn Geirionydd, east side.*

to duplicate part of *her* role. Taliesin even has to stomach Ceridwen rating the hideous Affagddu's skill above her own:

> *'Avagddu my son also...*
> *In the competition of songs,*
> *His wisdom was better than mine,*
> *The most skilful man ever heard of.'* [31]

Ogyrven, Ogma, Ogmios

As described in the *Book of Taliesin*, Ceridwen's cauldron contains the mysterious *ogyrven* or *gogyrven*. In one poem these are called: *'the various seeds of poetic harmony, the exalted speech of the graduated minstrel.'* [32] In another, Taliesin declares:

> *'May my tongue be free in the sanctuary of the praise of Gogyrven.*
> *The praise of Gogyrven is an oblation, which has satisfied them,*
> *With milk and dew and acorns.'* [33]

Ogyrven is again linked to *awen* and to cauldron in:

> *'High when came from the cauldron, The three awens of Gogyrven'* [34]

Ogma, an Irish deity credited with the invention of Ogam script, is thought to underlie the Welsh word *ogyrven*. Ogma is the patron of eloquence and literature and is often described as 'honey-tongued.' Resembling Taliesin, he is also called 'of the sun countenance'.

To the east, Ogma reappears as the Gaulish deity Ogmios, whose ceramic image, with solar rays streaming from his head, and carrying Sol's whip, was found at Richborough, Kent. Thus by swallowing the *ogyrven* 'seeds', Taliesin became one of a divine trinity, having allies east and west.

That wisdom comes in three-somes is central to the Celtic outlook, as seen in *The Triads,* the three drops of inspiration, *ogyrven* seeds, mother-goddesses and bardic chairs. So Taliesin says:

Opposite top left: *Bardic Chair and harpist; Dinorwic eisteddfod, Caernarvon, 1906–7.*

'I have been a string in a harp' – Taliesin, Book of Taliesin, *xv, 41–2.*

top right: *Cadair Brenhines, 'Queen's Chair', from the prehistoric site, Llys y Frenhines, Denbighshire.*

bottom left: *Enthroned goddess; a Celtic statue from Caerwent, Gwent.*

bottom right: *A Bardic Chair from the Colwyn Bay eisteddfod.*

Top left: *Base of a wooden tankard with central metal pellet as* ogyrfan *'grain'; from Trawsfynydd, Merioneth. AD first century.*

Bottom left: *The same tankard, with sheet bronze rim and bronze handle.*

Top right: *Handled ceramic beaker from a grave at Cwm-du, Breckonshire; circa 2,000 BC.*

Bottom right: *Yew and bronze medieval brewing bucket from Ty'r Dewin, 'Wizards House', Brynkir, Caernarvon.*

'*There are to me three chairs, regular, accordant,
And until doom they will continue with the singers.*' [35]

As if to counter-balance *Gogyrven's* solar role, the word is found again, deeply earthed in the name of the Welsh Giant, Ogyrfan, owner of the Iron Age hillfort, Caer Ogyrfan, near Oswestry. Folklore awards this giant five other fortress homes, all sited close to the English border, suggesting that, by brute force, and as the alleged father of Arthur's Queen Guinevere, Giant Ogyrfan might prevent the English language invading the heart of Wales.[36]

In plan, the Caer Ogyrfan enclosure suggests a gigantic head, with the unusual row of pits, aligned inside the entrance, adding 'teeth' to the giant's roar of defiance. His fort was incorporated into the fifth century line of Wat's Dyke, a British frontier ditch and bank, predating Offa's Dyke.[37]

Intoxication

Taliesin was grateful to find *ogyrven* seeds in his *geirionydd* potage, but if asked: 'What are *you* bringing to the language feast?' he could reply: 'fermentation skills, alcohol'. Many civilisations use intoxicating liquor to gain access to the 'other states' correlated with divine realms. Unsurprisingly, considering Gwion Bach's wine credentials, there are several allusions to the importance of alcohol in the medieval *Book of Taliesin*. Wine, mead, ale and bragget – he recommends them all, and often through a loose-knit flow of words, tumbling in free association, typical of near-drunkenness.[38]

Taliesin often sounds like a Mediterranean wine god, settled on the cold outer edge of the Roman Empire, and outliving its political collapse. He recalls:

'*Wine overflowing the brim, From Rome to Rossed.*' [39]

[Rossed was in Caledonia.]

The memory of Bacchus' grapes still crowns his brow. Having put his life-blood and soul into so many vintages, he is indignant if anyone fails to address the beverage with due reverence:

'*Why will you not recite an oblation
Of blessing over the liquor of brightness,
The theme of every one's rhapsody?
I shall be there according to custom*' [40]

As with the sacramental blood of Christ, converted into wine, Taliesin's divinity speaks through alcoholic liquor. He brings his own ferment to the Llyn Geirionydd language vat and can plausibly claim that Ceridwen's distilled drops, whether from cauldron or lake, are partly *his* achievement. By passing them back and forth between each other, mother and son collaborate to produce the perfect blend. One sip of its mellowness can dissolve the most intractable sex-tarian disputes.

In common with Ceridwen, Taliesin affirms the holiness of matter, as symbolised by sacred drinks. His is a non-dualistic viewpoint, encouraging sacred and secular joys to mix, while he sings:

> *'Pleasant the carousal that hinders not mental exertion*
> *Also pleasant, to drink together about horns.'* [41]

When, in the fifth century the wine supply from abroad dried up, Taliesin-Gwion adapted to the situation by 'becoming' mead, bragget, and beer. In common with the Nordic myth, where mead *is* poetry,[42] he also hints that he is the malted barley grain from which ale is fermented.

> *'I have been a grain discovered, Which grew on a hill.*
> *He that reaped me placed me Into a smoke hole drying me...*
> *'Let the brewer give a heat Over a cauldron of five trees.'* [43]

In Taliesin's *Song to Ale* he orders his brewer to use a lake as a mash tub for the malted barley:

> *'He shall steep it in the Llyn, until it shall sprout.*
> *He shall steep it another time until it is sodden.'* [44]

The process must not be rushed:

> *'Not for a long time will be finished*
> *What the elements produce.'* [45]

More than forty decorated ceramic 'beakers', holding about one pint and used around 2,000 BC for the ritual consumption of beer, have been found in the prehistoric monuments of Wales.[46] Alcohol carried the dead across the threshold to *Annwn*, realm of the gods. It was this pre-Roman tradition that Taliesin was determined to maintain, along with its Roman and post-Roman forms. He advocates *'Ale, when it is of an active quality'*,[47] rather than flat. Its bubbles were probably a sign of 'divine breath' contained in the brew.

He also repeatedly extols the wonder of mead:

> *'From the foaming mead-horns, with the choicest pure liquor,*
> *Which the bees collect and do not enjoy.*
> *Mead, distilled, sparkling, its praise is everywhere...* [48]
> *'And mead-horns intoxicating... The gift of the Druids.'* [49]

Opposite top left, top right and bottom left: *Llyn Geirionydd's north end* bala, *or 'outflow.' Always different, yet ever the same. This lake speaks volumes, and with a contemporary lilt, at its modern concrete exit sluice, leading to Afon Geirionydd.*

bottom right: *Afon Geirionydd.*

'I am not a mute artist. I am not a shallow artist.' *Taliesin,* Book of Taliesin, *xiii, 13.*

Druids, as poet-priest intermediaries between humanity and the gods, help to distribute 'Taliesin-as-mead.' Mead is fermented from honey combs, set in hollow trees or dark hives. In Wales, as elsewhere, bees themselves have yet to shed their folk reputation as supernatural agents.[50] Taliesin's mead-gold words ring out:

> *'And when there shall be an exciter of song,*
> *Let it* [mead], *be brought from the cell*
>
> *Let it be brought before kings*
> *In splendid festivals...*

The intoxication of mead will cause us to speak' [51]

'Outflow', *Bala*

Taliesin, the sometimes drunken pioneer of language, is willing to dive through incoherence and obscurity in his daring search for new sounds, rhythms, tropes, interconnections and meanings. Only by taking such risks will he be able to utter, and thereby *become,* the spirit flowing through everything. On rising, he can then break the surface, spouting words that glisten like a May morning.

In this manner, as a silver tongue of water, he shoots over the modern concrete spillway at Llyn Geirionydd's *bala* or point of 'outflow', where he can repeat:

> *'The Awen I sing, From the deep I bring it...* ' [52]
>
> *'I am a harmonious one, I am a clear singer...* '[53]
>
> *'The declaration of a clear song' Of unbounded Awen...* ' [54]
>
> *'Through the language of Taliesin It was bright day...* ' [55]

Llyn Geirionydd's weir-outflow resounds with tuneful *bwrlwm*, 'bubble, rippling, and gurgling' noises, similar to the *blerwm*, 'blabberer, chatterer' speech which Taliesin had imposed on Maelgwn's bards. But now, at the moment of his Lake Geirionydd departure, these infantile burblings declare a continuity with the loftiest utterances. Thus *berw*, 'seething, foam, jabber', also means 'poetic inspiration, muse, poetry.' Similarly, the outflow's rhythmic percussion, endlessly repeated, yet subtly varied, is both old as the hills that it has shaped, yet ever new, thereby matching poetry's inventiveness. As with Welsh *dwr byw,* 'running water, living water', novelty gleams in the timeless current of the poet's words.

Overlooking Llyn Geirionydd's *bala*, and only a hundred yards from that weir, stands the twenty feet high *Colofn Taliesin*. This stone pillar rises from three tiers of rugged steps and was erected in 1850 by Lord Willoughby de Eresby, to honour the great bard. Struck by lightning in 1976, the damaged shaft was restored, and a cross set incongruously on top.

Immediately behind the monument is a hillock named 'Hill of Songs', *Bryn Canidau*, beneath which Taliesin recalled: *'I am a harmonious one... a clear singer.'* [56]

Left: *Taliesin's Column,* Colofn Taliesin, 20 *feet high. Erected in 1850, damaged by lightning in 1976, restored 1994.*

Right: *A portrait of the Reverend Evan Evans, the author of the poem,* Glan Geirionydd.

Inspired by him, Welsh language bardic festivals were held annually from 1865 till 1890. Named *Arwest Glan Geirionydd,* 'Minstrelsy of the Geirionydd Valley', these gatherings were organised by William John Roberts of Trefriw.[57] He was the biographer of his uncle, Evan Evans of Trefriw (1795–1855). Evans' lyric poem *Glan Geirionydd,* written 'with a clarity and dignity of language and a smooth, melodic metre... delights in his childhood memories of the Geirionydd valley, and his communion with Nature there.' [58]

Unlike his uncle, Roberts was bitterly opposed to foreign 'contamination' of Welsh language, song and literature. Chosing a bardic name, *Gwilym Cowlyd,* after the stream whose waters merge with Afon Geirionydd, he awarded himself the additional title of *Prifardd Penant,* 'Chief Poet Positive', though his verse is considered to 'contain little of lasting value.'[59]

Roberts' exclusive stance failed to discourage some twentieth century Welsh poets who worked in English, Vernon Watkins for example, from seeking inspiration at Taliesin's lake. In 1938 Watkins cycled from South Wales on a pilgrimage to the Geirionydd valley. A draft of his poem, named *Taliesin,* composed shortly afterwards, contains lines referring to the replies of infants, from whom he had asked directions to the lake:

> 'Your name, your name on the tongues of children, Taliesin,
> Lost in the mist, a bard, I found your abode,

A blind man acclaimed on a blind road
By children learning to spell.' [60]

Indo-European exit

Having shot from the lake, the immortal Taliesin runs off in haste as Afon Geirionydd's turbulent stream. In this watery guise he snakes through tussocky pastures to where, by innumerably repeated journeys he has cut a sunless gorge. Its rocky sides echo his words as he rushes through:

> *'I am a serpent; I am love… I am not a confused bard drivelling… '* [61]

> *'And it is not known whether my body is flesh or fish.'* [62]

Glancing up, he sees the formidable overhanging ruins of the Klondyke lead ore-crushing mill, erected in 1900[63]. He bellows at those walls:

> *'All the sciences of the world collected together in my breast.'* [64]

After travelling for two winding miles downstream, singing: '*I am Taliesin, With a speed flowing as a diviner, Continuing to the end'*,[65] he swims into the river Conwy at Trefriw. There he is delighted to meet again someone who could appreciate his achievement in global terms, namely Dafydd Bryn Pyll.

During the 1880s, this 'tall, spare man with an aquiline nose and reddish hair' had run a steam ship service between Trefriw and Deganwy, a twelve miles voyage to the Conwy's mouth. Passengers shared the deck with his vegetables, which he grew from old buckets that stood in rows. In his youth, Bryn Pyll had often sailed round the world.[66]

Having at length retired to his homeland, he alarmed the Chapel elders by attending Sunday School at Deganwy, where he gave unofficial talks on Confucianism, Buddhism, Hinduism, and other non-Christian religions that he had encountered on his travels. A contemporary account describes how 'The entire Adult School crowded around him to listen, teachers included. But the elders were horrified and ordered him to discontinue his classes.' He obeyed, but announced that he would continue his talks 'in the commodious hold of an old hulk of his, moored alongside the quay at Trefriw.' To the fury of the elders, most of the enthralled Sunday school soon migrated there.[67]

Taliesin decided to attend Bryn Pyll's sessions. The rusty hulk's interior, ringing with animated talk, reminded him of Ceridwen's cauldron. As Sunday followed Sunday, Taliesin perceived that all that he had so painfully learnt by firsthand experience was known *and* practised already by innumerable 'foreign' communities. He gathered from Bryn Pyll's lectures that Ceridwen's 'sisters' included the Indian goddesses *Shakti,*[68] who embodies universal energy, and *Vac,* alias 'Speech', who was the deity of languages, human *and* divine.[69]

Taliesin immediately sensed that Ceridwen was his 'Vac.' He blurted out: '*I have been in India when Roma was built!*' [70] At this interjection, the sound of tittering broke out among the group, drowning Pyll's claim that Welsh *Awen* has a close parallel in Hinduism's *Atman*,[71] the cosmic spirit animating the 'World Soul', and that the mysterious *ogyrven* kernels of Wales were closely matched by the Hindu use of key syllables, or 'seeds', regarded as the ritually chanted essence of cosmic power.[72]

One afternoon, during the discussion following the main address, Taliesin's eye wandered towards the iron-plate ceiling. There he saw three water droplets, condensed from the company's collective breath in that crowded space. They hung like transparent ripe fruit, on a horizontal pipe. He was wondering which of the three would drip down first and on whom it would fall, when he heard Pyll's voice, speaking in a foreign language:

'*Tat tvuam asi,* meaning 'That thou art', is a mantra, encapsulating Hindu wisdom. It expresses the underlying oneness of things. *Tat*, 'That', is *brahman*, the universal principal. *Tvam*, 'Thou', is *brahman*'s individualised aspect. So, shipmates, the mantra declares that the single individual is identical with the cosmic Absolute; in other words, microcosm equals macrocosm.'

'That's me!' Taliesin shouted. 'That's what I've been trying t... .t... t... to... *CONVEY!* I'm not a boastful freak after all, but perfectly normal.' Pyll paused, nodded at Taliesin, and continued: 'Hindus believe that immortality involves the absorption of the individual into the unifying whole, just as a Welshman's *bod*, 'home', is synonymous with Welsh *bod*, 'being, essence, god-head.' We all know that, don't we?'

Dafydd Bryn Pyll loved his free-floating home, yet though deeply attached to Wales, and to one tidal reach of it in particular, he regarded Mam Cymru's beauty in an open-spirited manner as a local representative of global maternity. Following another Welshman, William Jones (who was the first person to recognise that the Welsh language belonged to a family of tongues, stretching from Ireland to the Bay of Bengal),[73] Pyll spoke of 'root words', shared across continents.

From Great Orme's Head to India's Cape Comorin, Taliesin now envisaged cruising this 'speech ocean.' He would hire a dinghy and sail to its many coasts, where he would enjoy rudimentary conversations on ground held in common. All his previous escapades could be seen as preparing him for this epic voyage. Yet half-fearing to do what he knew he should, he tried to whip up the necessary courage by singing:

> '*I am not a shallow artist...* ' '*The deep ocean is suitable...* ' [75]
> '*I will address the bards of the world...* ' [76]
> '*I got indeed in my bardic song All the magical arts of Europe
>   and Africa...* ' [77]
> '*Heroic numberer of languages, A conspicuous sea shoal of
>   goodly increase.*' [78]

CHAPTER TEN

GOLD AND GRAVE

Llyr Llediaith, 'Sea half-speech'

After finding a channel through the mussel banks of the Conwy Sands, Taliesin steered his boat towards the open sea. He intended to span the entire Indo-European speech-ocean, and to return loaded to the gunwales with the most ancient common roots of words. Even as he passed beneath the shadow of Penmaenmawr, that 1,300 feet high 'Great Stone Head' promontory, with its nearby Neolithic monuments,[1] he could taste in his imagination the exotic flavours of primal syllables buried, deeper than *Annwn*, beneath the Indo-European ancestral bed-rock, from which his own tongue had grown.

By contrast with his 'bag' voyage, he could also enjoy the reflected light from his own head. It lent:

> *'A complete billow of fire over the seas.'* [2]

In high spirits he remarked:

> *'Glorious the appearance of the torrent on top of the waves.*
> *The swans resort round the morsel on the face of the surges.'* [3]

His optimism was such that he imagined a new continent far to the west, whose inhabitants might say:

> *'I reckon – when I count at all – First – Poets – Then the Sun'* [4]

or: *'Nature is the incarnation of a thought, and turns to thought again, as ice becomes water or gas.'* [5]

'America! I must ask the famous Welsh-American architect, Frank Lloyd Wright, to build me two houses there and name them both 'Taliesin', after me, so that I can feel at home in that great country', said Taliesin.[6] Then he lowered his head to contemplate the vertical circulation of waters and saw:

> *'Three springs beneath the ocean… One generates brine to replenish*
> *the flood… the second without injury falls on us when there is rain*

abroad, through the whelming sky. The third will appear through the mountain veins, like a flinty banquet'.[7]

Meanwhile, from the outset of his voyage, the coastline of his native country was miming a range of animal utterances. For example, Anglesey's flatness gave off a monotonous insect humming, in contrast to the macaw-like consonants of Lleyn peninsula's mountain peaks and Cardigan Bay's turtle dove vowels. Mile after shoreline mile, the Welsh *Mam Daear*, 'Mother Earth', was clearly trying to say something coherent, but he was unable to translate her offsprings' medley into human speech.

Taliesin steered in closer in order to try again. However, as he entered the shallows, so the various voices were lost behind the boom of surf, a sound that Welsh legend attributes to a supernatural character called Llyr Llediaith. His name means 'Sea Half-Speech.'[8]

According to Welsh dictionaries, the seaward-sucked rattle of pebbles, followed by the hubbub of a breaking wave, is registered by the human ear as the sea's *llediaith,* 'corrupt or incorrect language, peculiar or affected accent, twang'. Yet Llyr's *llediaith,* 'half-, or semi-speech', contains other *lled* meanings, such as: 'wider, greater', and 'more abundant', drawn from the ocean's fecundity.

These connotations are in turn attached to agriculture, where *lled* is 'a width in mowing hay, or cutting corn with a scythe'. Thus Llediaith's noisy breakers are seen again across summer fields in the recumbent swathes of hay and golden corn. Because these swathes lie still and silent, *Triad 52* declares that Llyr Llediaith is then a prisoner of Euroswydd,[9] his 'Splendid Enemy', who is the land itself.

Buffeted by Llyr Llediath, Taliesin half understood that nature and culture are each other's 'prisoner' and that all languages are rooted in the pre-human sounds made by vocal natural 'characters' such as Llyr. They endlessly voice the world's original melodies, underlying every human tongue.

So engrossed did Taliesin become in the surf's hearty monologue that his planned voyage to India was jeopardised. On waves of Llediath's thunderous oratory, which grew louder as the beach approached, his frail boat was swamped. Then it capsized and was smashed against a wooden groin, while he was flung, like a drenched rag doll onto the dry sand above high watermark.

Border lines

'Where am I?' Taliesin asked on regaining consciousness. A sharp wind whistled. Herring gulls were screeching nonsense and marram grass was prickling at his face. On sitting up he saw the silhouette of a black bull being led inland on a rope by a man muttering in Welsh:

'Ynys Tachwedd, November Island; that's where; Slaughter Month, Year's End; the whole bleeding country slashed in two. You're for the chop, boyo!' Then man and beast disappeared. Taliesin had landed in a dangerous spot. Listlessly, he collected a

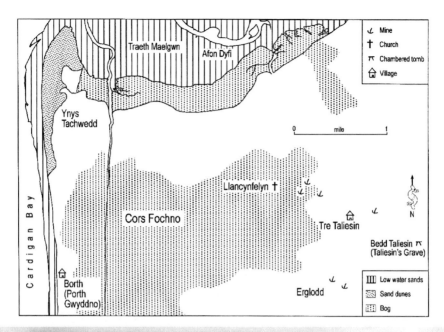

few driftwood sticks and lit a *coelcerth,* the traditional All Souls bonfire.[10] Hunched over its tentative flames, he expected the legendary black sow to join him – she that chases and gores the slowest person to run from the fire on that spirit night; but no pig came.

He looked around. To the north lay the wide mouth of Afon Dyfi, the east-west river, regarded as the boundary between north and south Wales. *Dyfi* is derived from the English word, 'division'. 'It seems that I have come to the 'great divide' and must choose between north's midnight and south's noon. Is it speech or silence, life or death for me?' Drizzle began to fall.

Then he heard the ghost of a fifteenth century bard, Deio ab Ieuan Du, who had lived nearby, reciting his *Greeting to Maredudd, On Having Survived Shipwreck in the Dyfi Estuary.* Deio followed this with a rendition of his *Thanks to Sion ap Rhys for the Gift of a Bull,* containing words now set into the royal badge of Wales: 'The red dragon will show the way.'[11] 'I hope so', Taliesin thought, while Deio's voice blew inland and faded out.

Afon Dyfi draws a frontier, perilous as that estuary's sands, across which incoming tides gallop to drown many who attempt a crossing, whether on foot or horseback. King Maelgwn had come here to start his conquest of south Wales. A chair, with waxed wings attached, was made for him, so that he could float on the in-rushing waters as they covered a stretch of sand on the southern side, now named *Traeth Maelgwn,* after his bird-like performance.[12]

By looking along the coast, Taliesin saw that he was only five miles from Sarn Gynfelyn, where he had landed on *Calan Mai,* six months earlier. Moreover, Gwyddno Garanhir, who ruled the submarine castle at its tip, had another base situated less than a mile from *Ynys Tachwedd,* named *Porth Gwyddno.* This, Gwyddno's mainland port, was near the modern village of Borth.[13]

Since Taliesin felt indirectly to blame for poisoning Gwyddno's horses at Llyn Tegid during the *previous* November, following the explosion of Ceridwen's cauldron there, he sensed that delayed retribution was now close at hand. The annual cycle's logic demanded the bard's death, in order to sustain the seasonal pattern on a divine foundation. Yet, being a coward, Taliesin was unable to wait passively for the final stroke. Instead, he decided to move inland and try to give Fate the slip.

Cors Fochno

He had taken no more than thirty steps to the east when he found himself floundering in *Cors Fochno* one of the greatest bogs in Wales. Neither land, nor sea,

Opposite top: *Map of Cors Fochno.*

centre: *Traeth Maelgwn, on the Dyfi estuary.*

bottom: *Cors Fochno bog.*

nor a fresh water lake, it is an unstable mixture of all three, and so perfectly matched Taliesin's precariously liminal condition nineteenth century attempts to drain the bog succeeded only at the margins.

Cors Fochno's saturated peat is over fifteen feet deep in places. The lowest level contains stumps of pine, alder and birch trees, part of a virgin forest, which flourished *circa* 3,000 BC, prior to a deterioration in climate.[14] Stacked above this 'submerged forest', and in strict chronological order (Nature being a proficient archivist) are the semi-decomposed remains of 5,000 summers' growth – the sphagnum moss and other bog-loving plants, including three species of the midge-trapping sundew, which flourished during those millennia.[15] Taliesin felt threatened by their sticky drops, which were said to possess magical potency.

With each squelching step he took, Cors Fochno's vegetable mortuary drew him in, as if urging him to admit that its rottenness was of *his* making. His solar head he had helped produce the life in whose filthy end he was now mired. By heel and toe, the former 'bright-browed' wanderer was puncturing *Calan Gaeaf's* fragile surface web of deer grass, cotton grass, heather and bog myrtle, so increasing the likelihood of drowning in filth. From the *Book of Taliesin* he intoned:

> *'The affair of Cors Fochno, he that will escape from it will be fortunate.*
> *There will be twelve women, and no wonder, for one man.'* [16]

Cors Fochno's quivering morass was presided over by *Yr Hen Wrach*, the inescapable 'Old Hag', the Mistress of life and death, sometimes called Ceridwen. She had Taliesin trapped. *Yr Hen Wrach* was said to emerge during the bog' frequent misty nights. She was over seven feet tall, and had a huge head. When she breathed on people who lived nearby, they caught the ague.[17] If seen, she would hiss like the adders that writhe through the marsh, and then vanish. Heather burning was carried out each February, in a futile attempt to drive her 'shivering sickness' away.[18]

Y Hen Wrach kept a gigantic toad, covered in warts bigger than ants' hills. The vile creature lived in the middle of the bog on a heap of its own excrement. It was 'the oldest animal in the world', according to several early Welsh texts.[19] This toad possessed oracular powers and could be consulted by anyone foolhardy enough to make the perilous journey to the 'faeces isle', sited near Cors Fochno's centre.[20] Like a terminally sick man determined to visit a fortune teller, Taliesin struggled there, resolved to hear the animal's predictions.

Llangynfelyn

The Giant Toad's 'dungheap isle' offered Taliesin better footing than the surrounding swamp. Indeed, it is solid enough to be capped by a small church, dedicated to the sixth century St Cynfelyn, a native of Ceredigion. He built and occupied a hermitage here. Church, hill, and parish are named Llancynfelyn, or Llangynfelyn, in his honour. The saint's feast day falls on November 1st.[21]

'That day again!' shuddered Taliesin. 'Cynfelyn's festival of turds must mark my demise. That being so, I will ask the holy man to hear my confession and beg him to

*St Cynfelyn's [or Cymbeline's] church on the island of
giant toad's excrement, Llangynfelyn.*

intercede with God for the absolution of my heathenish errors'. Then he fell to his
knees in the dirt and implored 'Oh Father Cynfelyn, son of Bleiddud, son of Meirion,
son of Tybion, son of mighty Cunedda, forgive me, for I have sinned'.

In reply, came the resounding *'urrwoomp, urrwoomp'* of a bittern, calling eerily from
somewhere across a marsh turned a flame red colour by the setting sun. Taliesin was
confused. He blurted: 'Is God a *bird*, nothing but a bittern, a *garanhir* crane, or
Avagddu, dressed as a cormorant? You atheistical fog-horning boomer, don't tell me
that Super-Nature is the only divinity still working!'

Then he heard voices radiating from within the church. They were chanting the
Gorchan, or 'Great Song' of *Cynfelyn,* which begins:

> *'Were I to praise, Were I to sing,*
> *The Gorchan would cause high shoots to spring*
> *Stalks, like the collar of Trych Trwrth,*
> *Monstrously savage, bursting and thrusting through*
> *When he was attacked in the river.'* [22]

Taliesin knew about *Trych Trwrth,* the mythic boar, with a golden comb adorning
the bristles of its head, which had often been pursued by King Arthur and his men.
They repeatedly chased it into the Severn.[23] But why did a Christian hermit choose
to recall this mythic event? Perhaps St Cynfelyn was a heretical follower of Pelagius,
the fourth century British Christian who denied the doctrine of original sin.[24] In *Cors
Fochno* beliefs of many kinds readily bed down together. Compressed as one, into

169

Top and bottom: *Tre Taliesin, a mining village on the east edge of Cors Fochno, named after the bard.*

Centre: Helyg Aur, *'Golden Willow'; the sun-faced house plaque of Taliesin's choice, seen in Tre Taliesin.*

clods of peat, they burned on local hearths with a welcoming glow and a hellish fug of smoke.

Cynfelyn had been a common name in Dark Age Britain. From Scotland to Cornwall there were lots of Cynfelyns. As indicated in Chapter Six, the name was derived from Cymbeline, alias Cunobelinus, the last pre-Roman British monarch. His *Calan Mai* phallic extension was visible at Sarn Gynfelyn, the place of Taliesin's May Eve landing. By contrast (and less than six miles from that proud *sarn*), at his *Calan Gaeaf* appearance he put on Llan Cynfelyn's winter cloak and intoned Llywarch Hen's impotent lament, while squatting on a dung-heap.

Tre Taliesin

On Llancynfelyn's hillock, Taliesin scanned the horizon, hoping to find somewhere better for a night's lodging. In the dusk he saw a light, flickering on the eastern edge of the bog. He strode off towards it, reasoning that 'It might be coming from *Neuadd y bardd*, 'Hall of the Bard', a place-name for which there is documentary evidence[25] and since I defeated all the bards gathered at Maelgwn's Court, the owners of this *neuadd* are sure to give me a bed'. ('A man's best candle is Reason' is a well-known saying of St Cynfelyn.[26])

Unfortunately the Hall had been demolished. By 1820 it had been reduced to the name of a tenement, which in turn was buried beneath part of a nineteenth century mining village, named *Tre Taliesin*, which in plain English means the 'family, home or township of Taliesin.' Could any two words offer a clearer invitation to this fugitive?

When a few yards from the first cottage, he paused by an enamelled metal sign, strapped to a pair of three feet-high poles set into the grass verge. Bending down, he slowly ran his fingers over its letters: T, R, E, T, A, L, I, E, S, I, N. Then he spread his arms along the sign's top edge and grasped its corners, as if to gather together long-lost relatives.

He could scarcely believe his good fortune. His breath came in rapid spurts as, with an accelerating stride, he paced the main street from end to end, crying out: 'Home! Home!' at each closed door that he passed.

Many of the dwellings had names, drawn from their immediate surroundings: *Min y gors*, 'edge of the bog', or *Is y coed*, 'under the wood', referring to the steep wooded ridge that rose behind the village. 'These people have deep roots here', the wanderer thought. Then he saw himself – a smiling solar head on a ceramic plaque, incorporating the name *Helyg Aur*, 'Golden Willows', attached to a cottage wall. 'That must be *my* place', he concluded, while continuing his walk.

Reducing his step to a contented amble, he noted that many of the houses bore titles drawn from his own adventures; for example, there was *Craig y Don*, 'Don's Rock', referring to the goddess whose 'chair' overlooks Llandudno. Nearby stood *Roman House* (named in English), stirring renewed thoughts of his Gwion-Bacchic connection. Across the street he saw Epworth House. Epworth, he recalled, was the birthplace of John Wesley, founder of Methodism, a cult given a harsh Calvinistic twist at Llyn Tegid.

The village showed how different strands in the nation's consciousness might be spun into a cable, strong enough to moor the great ship All-Imaginings to a bog-side quay. It was as if the entire contents of Taliesin's capacious head had been stored in, and were now unloaded from, this vessel. '*Tre Taliesin*, you are the craft of my soul!' he shouted. A dog looked round and barked.

Occasionally the outline of a female, peering out at him through lace curtains, but he saw no men. Like an Irish Otherworld, this was a place mainly for women. He asked a girl who was playing hopscotch on the pavement: 'Where is your father?' 'Down the mine, of course', she replied.

Despite its range of house names, Tre Taliesin was built as a single-minded nineteenth century mining village, set in an area of Cardiganshire noted for lead deposits, which in 1800 helped to make Britain the world's biggest lead producer. 142 tons of lead ore were extracted by Tre Taliesin's miners in 1855, while silver came from the Bryn Arian's small loads, worked beneath the steep ridge just east of the settlement. To the west, several vertical shafts, up to 240 feet deep, had been sunk through Cors Fochno into the underlying rock.[27]

As he stood at the domestic hub that capped this subterranean toil, Taliesin sensed a chance to escape his seasonal *Calan Gaeaf* death. He would simply detach himself from the inexorable mythic cycle to which he had always been bound, renounce his obligation to that archaic scheme, and instead begin a different *kind* of life, built on faith in linear progress. He would become a *miner.*

The gold miner

'Progress. *Cynnydd.*' Taliesin repeated the word in both languages. He enjoyed the sound, *and* its extra Welsh meaning, which is 'unlimited increase'. At Tre Taliesin he sensed that *cynnydd* was fast sweeping away all talk of 'conservation'. This profound change had left him 'out of date'. He was no longer required to balance the life-death seasonal accounts, or to mediate between human and supernatural domains, his previous tiresome lot. Instead, he could enjoy the rewards of technologically driven extraction, without bothering to make good the damage incurred. For him, *cynnydd*'s modern, individualistic rationalism was about to replace myth's thirst for repetition.

Gunpowder for blasting and coal for ore smelting, introduced into Cardiganshire *circa* 1700, had already produced quick fortunes for a few cunning entrepreneurs.[28] He would follow their example. So it was, that in the middle of Tre Taliesin, he finally cast off the lingering guilt over stealing a few drops from Ceridwen's yearly stew. With a sardonic laugh he shouted: 'What a fool I have been! It is time for me to join the real men, who take what they fancy from the earth, down to the core.'

That evening, Taliesin sat with miners in the village Temperance House, as they talked of pit props, lodes, methane gas, floodings and accidents. *Plwm*, 'lead', and *arian*, 'silver' were frequently mentioned. Then one man produced a crumpled copy of *The Mining Journal* and read out paragraphs in English, about the prospects for Welsh gold:

'It now seems the fashion to despise 'bunches' or 'pockets' of gold in quartz veins in 'poor little Wales... '[29] yet 'Wales contains all the necessary conditions for producing gold in large quantities, only requiring capital and energetic development to make it the richest gold country in the world.'[30]

'There you have it, straight from John L.M. Fraser, mining engineer of Dolgelly. And listen to this: 'Welsh gold mining is being established as a… remunerative enterprise… Shares… must inevitably have a big rise in price and the time is not far distant when a rush will take place to secure them.'[31]

Taliesin slipped away. Under a star-pulsing sky, he repeated under his breath the single word: *aur*, 'gold', as he hurried to a shaft-head near Llangynfelyn, where two men from Salford had spent £7,000 installing mine machinery.[32] There he struggled into an empty cage – scarcely more than a large bucket, which dangled from winding gear.

As dawn broke, and the cage was lowered to bring up night-shift men, he was deposited at the bottom of the shaft. From there, unobserved, he crept off, along a pitch-black, low-roofed gallery.

'Here I will find my true self at last', he thought. 'No longer a mere 'Shining Brow', Welsh *tal iesin*, I shall become rich, from head to toe. Even if there are no nuggets to be found, and the ore proves low-grade, it can be refined. Then I will possess an unalloyed, 24-carat fortune, to spend as I please. From an entirely secular golden palace I will outshine Apollo-Maponos and look down with pity on my demi-god past, incredulous that I could ever have been so gullible as to propagate such superstitious nonsense. This dark mine tunnel is the *Annwn* of the Future. Cleansed of gods by the power of reason, it will yield the ore to smelt into my mundane glory.'

Through a maze of cramped galleries, he then began to clutch and claw at the walls, feeling for the sharp texture of a quartz vein or lode, in which gold might be embedded. But none came to his hand. After searching for several hours, he did encounter the cubic shapes of *galena*, lead sulphide crystals. He was tempted to collect them, but knowing that alchemists had always failed to convert lead into gold, he slithered on without a pause. 'It shall be gold or nothing', he muttered. Yet hard as he looked, not one speck of that most precious metal glinted back at him from within the strata, to dispel his growing despondency.

He blamed his failure on a lingering mythic attachment. He was instinctively trying to out-shine Sol, or the Irish fire goddess Brigid. From ingrained habit, he had clung to obsolete hopes of progressing within a divine hierarchy, rising through mere demi-god's rank, to dazzle as a full sun deity. After admitting as much, he again renounced any sacred ambitions and instead resolved to concentrate exclusively on the concept of gold as a prosaic commodity. Only then could he gain access to the authentic currency of modern times.

To strengthen his determination, he focussed on a mental image of thirty-one fifteenth century English gold nobles, found in a hoard beneath *Cors Fochno* in June 1930. They bore the heads of Kings Richard 2nd, Henry 5th and 6th. They were in brilliant condition, and had suffered from no 'clipping.' Indeed, some exceeded the standard weight of 108 grains.[33]

Top left: *Mine chimney near Llancynfelyn.*

Bottom left: *Open mine-shaft at Tre Taliesin.*

'Money! How wonderful! Think of all those gold-crowned kings of Wales, depicted rising from the ship of state, as I did from my *Calan Mai* bag,' Taliesin mused, while continuing his search of the Llangynfelyn mine. Eventually, to ease an aching back he stood up and 'Ouch!' cracked his head on the gallery roof. On rubbing the bruise, an ingenious solution came to him in a flash.

He had no need to *look* for gold because he himself *was gold,* or rather he *generated* gold from his shining brow. Ever since Elphin had dragged him from the fish weir, he had probably been transmitting that precious metal from his own head, like a coin, stamped with a sungod-emperor's radiant crown.

'I am an artificer; I am a scientific one,' he chanted triumphantly.

To release his potential value, he only needed the tools to separate his gold rays from the body's dross. As with a Christian martyr, the more frequently his 'halo' was chopped off, the more vigorously it might spring up again. With this inexhaustible supply of metal available, he could then learn the coiner's art, and mint a million gold staters, guineas, or euros, with an image of his own head on each one. His wealth and influence would multiply exponentially. As King of Commerce, he could control the new age of *quantified* value and number-based accountancy. A bullionaire, he would flaunt his riches over all deities, and award Ceridwen the role of junior filing clerk.

Erglodd, *Aur Clawdd*

Taliesin returned, as fast as the labyrinth of narrow galleries allowed, to the shaft foot. Then, by clinging unseen to the side of the miners' cage, he was soon hauled to the surface, after which he hurried towards Erglodd, a district lying half a mile south of Tre Taliesin, where he had heard there was an ore-crushing plant.

'Excuse me', he said to a woman who was feeding chickens in the untidy Erglodd farmyard, 'I would like to use your gold-ore pounding stone'. The woman's eyes widened. Her jaw sagged. She dropped the meal bag and, with a scream, ran into the house, slamming the door behind her.

Amazed by this reaction, Taliesin was inclined to ignore the woman and wait for her husband to turn up; but since the man did not, he tapped on the door. It opened a crack, through which she hissed: 'Go away! I know why you've come. You are bringing the Third Stone. Don't deny it!'

Taliesin was even more surprised when she then grabbed his arm, drew him inside, and plonked herself beside him on a bench. In feverish tones she asked 'Don't you know the *prediction*?' When he shook his head, she reached for the topmost of three books, stacked horizontally on a low shelf behind her. In ascending order they were *The Holy Bible*, an almanac, and a second edition of Meyrick's *History of Cardiganshire*. From this she read aloud:

'In a field called *Lletty ngharad bach* ['Lodging of the little loved one'], belonging to Yurglawdd, are two stones, of which the vulgar say that when a third appears, the end of the world will be at hand. One of the stones is of a prismatical shape and has several circular interlinked excavations on its side and was doubtless used by the Druids in their sacrifices.'[34]

Putting the book down, she explained that the two stones had received repeated blows from a battery of Roman cam-operated trip hammers, like the one recently found at Pumpsaint, a Roman gold mine in Carmarthenshire.[35] Driven by a waterwheel, these iron-shod beams pounded up the lead and silver ores, dug from their mines in the immediate vicinity of Erglodd.[36] By repeated use, these hammers left overlapping bowl-shaped indentations in their 'anvil' stones. Taliesin had noticed just such a relic, lying by the front gate.

To Taliesin the stone looked more like a child's stone coffin, laid against a church wall. 'Yes', the woman confessed, 'we uprooted it from the field and placed it there, hoping to destroy the prediction. The Romans used the second stone – the one we've filled with earth and converted into a flower trough – to beat up their silver ore, in the same way as the lead.'

What she could not have foretold was that in the dry summer of 1976, an air photo revealed the presence of a Roman fortlet, only a few yards from where they sat.[37] It had a ditch (Welsh *clawdd*, hence the place-name element Er*glodd*), plus ramparts, and typically rounded corners. Traces of this fortlet still stand at the head of a silted

Top: *The Erglodd stone at Erglodd farm; three feet long; dimpled by Roman ore crushing tilt hammers.*

Bottom left: *The second Erglodd stone, adapted as a plant trough.*

Bottom right: *Carreg Pumpsant, Dolaucothy, Carmarthenshire; another gold ore-crushing anvil stone, subsequently venerated as commemorating 'five Welsh saints on November 1st.*

tidal creek. From there, as archaeologists assert, refined silver and lead were exported.

'And that brings us to you, the talking Gold Head', the woman said, while shrinking to the far end of the room as her initial terror welled up again. 'I suppose you've brought the third stone with you. Where are you hiding it?'

In fact Taliesin *had* intended to carry to Erglodd the solitary prehistoric megalithic which stood in a field, due east of Tre Taliesin's village mission room, at OS grid reference 660917. He regarded that pillar as an effigy of his own earthly component. Made of local grit, this menhir was six feet tall and over twelve feet in girth, but by 1910, according to Sansbury's survey, it had disappeared.[38]

Before he could answer the housewife's question they heard the scuffling sound of the returning husband, removing his boots outside the door. 'We have a visitor', she said as he entered. 'Don't tell me. I'll guess: *Taliesin.* We've been expecting you for ages. Come about your gold, eh? Well you can't crush it here. We've got no hammer-stone for you; so clear off.'

'Ieuan! He is our guest. We can't send him away,' his wife protested: 'The farm is not named 'Gold Ditch', *Eur Clawdd*, for nothing. Our 'destiny bard' has come to tea. He will turn himself into Welsh *aur*, 'gold, gold coin.' His *aur* is our fatal 'money, fine, splendid, beloved, darling, treasure'. We can't deny him a simple stone on which to lay his *tal iesin.* He wants to trim it up to make sovereigns!' Then she let out a prolonged cackle, like a black hen that had laid an egg.

'But look at his head! What colour do you call *that?*' the farmer demanded of Taliesin. 'Why, gold, Sir', the poet replied, attempting a smile. 'Yes, but of what sort? There's green gold, white, orange, and red gold. Which are you?' Taliesin did not answer. 'Tell me this then', the farmer continued his aggressive interrogation: 'Where do you come from?'

'I am from Llanfair Caereinion in Powys', Taliesin was surprised to hear himself reply, since his father's house stood so many travels away. 'And? Come on, come on; where else?' The man was leaning over the demi-god. 'Er, from the womb of Ceridwen, I think', Taliesin faltered. 'And, And? You take me for a fool? We all *know* where you're from. We ought to; you've been boasting about it for long enough. There's not a person in Wales who *doesn't* know by now. You are *from the sun*!' he roared, straight into Taliesin's face. *'You* are Sol's agent on Earth.'

Taliesin blushed crimson. 'Please, all I ask is the use of your tilt hammer, so that I can strike off my head's gold swarf and separate it from my mortal dross. Then I can play with those shavings forever in the global economy. I'm a child at heart; I enjoy that sort of game; and you can have shares in my new multi-national company'.

'For ever? Are you sure? Didn't Ceridwen teach you the elementary solar facts?' the man asked. 'Once set free, those red-gold curls of yours will become the flares of a dying sun. *You,* my friend, are a Red Giant-in-waiting, intent on performing his ruddy death throes, with a money market dance that will herald our planet's extinction. On that all the papers are agreed. I'll bet a thousand guineas that as your business expands, so the inner planets, including Earth, will fry. Oceans will boil away. There will be nothing left but cinders. The craving for gold that is about to kill *you* is also stoking the sun to *its* inflated demise. He paused, inhaled, and added:

'You, Taliesin, our home grown, gold-headed, solar demi-god, *are evil.* You will bring Hell fire from Heaven to Earth.'

'But I've now renounced all far-flung ideas about Heaven and have abandoned mythic acts entirely', Taliesin protested. 'Now I only believe in hard cash, science, and human progress'.

'Quite so', replied the farmer, 'and this very conversion of yours has stirred the *Erglodd* prophecy from sleep. While you were content to run round for ages in mythic circles, we were safe; but now that you've turned scientific and strictly *chron*ological we're lost, doomed to the one-way terminal event that you now propose and personify.'

While he was speaking, his wife crept up behind the bewildered Taliesin and quietly pushed a kitchen knife through his back. The blade sank in to the hilt. It was easier than sticking a *Calan Gaeaf* pig. The victim groaned and fell to the floor. A pool of blood red wine (or wine-red blood) quickly spread around him as he tried to say:

> '*The strong-handed gleamer, his name, With a gleam he rules his numbers. They would spread out in a flame, When I shall go on high.*'[39]

He may have been referring to the Welsh *Tan-wed* or 'fiery apparition', of which J. Lewis wrote in 1656: 'Such a phantom 'spear' moves or shoots directly, and level, as if to say: 'I'll hit'! 'No man seeth its rising or beginning. It lighteneth all the air and ground where it passeth. After three or four miles, sparkling, it falls to ground… as a prophecy of death to the Freeholder.'[40]

Taliesin took one sip of his own fast-congealing blood before gargling 'Jesus Christ'! Then he spluttered, choked, and died.

'Why did you do that?' the husband asked his wife. 'We *needed* him, woman. He was our gilded weather vane, our forecaster, which ever way the wind blew; and I was *enjoying* the discussion.'

She replied: 'I thought you wanted him killed in one piece, to thwart his third stone intentions. And because I've stopped him dead, we have probably postponed the red giant sun's arrival by some three billion years – if, as you maintain, the pair of them *were* working together'.

'Take hold of his legs, then' said the man. 'We must bury him before his nasty friend, *Y Hen Wrach* finds out.' The woman answered: 'No need to worry about *her*. You heard him. He said he had resigned from *Y Tylwyth Teg*. So now he's just a mortal corpse, plain history'.

Bedd Taliesin, Taliesin's grave

For centuries popular belief has identified *Bedd Taliesin*, 'Taliesin's Grave', with an Early Bronze Age chambered cairn, built between 2,300 and 2,000 BC.[41] Prior to that date, burial in what is now Wales was communal rather than, as here, a tomb intended for one individual. By contast, *after* 2,000 BC, cremation replaced burial until at least 600 BC.[42] Therefore if Taliesin was carried into the tomb when it was newly constructed, he must have died towards the end of the third millennium BC. On the other hand, as Lynch reports, 'many [such round cairns] were re-used' in prehistoric times.[43]

Bedd Taliesin is now regarded as one of over thirty 'structured round cairns', surviving from that era in Ceredigion and Merionethshire.[44] It stands 710 feet above sea level, on the fringe of open moorland at a spot called *Pen Sarn Ddu*, 'Black Road's Head', and just over a mile north-east from Erglodd, at OS grid reference 67149120. *Moel y Garn*, 'Cairn Mountain', rises 1,377 feet to the east of the monument.

There, bright Taliesin was laid in the dark ground, and so denied the splendid view over Cors Fochno to the Dyfi estuary that greets today's visitors to his tomb. His only contact with the living might come at Hallowe'en, when, tradition states, wind blowing over dead feet, 'bear sighs to the houses of those who will die in the coming year.'[45]

The low, plum-shaped mass of turf-covered cairn-rubble is today little more than three feet high. Aligned north-west to south-east, it is 42 feet long by 40 feet across. Sticking up through the mound, ten 'orthostats', remnants of a ring of free standing stones, are visible, arranged on a six yard diameter. Some of the missing stones from this internal circle were, as Wyndham found in 1781, 'plundered within these few years... and converted to gate posts.'[46]

The barrow's central chamber or cist aligns to the south-east. It is six feet long, but less than two feet wide, the side slabs having leant inwards with time. These slabs are about 18 inches deep.

The chamber's massive capstone, nearly six feet in length, has been levered slightly to the north of its original position.

A dramatic eighteenth century drawing of this stone and mound, is inscribed 'Gvaith Taliesin'. The Welsh word *gwaith* could be intended to refer to Taliesin's 'works or compositions', or to his life's 'journey, travels.'[47]

The Welsh scholar Edward Lhuyd's account of the monument, written in 1695, runs: '*Gwely Taliesinus* in the parish of Llanfihangel Geneu'r, by its name and tradition of the neighbours concerning it, ought to be the grave of the celebrated poet, Taliesin *ben beirdh* ['chief bard']... This grave or 'bed' [for that is the significance of the word *gwely*], seems also to be a sort of Kistvaen, 4 foot long and 3 in breadth, composed of four flat stones, one at each end, and two side stones; whereof the highest is about one foot above ground... I am far from believing that ever Taliesin was in'terred here.'[48]

The disparity in dates between what Lhuyd recognised as an 'old heathen monument' and a post-Roman bard was obvious. Even so, Taliesin's undertakers *could* have re-used a Bronze Age structure, previously emptied either by time's decay or by grave robbers.

In the eighteenth and nineteenth centuries, numerous antiquaries visited Bedd Taliesin.

On 8th September 1846, during the first annual meeting of the Cambrian Archaeological Society, a party, including the Dean of Hereford (who would later search for a gold equestrian statue beneath Silbury Hill, Wiltshire[49]), arrived at the monument in three carriages. After measuring it, 'some very curious and interesting notices of the history of Taliesin, from the manuscripts collected by Iolo Morganwg', were read. These were unanimously considered to be 'highly corroborative of the tradition of Taliesin having been interred under the cairn that bears his name.'[50]

As for local opinion, in 1911 the Rev J. C. Davies wrote:

'The people of North Cardiganshire believe *to this day* that Taliesin was born and buried in their district.' In 1931 Professor M. Williams brought a group to the monument and declared: 'We believe that we have visited Taliesin's final resting place today, which makes us proud to be Cardiganshire folk.'[51] Davies thought 'The bones and human skull unearthed there [in *Bedd Taliesin*] were probably the remains of the great ancient poet.'[52] Yet there *were* no bones, but only a skull 'found there some years ago', according to the Rev T. Rees' account of 1819.[53]

A 'large skull', remarked upon by other authorities, and dug from the cist before 1800 was subsequently lost. Yet in 1977, Juliette Wood of Linacre College Oxford, 'was told by two local farm workers that a skull had been discovered at *Bedd Taliesin* 'a few years ago', and that it had been sent to the Welsh Folk Museum at St Fagan's, near Cardiff.'[54] In 2005 that museum could find no record of having received the item. Perhaps Ms Wood was misled.

Opposite top left: *Bedd Taliesin, OS Grid reference SN 672913, looking north-west to the Dyfi estuary, with bagged hay, end of another grass cycle.*

top right: *Bedd Taliesin, looking northeast up Pen Sarn Ddu, 'Black Head Road.'*

centre left: *Bedd Taliesin.*

centre right: *One of the 'ring stones' of Bedd Taliesin protruding through the mound.*

bottom left: *An enigmatic wooden figure; from Strata Florida, Cardiganshire.*

bottom centre: *Plan of Bedd Taliesin chamber and grass covered cairn.*

bottom right: *Gwaith Taliesin; a late eighteenth century drawing of the burial chamber in Llanstephan MS 193, National Museum of Wales.*

While Lhuyd, Wyndham and Meyrick found reasons to call Taliesin's connection with this tomb 'entirely fabulous', as 'Gwion-Bacchus' he had links to many graves. Given the strong Welsh sense of continuity between Roman Britain and their post–Roman culture, Gwion-Taliesin, like Bacchus before him, was probably still 'widely recognised as a grave guardian, a patron of the dead and host to the revels in Paradise.'[55]

The marble figure of Bacchus, with a wine-cup and grapes, buried in a Roman grave at Spoonley Wood, Gloucestershire, is one of many instances where he acted as 'a protective deity to an individual entering the nether world and a host to the revels there.'[56] Similarly, the mortal Taliesin could expect help from his Gwion-Bacchic self, when, as one, they journeyed downwards into Bedd Taliesin, hoping to drink out of the two-handled *cantharus,* or wine cup.

In some ways this vessel continued to haunt Wales in post-Roman times. For example, one night around 1840, a horseman riding near Maentrog, Merioneth 'beheld a living thing in the form of a bowl, rolling towards his horse's hooves. The man said a paternoster whereupon the bowl gave a flash, and a peal of laughter rent the air. Looking back, the rider saw an imp, bounding with great leaps along Cwm Bychan, where it rolled about among a circle of Druid stones.[57]

Having now discarded such stories, when *we* peer into Bedd Taliesin's cist there is nothing to discover but emptiness. Even in 1847 Guest could report only that the soil, which had been recently dug from the cist, was of a different colour from that of the surrounding earth.[58] By then, the mortal remains of the sixth century Welsh bard named Taliesin, if indeed he had ever rested in this acidic ground, was converted into a mere red wine stain on the earth's table cloth. This total merger of body with tomb is echoed by Taliesin's words: *'I am a cell, I am a cleft.'* [59]

Lost is the supernatural character, whose recurring existence was for centuries sustained by folk belief, expressed in his *Chwedl Taliesin* folk tale, *and* by the medieval poetry attributed to him. An empire of secular materialism has rendered faith in a living universe, inspired by divine play, largely obsolete in Wales, as throughout the Western world. Consequently Taliesin has received a double death sentence – as an immortal demi-god, *and* as a mortal bard, with both executions carried out.

Perhaps his last manifestation was as a *canhwyllan corff* or 'corpse candle', an uncanny light, often seen in Wales. Known elsewhere as Will o'the Wisp, Jack o' Lantern or as the Roman *ignis fatuus,* this flickering, pale bluish light was said to disappear when approached. If small, it foretold the death of an infant.[60] A bigger light meant the immanent death of an adult. Yet these flames were probably nothing more than marshland methane, ignited by natural interaction with the phosphoretted hydrogen that is generated by wetland decay.

CHAPTER ELEVEN

FIVE LIGHTS TO HOME

Gwely Taliesin

> *'Cold death, the destiny of the ready muse.'* Book of Taliesin, xii, ll. 9.

During his lifetimes Taliesin often voices an abhorrence of death, while the god Gwydion ap Don speaks of *'severe afflictions after death-bed.'* [1] Taliesin begs: *'May I not fall into the embrace of the swamp, Into the mob that peoples the depths of Uffern.'* [2]

There the terrors of an inescapable 'Cors Fochno' combine with his own putrifaction. The ground gives way, threatening to suck him into a Christian Hell, Welsh *Uffern*. With the entire planet at risk of a similarly vertiginous drop, he asks:

> *'Or if the world should fall, On what would it fall?'* [3]

But as his mouth is gradually stuffed with earth, it is left to his ghost to say:

> *'In the deep below the earth… There is one who knows what sadness is, better than joy'* [4]

and to submit once more to death's universal claim:

> *'Death, having a foundation in every country, is shared.*
> *Death above our heads, wide its covering.'* [5]

Yet *Bedd* Taliesin, Taliesin's 'Grave', has for centuries also been known as *Gwely* Taliesin[6]; and *gwely* means 'bed, mattress, sleeping place, resting place of an animal, marriage bed of procreation and childbirth'. In Gwely Taliesin the demi-god may be dead, or at rest, preparing to get up again.

Britain's prehistoric inhumations are often arranged in a foetal or prenatal position, with knees drawn up to the chin, indicating that 'Mother Earth' is pregnant with the dead, who she will give birth to again as future generations.

The grey slabs of the Gwely Taliesin cist may accordingly describe her vulva, a gateway leading to *and from* her endless life cycle. Into her dark 'bed chamber' Taliesin had descended. If his death was inevitable, so too, as the offspring of Ceridwen, *Mam Daear's* agent, was his rebirth. His recovery was certain as sunrise.

Even before his interment he confidently states:

> *'I will declare when I am in the gravel.'* [7]

Speaking of himself in the third person, he goes on:

> *'He will compose, he will decompose, He will form languages.'* [8]

He will be better equipped to do so, having mingled with his beloved poet-ancestors:

> *'Company of poets above, Company of poets below;*
> *My darling is below, 'Neath the fetters of Arianrhod.'* [9]

As the moon deity, and queen of the night, Arianrhod traps the solar demi-god below ground at dusk. Her sickle marks the end of his days. When Taliesin said: *'I have been three periods in the prison of Arianrhod'*, he may be referring to three of her four lunar phases. By contrast, his eventual revival and release is possible if synchronised with the full moon, when her shape and brightness most closely matches *his* round solar head.

This also fits the British folk tradition that links a full moon with the birth of a new harvest at Lammas – *Gwyl Awst.* Then Taliesin longs for *'Arianrhod of laudable aspect, dawn of serenity'*,[10] because at each full moon close to August 1st, he is again a golden 'first fruits' child of the harvest goddess, and can jump from the earth, shouting:

> *'I have been dead, I have been alive.'* [11]

Revivings

Today, a few stones belonging to Gwely Taliesin's internal ring of megaliths are still visible, sticking through the cairn-mound. Despite eighteenth century damage, enough remains of this circle to suggest a solar-lunar-seasonal round dance, in which life, death and rebirth together poke up their stoney fingers, to bring underworld, surface plain and sky into a united rotation. (In 1810, Meyrick saw arcs of *two* concentric stone circles protruding from the mound, 27feet, and 31 feet in diameter.[12])

Whether in architecture, jewellery or dance, the ring was (and often still is) a potent symbol. It expresses and encourages continuity, and reconnects surface to subterranean powers. At Gwely Taliesin's damaged megalithic ring (or rings) we are invited to 'fill the gaps' by joining hands with the ancestors who, as a matter of fact, gave us our flesh and bones. Then, for us, as for Taliesin, 'reality' will incorporate a wheeling inheritance of coitus, parenthood and mortality, of at least four thousand years' duration. Indeed, by its name and form, the monument suggests a universal companionship. Then, as Taliesin implies in his *Song to the Little World*, past and future may roll into an 'eternal present':

The Welshpool bronze skillet handle's images of Bacchus.

Left: *As an old man.* Right: *As a youth.*

'*The beautiful I sang of, I will sing. The world one day more…*
The world, how it comes again, When it falls into decay,
Again in the enclosing circle.' [13]

If the *historical* bard must be evicted from Gwely Taliesin on chronological grounds, fable and legend make a strong case for his continuing *mythic* residence here. As an *a*-historic character, 'there existed a core of genuine tradition', linking him with the site, writes Wood.[14] In order to commune with his enduring spirit, people were tempted, at the risk of losing their sanity, to enter Taliesin's bed. 'The popular superstition is that should anyone sleep in this bed for one night, he [or she?] would the next day become either a poet or an idiot', wrote Meyrick in 1810.[15] This indicates Taliesin's willingness, indeed *eagerness,* to share his hard-won insights with future poets. To be experienced anew, the mythic round always needs fresh input.

Taliesin serves the need for communion between human and divine realms, also reflected in the ritual beer beakers found in Early Bronze Age barrows, *and* by the shallow bronze wine bowl or *patera,* carefully deposited in a bog at Welshpool, Montgomeryshire during the first century AD. Laid within a larger bronze cauldron, this *patera*'s handle displayed 'prototype' images of Gwion Bach as the young Bacchus, *and* as old man Bacchus.[16]

On contemplating this image of his young self, garlanded, and with silver-inlaid eyes, Taliesin's mind drifted seven miles west from Welshpool, to Llanfair Caereinion, his childhood home. Suddenly, he was gripped by an intense longing to go to his native village again, to re-cross the threshold into a half-human infancy, and to sit in his dead father's chair.

He therefore slipped out of *Bedd Taliesin* and headed towards Pumlumon, Wales' central mountain. From there he hoped to make the long descent eastwards to the farm of his infancy. As he climbed the track onto rough moorland he repeatedly chanted: '*Hominibvsbagisbitam*', the fourth century inscription, carved beneath his marble Bacchus statue, found in Londinium's Mithraic temple. The compressed Latin means: '[You give] life to men who wander.'[17]

The maidens

Two miles due east from his grave, Taliesin came upon a prehistoric stone ring called *Cylch Derwyddol*, 'Druid's Circle.' In 1846 it consisted of 'about seventy six upright stones, forming a circle 228 feet in diameter', sited at Ordnance Reference SN 69949106, against the foot of *Moel y Carn*.[18] A survey by J.H.S.E. in 1873 could find only forty stones, with sixty as the estimated original number (and some of these all-but submerged by accumulating peat), arranged on a 180 foot circumference.[19]

Uncertainty surrounds the *Cylch Derwyddol's* circle's name. J.E. heard it called *Cae yr Arglwyddes*.[20] 'Field' of the 'Maiden, Sweet-heart, Lady, or Woman ruler', are the Dictionary's options for *arglwyddes*. Had Taliesin passed this spot at *Calan Mai*, during any year prior to 1800, he would have witnessed the traditional ascent of valley dairymaids to the uplands, where they remained till *Calan Gaeaf*, to milk the herds and flocks that they drove before them.[21] Traces of the *hafodtai*, or 'summer huts', where they slept on the mountains, can still be found.

From the Hebrides to Cornwall, stone circles, erected in antiquity on the edge of highland pastures, probably had ritual importance as May Day dancing grounds. Within these sacred enclosures, performers urged new vegetation to rise from the underworld by their prancings; hence '*The Merry Maidens*' and '*Nine Maidens*' – names of two Cornish megalithic rings.[22] Such superhuman dancers are seen again in the nine maidens, whose breath helped kindle the cauldron belonging to the Lord of *Annwn*, which Taliesin brought from the Otherworld, as described *The Spoils of Annwn*.[23]

In Wales, young women drew on the power of their supernatural equivalents, whose acts they mimed. One such was Creiddylad, daughter of the god Llud Silver Hand, 'the maiden of most majesty that ever was in the Isle of Britain'.[24] She combines Welsh *craidd*, 'centre, middle, heart, essence', with Welsh *ladi*, 'lady.' Creiddlylad was *Y Ladi Wen*, 'The White Lady', seen in her youthful aspect.

The leading dancer could also play the part of Ceridwen's beautiful daughter, Creirwy. She was her mother's *crair*, 'darling', and her *bwy*, 'lively treasure.' 'A shapely maiden... of the hue of snow',[25] this Creirwy was her mother in maidenly form entering into a human May Queen shape for the occasion. Creirwy's 'sister' was St Guennole, the 'swallow', (Welsh *guennol*). The swallow's arrival in late April installed that bird, along with the cuckoo, as *Mai*'s emblem and winged spirit.[26]

Standing in *Cae yr Arglwyddes*, Taliesin thought of the toilsome life of his own yeoman father, and how a herdsman's success depended on a divine maiden raising new grass, assisted by these girls and their musicians. As a bishop of Bangor

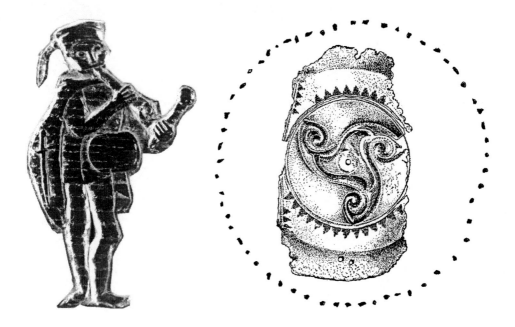

Left: *May Day musician, from a sixteenth century oak chest carving, Lancaster museum.*

Right: *Plan of the 'Field of the Maidens' stone circle with copper alloy shield boss from Tal y llyn, Merioneth; late Iron Age.*

complained in 1580, 'upon... hollidaies multitudes... do meet on the side of some mountaine, where theire harpers and crowthers singe them songs... and in hearinge some parte of the life of Talaassyn [Taliesin].'[27]

Taliesin was also required to light the May Eve 'need-fire' from his bright brow, symbolising summer sunshine, warming the chilled earth. Quartered oaten cakes were then cooked in the bonfire and shared out. Those who by chance picked a burnt piece were obliged to jump over the flames. Thus by their acts people joined hands with the elemental play of the gods.[28]

Cow, calf and five beacons

With the sound of glee in his ears, Taliesin left the *Arglwyddes* circle and trudged all morning towards the sprawling summits of Pumlumon. As he advanced, what at first he took to be a trick of the light became a far off dazzling object, which shone out from the moorland's sombre immensity and held his attention. On drawing nearer, the 'mystery' gradually enlarged and resolved into a six feet high boulder of white quartz, with a diminutive stone of the same rock, lying close to its foot. He had arrived at *Fuwch Wen a Llo*, 'The White Cow and Calf.' They are so named on the 1999 *Explorer* map, at OS Grid Reference SN 815904.[29]

Fuwch is a variant of Welsh *buwch*, 'cow'. In a seventeenth century letter describing this pair of rocks, Thomas Harper writes that 'the most eloquent poets have descanted most eloquently upon *Y burch Yvenn-a'r llo*'.[30] Throughout the British Isles, white cows were venerated. A legendary animal, linked to Shropshire's Mitchell's Fold prehistoric stone circle, 'gave a paleful of milk to all and sundry',[31] while in Ireland people sang of a magic beast that appeared on May morning:

> 'There is a cow on the mountain,
> A fair white cow;
> She goes east and she goes west,
> And my senses have gone for love of her.
> She goes with the Sun,
> And he forgets to burn,
> And the moon turns her face
> With love to her… ' [32]

Long before the advent of pastoralism, Pumlumon's *Fuwch* and her calf sat on the ridge (which is still named *Esgair Fuwch Wen* in her honour), as herds of wild cattle and deer made the yearly trek to their summer grazing grounds. In their hoof-prints followed countless generations of dairymaids, tending their black Welsh cattle. These young women probably saw the *Fuwch* rock as a 'Queen Cow' of the Otherworld, greeting them on May Day. She was a supernatural effigy and the pivotal figure of adoration in their mountaintop ceremonies. Presiding over heather, moss, rushes, red kites, hares, calves and human cheese production, she embodied that 'Great Spirit', more valuable than gold, drawing all life together.

Nature has given this *Fuwch Wen* a suggestion of horns, a dark eye, and 'a smile', Welsh *gwen*. *Gwen* is also 'a favour, goodwill, prayer, wish, a gleam of sunshine' and 'sacred song'.

From a huge white head, this smile is directed at her *llo*, or calf, with which Taliesin identified. Transfixed, he mumbled: 'Fair *wen*, 'holy, white one', my c*ariad*, 'love', I come to your *cariad-wledd*, 'feast of charity', for you are *cired*, 'generosity, bounty''.

Midway through this fulsome greeting, he recognised the white cow as *Mam Ceridwen*, in bovine form. Face to face with him, she confirmed his double attachments. As the mother of his second birth, he had acquired a share in her Otherworld. Equally, as *Gwion Bach*, son of a Welsh yeoman, he belonged to this earth. Consequently, although the two feet high 'calf' stone juts diagonally into the air, it remains firmly earth-bound. Loyal to both realities and to both *kinds* of stock, he felt himself drawn twice over into the Cow and Calf double image. Ceridwen had balanced it with evident ease between the two worlds, as procreation's divine, yet tangible, icon.

Opposite: Yr Fuwch Wen a'r llo, *'The White Cow and Calf'; two quartz boulders on Pumlumon, Wales' central mountain. The 'cow' stands six feet tall. She is the Otherworld white cow known to Welsh and Irish folklore. As Welsh* ceridwen, *'dear white ', she grazes between worlds. Her calf can be Gwion Bach.*

Twin Bronze Age cairns, one damaged, at Cwm Biga, Pumlumon;
15 feet tall and 33 feet apart.

Emotion overwhelmed Taliesin, the accidental pilgrim. It lit up his head, which glowed with surplus heat. Wanting to put the burning sensation to some use, he ran between the prehistoric cairns that adorn each of Pumlumon's five mountain lobes, and re-lit a *Calan Mai* beacon fire on each, thereby recovering Pumlumon's name and purpose; Welsh *pum*, 'five', plus Welsh *lumon*, 'beacon.'

As Harper noted, from Pumlumon 'one may view most part of ye counties of Wales except Anglesey'.[33] Scattered throughout those counties, innumerable families re-sanctified their domestic hearths with May fire, in response to those lit on Pumlumon's central hearths.

'*They would spread out in a flame, When I shall go on high,*'[34] Taliesin sang, while from the sacred mountain, he 're-ignited' the nation, north, south, east and west. Simultaneously, on Ireland's central Hill of Uisnech the four provinces of *that* country were re-united by a comparable May-Eve *Beltaine* blaze.[35]

Anemometer on Pumlumon, measuring what the Mabinogion *states 'is the highest wind in the world.' Meteorological staion AD 2002. It mimics the Four Quarters, crossing at a divine heart, and scatters Taliesin's wind-blown dust. 'And he is coeval with the five periods of the five ages,' says the early medieval* Song of the Wind, *where wind is the inspired and expiring breath of changes.*

That the Gwion-Taliesin story is involved from start in a five-fold pattern appears in an archaic name for Llyn Tegid – *Pimblemere*, or *Pemblemere*, which is derived from the 'five' (Welsh *pum*) parishes around its shores.[36]

'Having served my country high and low, I deserve a *rest* in my father's home,' said Taliesin to the four quarters or cardinal points, as the fires he had lit spat and crackled. Then, imitating 'The Three Sisters', the Rivers Severn, Wye and Rheidol, that rise on Pumlumon,[37] he slowly began to meander downhill.

He had scarcely meandered a mile before he spotted an old acquaintance. It was Cai from Llyn Tegid, now standing on the open moor.

'Cai! Cai! It's me! Taliesin'. Cai and another knight, Bedwyr, were dressed in full meteorological station 'rain gauge' armour. They dripped internally. Taliesin approached the wired-off enclosure and greeted them:

'Good to see you, Cai. So you're in the environmental business now! I've done some wind measuring, as a sideline. We all have to change with the times to some extent. But how you've shrunk! When we met under Llyn Tegid you were taller than a tree'. Taliesin held out his hand, but the 'Cai instrument' did not respond.

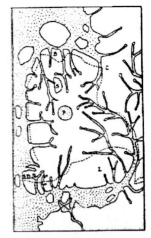

Pumlumon and the Four-plus-One pattern in Wales

Pumlumon, marked 'P' on Gough's fourteenth century map of Wales. The mountain's name means 'Five Beacons' or 'Five Lights', symbolising the four quarters around Wales' sacred centre. Four plus One makes Five. The hill of Usinech in Mide performed a similar role for ancient Ireland.

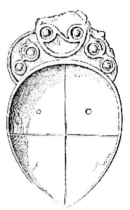

Bronze plate from Llyn Cerrig Bach, Môn; Iron Age (after Fox).

Bronze spoon from Castell Nadolig, Ceredigion. Four inches long. Gold nipples enhance this goddess image. (Ashmolean Museum)

Celtic figurine amulet from Rhagatt, Merioneth; third century AD.

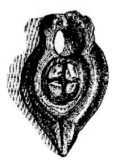

'I'm Taliesin. You *know*: 'Bright Brow.' Don't you recognise me?' 'Never heard of you,' Cai replied, as more rainwater dribbled down a funnel into his belly flask. 'Ah, yes; of *course* not; I was Gwion Bach then,' the demi-god recalled. 'Well, 'Bright Gwion', why don't you *bach* off?' Cai snarled. As Taliesin slunk away he considered abandoning his 'shininess' in order to improve the chances of being recognised among the friends of his infancy, if he could find them.

Llanfair Caereinion

After dropping off the mountain, Taliesin had intended to hitch lifts from Llanidloes to Newtown, before thumbing along the lane which led over the hills to his native parish. Although at first there was plenty of traffic, however hard he peered into the drivers' eyes as they whizzed by, they looked straight through him, as if he was invisible. So he left the roads and instead followed a midsummer sunrise course, leading into woods and across crumbling field walls and through blackthorn hedges. Any weariness was offset by the excitement he felt on approaching the land of his infancy.

At noon he came to a Roman fort, *Y Gaer,* [38] and, soon after that, a view of the Afon Banwy valley opened at his blistered feet (Welsh *banwy,* 'piglet, wife, daughter'). With joy he admired its snakey green tract, running from a *Carnedd Wen* source towards confluence with the Severn at Welshpool. Below, and straight in front of him, perched on the river's steep bank, rose the *Llan Fair* church tower. Our Lady's 'keep-safe' against English raiders still soared above a cluster of cottage roofs.

Looking left, he could make out the hunched mass of Moel Pentyrch, the mountain under whose evening shadow his father's farm lay. Towards that homestead he set off at a brisk trot and did not pause till he came to the farm. But the house had gone. The building he knew by heart had vanished. In its place was another timber-framed dwelling, itself about to collapse. Saplings had sprung up, blocking off the frontage. Walls leaned. The place was uninhabited,[39] silent as his dead father.

For at least an hour Taliesin hovered before its rickety front gate, as if clutching the rail around a demolished family vault. Only slowly did he come to accept that his intention to rejoin humanity was turning bad. Over the scene lank cobwebs wrote the word 'mortal'. His homecoming had failed.

Opposite top: Craig yr Eglwys, *'Church Rock', Pumlumon; divinity in the wilderness.*

top right: *Taliesin as an engraved solar angel; Ceredigion tomb-stone, 1768.* 'And my native land is the land of the cherubim… And I was moved through the entire universe.' *Taliesin, (Ford 1977, p173)*

bottom left: *Cai and Bedwyr as rain gauges; Pumlumon weather station raingauges, 2002.* 'I am steel. I am a druid' *Taliesin,* Book of Taliesin, *iii, 10.*

bottom right: *The infant Severn, Welsh* Hafren, *bursts from her Pumlumon home.*

Ffynnon y Wrach, the hag's spring

Sunk as he was in despondency, it took some time for Gwion T. Bach to register the faint voices, floating down from Moel Pentyrch. He blinked, yawned, tilted his head, frowned, and started to climb the mountain towards them. A few paces north of the summit he found people gathered around a rushy pool. Each Trinity Sunday, the first after Whitsun, they met at this breezy spot to drink sweetened water from a well named *Ffynnon y Wrach*, 'The Hag's Spring'.[40]

'Her again,' groaned Taliesin. 'That *gwrach* was here, overlooking my birth, casting her shadow on my cradle.' Then a second thought hit him. 'Was she, *Y Wrach*, my father's wife or paramour, whom none of the twenty-four *Chwedl Taliesin* manuscripts dare mention, let alone name? Was this *ffynnon* water, oozing from her 1,200 foot-high 'breast' my only milk? Are my two mothers one and the same? Am I Ceridwen's brat twice over?' He suspected that all the answers would be 'Yes'.

Of the many games played at the annual *Ffynon y Wrach* gatherings, a favourite was pitch and toss. The competitors each threw a silver half-crown at a mark. Next, the person whose shot landed nearest gathered all the coins into a hat, which was then inverted. Those coins showing 'heads up' were awarded to the winner.[41] 'Why half-crowns only?' Taliesin enquired, at which the company laughed, since to them the answer was more obvious than a full moon. 'Silver Head!' they shouted at him, in good-humoured banter.

Meanwhile, the older people sat around, retailing the year's news, both local and from far afield. Then, as tradition demanded, someone began to recite from memory a tale about the legendary hero and founder of Llanfair Caereinion, Einion Yrth. Einion was imprisoned after a battle and presumed dead by his wife. Many years later she prepared to marry again. On the eve of her second wedding an old stranger arrived and asked to play on Einion's Harp, the sole memento of her former husband. On sweeping his fingers once across the strings, she instantly recognised the decrepit stranger as Einion. Amid much rejoicing, the pair resumed their marriage and continued to live at Llanfair Caereinion.[42] On hearing the tale again, tears ran down Taliesin's cheeks. He wept for the power of music beyond words, and because he had failed to re-enter his own old home.

Opposite top left: *Ruined abandoned house at Gelli, Llanfair Caereinion.*

top right: *The path up Moel Pentyrch, the Dragon's mountain, leading to* Ffynnon y Wrach, *the 'Hag's Well.*

centre right: *Medieval 'sheela-na-gig' stone carving, Llandrindod Wells church, Radnorshire; now in the town's museum.*

bottom left: *Engraved medieval slate from Trewyn, Montgomershire., showing a ploughman with ox-team, whip, and seed basket. Gwion's father is in the rock.*

bottom right: Ffynnon y Wrach, *the 'Hag's Well.*

As was the custom, an old woman then retold the *Hanes Taliesin* story, starting from where Gwion, their uncanny neighbour, had set out. Taliesin stopped himself from correcting some minor errors in her account, because he realised that the legend enjoyed a flexible life.

For her 'to burrow' (Welsh *tyrchu*), into Gwion Bach's past on Moel Pentyrch made an opening to the future. Therefore, when the woman ended her yarn, a reputable wizard, Moses Morgan of Brynglas, prognosticated for the year to come.[43]

The dragon or *wiber,* over whose lair they sat, was not mentioned. Yet as recently as 1890 an old woman had assured the rector that she had seen smoke coming from its den, generally considered to be the deep hole, leading into the contorted crags of the mountain's east wall. The *wiber* emerged to attack man and beast, for this long-tailed, two-footed dragon with scaly wings lived on animal and human blood. It was *Y Wrach*-as-Devourer – Death on the wing.[44]

Some reports claim that the creature was killed after flying at speed into a red pole, studded with iron spikes, made to attract it.[45] However, those who travel in Wales know that it survived the crash.

Indeed, it flaps vigorously from flagpoles in every corner of the country. It also rides, stuck to the rear windows of cars, and finds its way onto letter headings, T-shirts and postcards. The 'Pentyrch dragon' swarms over Wales as an image of Creation's vigour, fecundity, inventiveness and cruelty.

Sitting alone on Pentyrch, the Trinity crowds having dispersed, Taliesin heard the dragon's blood-curdling shriek, followed by a series of loud snortings, as its white breath shot skywards. This display came from the direction of a light railway terminus, close to the east fringe of the township, where steam train enthusiasts re-opened the derelict line to Welshpool. Flames, for so long trapped as sunlight in the trunks of fossilised Carboniferous forests, were resurrected from a boiler's mouth.

'The dragon will flow around, above the places.' Book of Taliesin, *xliv, ll. 10-11.*

Opposite top left: *Megalith at Llanrheaedr ym Mochnant, Montgomeryshire, formerly draped in red to attract a dragon.*

Top centre: *The 'Welsh dragon'.*

top right: *St Mary's holy well at Llanfair Caereinion; it lies beside her church.*

left centre: *Railway yard at Llanfair Caereinion. Black coal plus dead leaves equals gold flames.*

'A ruddy wind will be brought out of the cinder,
Until the world is as desolate as when created.'
Book of Taliesin, *v, 44-7.*

bottom: *View of Llanfair Caereinion.*

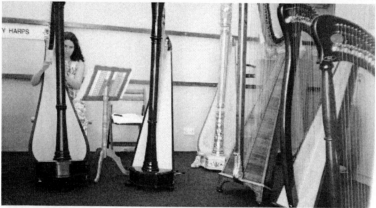

That fire was another aspect of Taliesin's 'Shining Brow' legacy, which he shared with the dragon, as it shunted an old-new Iron Age onto the universal turntable of arrivals and departures.

Departure: Taliesin got to his feet, determined to move out of the parish. He wanted to escape from the drudgery of re-staging his adventures yet again. Even the hardiest actor can grow weary of a show that never closes and is glad to hand over his part to an understudy. 'And if I *have* no understudy, let the play end for good. Everyone in the world must know the plot by now'.

However, numerous studies in Comparative Religion indicate that it is hard, if not impossible, to bring down a final curtain on any myth, once it has become indelibly scripted into the collective psyche. This is well understood in Llanfair Caereinion. It was here, between 1830 and 1835, that R. Humphries and E. Jones compiled and printed the very first 'Welsh Language Encyclopedia', *Geirlyfr Cymraeg*. This massive work paid particular attention to the mythic foundations of the world's great cultures, 'holding in *impartial* [my italics] examination... Paganism, Deism, Judaism, Mohamedism and Christianity.' There was also a section on Atheism, anticipating the effect of Taliesin's proposed disappearance from the scene, along with his divine associates.[46]

Taliesin was finished with make-believe divine revelation. Instead of another holy day, he set out to find a refreshingly secular holiday. In place of endless re-Creation duties, he was looking for simple recreation. With that in mind, after declining the offer of a water bottle from Our Lady of Llanfair's churchyard holy well, he walked out of his native village, vowing never to return. At a brisk pace, he headed for Llyn Tegid, to participate in the water sports listed in its latest tourist brochure.

Opposite top: *Maes yr Eisteddfod at Llanfor, near Bala, August 1997.*

centre: *A Welsh harp tent at the 1997 Eisteddfod.*

bottom: *Archdruid, herald, and flower dance girls approach* Maeni yr Orsedd, *'Stones of the Throne', Bala.*

CHAPTER TWELVE

MAGIC ARTS

Bala Eisteddfod

When Taliesin approached the Bala town end of Llyn Tegid during the first week of August 1997 he was amazed to see a vast encampment of tents packed tightly together on the flood plain a mile downstream from the Dee's Bala outflow. His visit had by chance coincided with the Welsh National Eisteddfod. With no money for the entrance fee, he sneaked into the field through a thorn hedge and found himself inside *Maes yr Eisteddfod,* the 'Field of the Eisteddfod',[1] which was devoted to the great game of Art.

Around a huge performance marquee, *Theatr y Maes* (through the canvas walls of which seeped waves of choral song), the site was laid out like a Roman city. Its grassy avenues were lined by close-set booths, where embroidery, hot dogs, hand-carved bowls, jewellery and metalwork, Welsh novels and poetry, and one stall containing nothing but harps, were crowded together. For eight days people came to perform, listen, buy, or browse; nearly 200,000 in all.

Mesmerised, Taliesin drifted through the throng into a tent displaying recent examples of Welsh Fine Art. Ignoring the images, he moved systematically around the exhibition, reading the artists' printed statements. One of these was by Iwan Bala, a Bala-born 'son of Penllyn's rich soil'. The text read: 'It is the imagination of Taliesin, rather than any particular visual style, which seems to chararacterize the visual arts in Wales. What transforms the silent marks on the canvas is the use of metaphor and symbol, just as the poet transforms words. The Taliesin tradition has enabled us (visual artists) to re-invent and transfigure. We still live in the shadow of the old gods.'[1]

Taliesin was stunned. He swayed, blacked out, and crashed to the ground. When his eyes re-opened an attendant was looking down at him. 'I am OK,' the ex-demi-god said, mustering a confident colloquial tone. 'I'm just fed up because they won't let me die out.' 'You need some fresh air – stuffy in here' said the steward.

Under a deep blue sky Taliesin then staggered to Bala town. Near the industrial estate he was surprised to come across a ring of twelve massive stones. It looked prehistoric, but in fact had been recently set up. This megalithic circle, reinforced by a temporary amphitheatre of chairs and benches, was the focus of the *Eisteddfod* rites. An audience dressed in summer frocks and open-necked shirts waited patiently. They had come to witness the Crowning of the Bard, an honour awarded to the Welsh poet who had composed the best work in free metre that year. The assembly gave substance to the word *eisteddfod*, 'sitting together.'

Much of the ceremonial was unfamiliar to Taliesin, for it had been largely re-invented around 1800, after a long lapse, by the poet-scholar Iolo Morgannwg, who had organised a gathering of bards, or *gorsedd*, (literally a 'high seat') on Primrose Hill, London, in 1792. At the 1819 Carmarthen Eisteddfod, some of the costumes that Taliesin now saw, based on imagined pre-Christian designs, had first re-appeared.[2]

At 10 o'clock, from a gathering place somewhere in Bala town, a long procession wound into the arena, entering between the twin *Maen Porth* 'Gatestones' and *Maen y Cyfamod*, the 'Covenant Stone.' It was led by a man in white; white shoes, white gloves, white head dress and white garments, reaching to the ground. His knobbed staff of office was decorated with serpents. Behind him stood two bearded, burly men in red, carrying elongated trumpets, hung with the red dragon flag of Wales.

Then came *Plant y Ddawns Flodau*, the 'Flower Dance Children' – twenty-four little girls in peacock blue tunics, carrying garlands, and with flowers in their hair. On their heels sauntered the 'May Queen', beautiful as Creirwy, dressed in white, with a red cloak, embroidered in gold, and wearing a gold crown. She presented the Archdruid with a bunch of flowers 'from the land and soil of Wales.'

Behind her two white-robed handmaidens walked a stately maternal figure, combining the attributes of *Dea Nutrix*, *Mam Daear*, Minerva and Ceridwen, as if emerging again in glory from an under-lake home. Against her bosom she carried a large drinking horn, silver-mounted at tip and lip, from which she urged the Archdruid to drink the 'wine of welcome'. 'That's me!' Taliesin was tempted to shout. Two white-cloaked boys, her token offspring, attended the woman. Taliesin felt jealous.

Next, a tall banner swung into view, supported by six youths, with black and white 'Iron Age' patterns on their red costumes. The banner was emblazoned with a dazzling sun, from which three rays shot down to touch a correspondingly black sphere, representing, Taliesin supposed, Afagddu's realm. (Soon there might be new sun flowers in bloom outside the cottages of Tre Taliesin.) 'Concentrate!' he told himself, for the event was unfolding rapidly. A marshal of the Bardic Order strode by, rod in hand, ahead of the banner, which was followed by thirty or forty blue-robed bards. Were they all renowned poets? If so, who were the men clothed in white, wearing white hoods, he asked. 'Druids,' his neighbour replied. 'And that other cohort, completely dressed in green?' 'Ovates'. 'What are ovates?' 'Soothsayers. Ssshh!' answered the man, growing tired of the questioning. Taliesin counted altogether two hundred cassocked figures of different sorts, as they entered and sat in crescentic tiered ranks behind the Logan Stone, on which the Archdruid eventually stood.

Top left and right: Plant Ddawns Flodau, *the'Flower Dance Children' lead in the 'May Queen', followed by the maternal figure of 'Summer' and her two boys.*

Left centre and bottom: *Bards enter and assemble in the circle, with the Archdruid at the centre.*

Bottom right: *The Eisteddfod banner, with rays of equinox and midsummer.*

The richness of the unfolding pattern resembled a June meadow, complete with nodding flower heads and bees, giving an airy buzz of spoken address and response. As an onlooker, Taliesin was content merely to note how 'sense' emerged from 'sight', and that an archaic story was being reborn from these icons in motion. 'I *see* what you *mean*,' was his silent thought, as he enjoyed his overdue break from words. Nevertheless, he shortly whispered to his unknown neighbour:

> *'I sang before a renowned Lord where the Severn winds;*
> *Before Brochfael of Powys who loved my muse.'* [3]

'And, did you know that John Williams named his literary journal *Taliesin* after me, following the success of the 1858 Llangollen *eisteddfod* ? Mind you, it folded after only two years. Yet here I am.'

Then Taliesin put out a hand to brush against the Archdruid's white and gold vestments, as they wafted by, in order to check that the man was not a hallucination. After doing so, he realised that the imagination can speak through purely visual symbols, and began to regard the easily mocked fancy dress of Welsh Eisteddfod ceremonial as a necessity. The special clothes, along with the heightened words and music, helped to shape a new magic, designed to re-invest Wales with ageless mysteries.

The climax to the Bala event came with the enthronement of a bard who had composed the best long poem that year. Grasping his bound-up word-harvest, he sat in the very lap of the muse, from whom his inspiration had been born. 'That is Ceridwen in her *cadair* or 'chair' shape,' Taliesin sensed. He could think of nowhere better for a new poet to be placed in such a chair than here, close to the Bala outflow, where the sacred river Dee, alias the great goddess Don, continually emerges from Ceridwen's lake.

Afon Dyfrdonwy

The Welsh word *cerdd*, 'poetry, music, craft, art', also means 'to spring forth, to run, to flow', and thereby draws rivers and arts into metaphorical partnership. Welsh tradition tends to regard their related streams as emanating from a unifying divine source. So the Dee and the Arts reflect upon another's intrinsic sanctity. That being the case, when the Bala circle ceremony ended, Taliesin walked half a mile to the Dee's outflow, intent on paying his respects to her ineffable current.

He recalled that her name comes from Latin *dea*, 'goddess', while the Welsh title of the same river, *Dyfrdwy*, means 'Water of the Goddess.' But as Gruffydd has shown, *Dyfrdwy* is a contraction of *Dyfrdonwy*, which specifies the Welsh goddess Don as that waterway's *genius loci*.[4]

Don, an ancient and powerful deity, acknowledged throughout Europe, is personified by the Russian, English and Scottish rivers of that name. In her alternative forms, Dan and Danu, she is Bulgaria's Danube,[5] while the Irish *Tuatha de Danaan* is comprised of her offspring-gods. Similarly, Rhys has shown that Don was the founding mother of the entire Welsh pantheon.[6]

Right: *Plan of the prehistoric and medieval*
hafotai, *or summer-time settlement near*
Moel Caws

Opposite top left and top right: *Two natural*
images of the goddess Don at Moel Caws?

Opposite centre: Welsh black cattle on Moel
Caws, summer 2004.

Opposite bottom: *Stepping-stones over the*
Dee's headwater, with Moel Caws,
('Cheese Hill') rising behind.

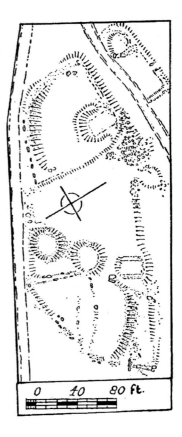

The *Dyfrdonwy* is the spinal chord of Don's Wales. Compared to her, even Ceridwen is of secondary importance, being but one small bead strung on Don's river necklace. This might explain why folk opinion is unanimous in believing that when the Dee runs through Llyn Tegid its river water can always be distinguished from that of the lake.[7]

On the other hand, *Peryddon*, an alternative and now obsolete name for Llyn Tegid, still employed in 1596, suggests that Don once claimed the largest lake in Wales in its entirety, as her own Welsh *peir*, or *pair*, her 'cauldron.' Then Llyn Tegid was literally *Peryddon*, 'The Cauldron of Don', while the river Dee's estuarine mouth could be (and was) called 'Aber Peryddon'.[8]

Seen as her divinely created 'artefact', the 'lake-cauldron' is at least half a mile across at the rim. Tegid and his wife, who lived at its reputedly unfathomable bottom, were probably regarded as ingredients in Don's original brew. Thus Ceridwen, being on the receiving end, learnt her magic art directly from Don, and eventually matched Don's *Peryddon* with her own vessel – the *Peir Awen*, or 'Cauldron of Inspiration.'

At Llyn Tegid, Ceridwen happily serves as Don's local agent. While Ceridwen was in charge of collecting plants for the brew, she in turn relied on Don's river water, passing through the lake, to provide the basis of her liquor. The quintessence of

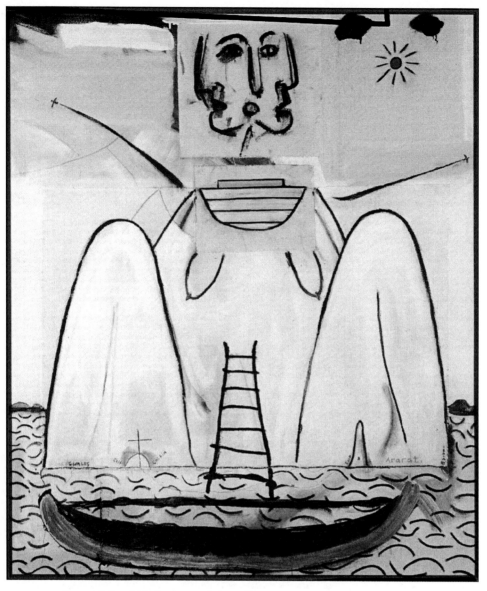

Ararat [Gwales], by Iwan Bala; oil on canvas,150x 135cm. 1997.

wisdom contained in the 'three drops' that splashed onto Gwion Bach was therefore derived from both Ceridwen *and* Don, as he himself obliquely implies:

> '*I was in the Court of Don before the birth of Gwydion*' [9]

and '*I am called skilful in the Court of Don.*' [10]

The river *Dyfrdonwy* or Dee has its source in a swamp, named *Daear sinc,* beneath *Dduallt,* 'Black Cliff'. (OS Grid Reference SH 812274). This 2,000 feet-high ridge stands six miles south-west from Llyn Tegid. The place name joins Welsh d*aear,* 'earth', to *sinc,* 'cesspool' or 'wash-tub', and brings together the functions of excretion and cleansing, as twin aspects of Don's comprehensive metabolism and endless labour.

Substantial remains of a prehistoric settlement, which continued in use during the medieval era, have been discovered overlooking these headwaters at Moel Caws, 'Cheese Hill'.[11] Here Don emerges in her summer pasture role as the great provider.[12] Traces of her beneficence are retained in the Welsh language: *donhaf,* 'to endow' (*don,* plus *haf,* 'summer'), *doniad,* 'giver' and *doniaf,* 'to bless.' The first cheese of the summer had religious significance in Wales. It stood for a New World, as did the cheese traditionally presented to a newly-married couple. When made at *Moel Caws* it emerged as the 'first-born' of Dyfrdonwy's holy catchment area.[13]

Otherworlds

Wishing to taste this cheese, Taliesin climbed between what he took to be two natural stone effigies of Don's head as he made his way to the rocky summit of *Moel Caws,* where herds of black cattle graze to this day. There he felt he had arrived in paradise. Four miles off lay the shimmering surface of Llyn Tegid, joined to his viewpoint by Don's umbilical chord, her sacred river. In the far distance he could see the fertile Vale of Ederion, with the Dee running on towards Chester and the oceans. Content at last, he decided to give up wandering. He would stay on *Moel Caws* indefinitely.

But having savoured this resolve through the length of a warm afternoon, he was obliged to admit that a new and unexpected need had crept into his mind. He found himself wanting to see Iwan Bala's paintings, which were still hanging in the *Eisteddfod* field.

By the time he got there, the Fine Art tent flap was about to be laced shut for the evening, so he slipped in quickly and concentrated his gaze on one work entitled 'Ararat [Gwales], 15 x 130 cm, oil on canvas, 1997'. What struck Taliesin was the rawness of the image, as if it had been hastily caught in the act of boiling over.

Ararat-Gwales is an 'end-game', in which ragged bits of cloth, debris from abandoned or failing myths are here stuck together, to suggest the possibility of a new, integrated life. In this array, Noah's ark is a postage stamp, glued near Mount Ararat's summit. That mountain doubles as the torso of a naked giantess who is also the artist's wife. Her drawn-up knees are the two Arenig peaks that look down on a Llyn Tegid in which her feet and buttocks are submerged. This gross female is 'Ceridwen rising', or *Mam Cymru,* 'Mother Wales', about to give oceanic birth to fresh imaginings.

She squats as the magic Otherworld islet of Gwales,[14] alias Grassholm, which lies ten miles off the western-most cliffs of Pembrokeshire. There, according to the *Mabinogion,* the dark god Bran's head lived on, after it was struck from his body. Bran is the brother of white-breasted Bronwen, who sits on her Cadair Bronwen mountain cairn, 2,430 feet high (OS Grid Reference SH 077346), above Llyn Tegid.

In Iwan Bala's picture, Bran's three faces draw the past and future into a fully laden present.

Welsh *gwal*, 'couch, bed', plus its feminine *es* suffix, spells Gwales, a bed of procreation and death, where the giantess is about to give birth into a smashed cauldron, perhaps Ceridwen's broken cauldron. This bloody slop basin is also a barge, ready to carry a passenger to an endless dream, on whose shore the graffiti of old beliefs have not yet washed away. A rickety ladder gives access from the barge to the island-belly. Way beyond words, the painting spoke to Taliesin.

'Must *I* float offshore again?' Taliesin asked. 'Yes, you must; we're closed,' said the exhibition steward, looking at his watch. 'Then I'd better be going,' said Taliesin, taking a deep breath. 'King Arthur wants me to join his crew on a voyage down to *Annwn;* treasure hunting. Let the arts be my compass, eh? After that, if I survive, I might be allowed to enter the revolving castle, Caer Sidi. It caters for demi-god misfits like me and lies somewhere between *Annwn* and what passes for reality in this country. Ynys Enlli, Bardsey Island in English, that is where they reckon Caer Sidi is sited; sea-cradled, beyond the whirlpool of divisions, off Lleyn's furthest tip. Ah, well, thank everyone in Wales for me, will you? I've enjoyed my stay, on the whole. Yes... I'll say 'Goodbye', then.' The steward nodded in acknowledgement and zipped the tent shut.

Ynys Enlli, Bardsey Island

> *'Do the skilful in song know where the powerful artist is concealed?'*
> *Book of Taliesin*, xx, st.ii, ll. 8–9

As Taliesin's *Preiddeu Annwn* poem makes plain, of the three full boatloads that sailed with Arthur on his voyage to find the treasures of Annwn, only Taliesin and six others survived the hazardous trip.[15] They were then able to reach the mysterious 'between worlds' destination of Ynys Enlli. When in Annwn, they had looted a precious cauldron, studded with pearls around the rim, *'concerning which my first utterance was spoken'*, says Taliesin.[16] This pot had been forged or *'kindled by the breath of nine maidens.'* [17] That being so, on Enlli they act as his nine muses. Their breath, when inhaled, gives Taliesin the gift of supremely inspired speech from the most profound magical realm, *Annwn*.

This additional infusion combines with his other source of inspiration 'from the cauldron of Ceridwen',[18] to equip him with exceptional insight.

> 'And around the lands of Enlli the Dyfi has poured
> Raising the ships on the surface of the plain.'
> Book of Taliesin *xiv, 18–19*.

Opposite top: *A Bardsey sunset; Taliesin's solar eye winks at Caer Sidi.*

bottom: *The moonlit isle,*Ynys Enlli, *alias Bardsey. To Taliesin, the moon is*
           'Arianrhod of laudible aspect, dawn of serenity.' Book of Taliesin, xix.

'I am the depository of song... ' [19]

'I will sing a wise song, the song of the host of harmony.' [20]

'I sing in perfect metre, which will last to the end of the world.' [21]

'Ye intelligent druids... What is there earlier than I that sing of?' [22]

From the top of Bardsey-as-*Caer Sidi*, where his *'song was heard in the four turreted fort, fully revolving'* in time with the sun and moon, he scans mainland Wales and contemplate his contribution to its fabric:

'I have supported an earthly scene, In the water of law and the multitude, in the element of lands... ' [23]

Yet by his scrutiny across eons, he knows that Wales and the whole world is prone to periodic submergence he asks:

'What fountains break out above the cover of darkness?' [24]

He watches, as *'the land becomes ocean'*, before re-emerging once more, exclaiming:

'The world how it comes again, When it falls into decay, Again in the enclosing circle.' [25]

Its re-incarnation reflects *his* death and revival as super-natural events. On considering this cycle he recalls:

'I travelled in the earth... I made a circuit,
I slept in a hundred islands. A hundred caers I have dwelt in.' [26]

Yet on Ynys Enlli the indefatigable traveller is content to rest beside the fountains of water and of sparkling wine, which are notable features of Enlli. Indeed, he has settled in *'A place of complete benefit, And bards and blossoms.'* [27] Dozing there, he wonders if he will dream up another round of travels, another world tour, beginning at a Llanfair Caereinion farm. But in his quiescent state, the urge to rush about has given way to deep contemplation as he wonders:

'Do you know what you are When you are sleeping?
Whether a body or a soul, Or a secrecy of perception?' [28]

Eventually rousing himself, he decides to invite Merlin to stay with him on Enlli, since that wizard of a thousand faces is said to be his third self.[29] Re-united, they will recuperate. The isle is shaped, they imagine, as a goddess of knowledgeable fruitfulness, seen in a mountainously pregnant condition. Through her *'radiant door'* [30] they will witness the rebirth of each sacred dawn, season by season, while Taliesin sings to his cousin-suns, the ever circling stars.

CHAPTER NOTES

Introduction pages 4 to 7

1 Ford, *The Mabonogi*, 1977, 159–181
2 Guest, *The Mabinogion*, 1877, 471–494
3 Ford, 'A Fragment of the Hanes Taliesin by Llewellyn Sion', 1975, 451–460; Ford, *The Mabonogi*, Los Angeles, 1977 (includes *The Tale of Gwion Bach and The Tale of Taliesin*, pp.159–181; transl. from E. Gruffydd, *Chronicle of the World*, 1548).
4 Skene, *Book of Taliesin*, 1868, vol.1

Chapter 1 Setting Out pages 7 to 11

1 Ford, 'A Fragment of the Hanes Taliesin by Llewellyn Sion', 1975, 457; and Guest, *The Mabinogion*, 1877, 472
2 Ford, 'A Fragment of the Hanes Taliesin by Llewellyn Sion', 1975, 457
3 Jarman and Rhys-Hughes, *A Guide to Welsh Literature*, 1976, 55
4 Skene, *Book of Taliesin*, 1868, poem 33, vol.2, 6–7
5 Coleridge, *Kubla Khan*, ll. 40
6 H.F.S. Vaughan in *Archaeologia Cambrensis*, 1876, 201
7 Pennant, *Tours in Wales, 1778–1781*, 1883 edn, vol.2, 203
8 Ford, *The Poetry of Llywarch Hen*, 1974, st. 81, vol. 11.2; and *Archaeologia Cambrensis*, 1884, 309–10
9 Morris-Jones, 'Taliesin', 1918, 172
10 Morris-Jones, 'Taliesin', 1918, 176
11 Morris-Jones, 'Taliesin', 1918, 157 and 162

Chapter 2, Llyn Tegid pages 8 to 22

1 F. Durrenmatt, *Der Doppelganger*, Zurich, 1960
2 Seen in 2005.
3 Seen in 2004.
4 Erected *circa* AD 2000.
5 Hyde-Hall, *A Description of Carnarvonshire, 1809–1811*, 1952, 313
6 S.R. Glynne, *Archaeologia Cambrensis*, 1884, 334
7 Baring-Gould and Fisher, *The Lives of the British Saints*, 1907–13, vol.1, 208; vol.3, 165
8 Bartrum, *A Welsh Classical Dictionary*,1993, 423
9 Rowlands, *Early Welsh Saga Poetry*, 1990, 70
10 Craddock, *Letters from Snowdon*, 1770, 80
11 Jenkins, *The Reverend Thomas Charles of Bala*, 1908, vol.2, 88
12 Jenkins, *The Reverend Thomas Charles of Bala*, 1908, vol.2, 90

13   Jenkins, *The Reverend Thomas Charles of Bala,* 1908, vol.2, 89
14   Jenkins, *The Reverend Thomas Charles of Bala,* 1908, vol.2, 90
15   Rhys, *Celtic Folk-Lore, Welsh and Manx,* 1901, vol.2, 38
16   R. Fenton in *Archaeologia Cambrensis, Supplement,* 1917, 90
17   Trevelyan, *Folklore and Folk-stories of Wales,* 1909, 254
18   Owen, *Old Stone Crosses of the Vale of Clwyd,* 1886, 73
19   Owen, *Old Stone Crosses of the Vale of Clwyd,* 1886, 38 and 66
20   Owen, *The Customs and Traditions of Wales,* 1991, 72
21   M. and J. Stutley, *Dictionary of Hinduism,* 1977, 161
22   Knappert, *Indian Mythology,* 1991, 57
23   Pennant, *Tours in Wales, 1778–1781,* vol.2 214
24   Jones, *The Holy Wells of Wales,* 1954, 129
25   Rhys, *Celtic Folk-Lore, Welsh and Manx,* 1901, vol.2, 376–7
26   Ward, *The Lakes of Wales,* 1931, 219
27   Nennius, *British History and the Annales of Wales,* 1980, 40
28   Dames, *The Avebury Cycle,* 1977, 173
29   Rhys, *Celtic Folk-Lore, Welsh and Manx,* 1901, vol.2, 378
30   *Bye-Gones,* 1873, 187
31   Davies, *Folk-lore of West and Mid-Wales,* 1911, 89–90; and *Zeitschrift fur Celtische Philologie,* 53, 74–5
32   *Bye-Gones,* 1904, 272
33   Rhys, 'Welsh Fairy Tales', 1882, 74
34   Rhys, 'Welsh Fairy Tales', 1882, 82–4
35   *Bye-Gones,* 1898, 492; *Bulletin of the Board of Celtic Studies,* vol.30, 1982, 152
36   H.J. Fleure, *Journal of the Royal Anthropological Institute,* vol.46, 1916, 113–118
37   Rhys, 'Welsh Fairy Tales', 1882, 84
38   *Bye-Gones,*1886, 209
39   Trevelyan, *Folklore and Folk-stories of Wales,* 1909, 13
40   Trevelyan, *Folklore and Folk-stories of Wales,* 1909, 40

Chapter 3 Under the Lake pages 23 to 42

1   Jones and Jones, *The Mabinogion,* 1993, 155–157
2   Jones and Jones, *The Mabinogion,* 1993, 90
3   Bromwich, *Trioedd Ynys Prydein,* 1961, 303–5
4   Jones and Jones, 1993, 90
5   Nash-Williams, 'Roman Stations at Neath and Caer Gai', 242–6
6   Jones and Jones, 1993, 90
7   Rhys, 'Welsh Fairy Tales', 1882, 86–93
8   Frye, *Creation and Recreation,* 13
9   Frye, *Creation and Recreation,* 13
10   Rhys, 'Welsh Fairy Tales', 1882, 90
11   Rhys, 'Welsh Fairy Tales', 1882, 91
12   Dames, *The Avebury Cycle,* 1977, 85–8
13   Rhys, 'Welsh Fairy Tales', 1882, 91

14 Rhys, 'Welsh Fairy Tales', 1882, 92
15 Rhys, 'Welsh Fairy Tales', 1882, 92
16 Trevelyan, *Folklore and Folk-stories of Wales*, 1909, 93
17 Rhys, *Welsh and Manx*, 1901,vol.2, 441
18 Knappert, *Indian Mythology*, 1991, 277
19 Dames, *Merlin and Wales*, 2002, 169–70
20 Guest, *The Mabinogion*, 1877, 471
22 Jones and Jones, *The Mabinogion*, 1993, 86
23 Cynddelw, *circa* 1190, H. 125, 26
24 Trueman, *Geology and Scenery in England and Wales*, 1949, 214
25 Ford, *The Mabonogi*, 1977, 163
26 Guest, *The Mabinogion*, 1877, 472
27 Ford, 'A Fragment of the Hanes Taliesin by Llewellyn Sion', 1975, 457
28 Guest, *The Mabinogion*, 1877, 472
29 Ford, *The Mabonogi*, 1977, 163
30 Ford, 'A Fragment of the Hanes Taliesin by Llewellyn Sion', 1975, 458
31 Ford, *The Mabonogi*, 1977, 162
32 Ford, *The Mabonogi*, 1977, 163
33 Ford, *The Mabonogi*, 1977, 163
34 Guest, *The Mabinogion*, 1877, 472
35 Dames, *Mythic Ireland*, 1992, 174
36 Guest, *The Mabinogion*, 1877, 472
37 Ford, *The Mabonogi*, 1977, 162
38 Guest, *The Mabinogion*, 1877, 500
39 Trevelyan, *Folklore and Folk-stories of Wales*, 1909, 198–202
40 Trevelyan, *Folklore and Folk-stories of Wales*, 1909, 149
41 T. Lyttelton, *Collected Works*, 1756, 718
42 Bromwich, *Trioedd Ynys Prydein*, 1961, 107
43 Bromwich, *Trioedd Ynys Prydein*, 1961, 308
44 Ashmolean cat. no. 1927.2732
45 Ford, *The Mabonogi*, 1977, 163
46 Guest, *The Mabinogion*, 1877, 472
47 Douglas, *Purity and Danger*, 1966, 13 and 16
48 Leach, *Culture and Communication*, 1976, 62
49 Leach, *Culture and Communication*, 1976, 63
50 Dames, *Mythic Ireland*, 1992, 201–3, 219–20

Chapter 4 The Pursuit pages 43 to 58

1   Guest, *The Mabinogion*, 1877, 472
2   Ford, 'A Fragment of the Hanes Taliesin by Llewellyn Sion', 1975, 458
3   D.W. Nash, *Taliesin*, 1858, 156
4   Rowlands, *Early Welsh Saga Poetry*, 1990, st. 3–9; and st. 19
5   Trevelyan, *Folklore and Folk-stories of Wales*, 1909, 47–51
6   Dames, *Merlin and Wales*, 2002, 146–7
7   Trevelyan, *Folklore and Folk-stories of Wales*, 1909, 64

8   Baring-Gould and Fisher, *The Lives of the British Saints*, 1907–13, vol.2, 331–5; and *RCAHM Merioneth*, no. 179

9   Trevelyan, *Folklore and Folk-stories of Wales*, 1909, 206

10   Gwynn-Jones, *Welsh Folklore and Folk Customs*, 1929, 147

11   Gwynn-Jones, *Welsh Folklore and Folk Customs*, 1929, 157

12   Owen, *Old Stone Crosses of the Vale of Clwyd*, 1886, 142

13   Jones and Jones, *The Mabinogion*, 1993, 180

14   Jones and Jones, *The Mabinogion*, 1993, 112

15   Jones and Jones, *The Mabinogion*, 1993, 113

16   *Archaeologia Cambrensis*, 1876, 183

17   Trevelyan, *Folklore and Folk-stories of Wales*, 1909, 413

18   *Bulletin of the Board of Celtic Studies*, 30, 1982, 149–153

19   *Bulletin of the Board of Celtic Studies*, 30, 1982, 151

20   Thomas, *Antiquae Linguae Britannicae, Thesaurus*, 1753, 41

21   Guest, *The Mabinogion*, 1877, 473

22   Ford, 'A Fragment of the Hanes Taliesin by Llewellyn Sion', 1975, 458

23   Douglas, *Purity and Danger*, 1966, 14

24   Owen, 1991, 12.

25   *Bye-Gones*, 1928, 118

26   Bromwich, *Trioedd Ynys Prydein*, 1961, Triad 26w

27   Hutchinson, 'Bacchus in Roman Britain', 1986, 168

28   De la Bedoyere, *The Golden Age of Roman Britain*, 1999, 99

29   Thomas, *Geiriadur Prifysgol Cymry*, 1950, vol. I

30   Wheeler, *Prehistoric and Roman Wales*, 1925, 291–2

31   Davies, *A History of Wales*, 1993, 71–2

32   Rainey, *Mosaics in Roman Britain*, 1973, 32

33   Boon, 'Backhall Street Mosaic, Caerleon', 352

34   Bromwich, *Trioedd Ynys Prydein*, 1961, 214

35   Hutchinson, 'Bacchus in Roman Britain', 1986, 126

36   Craddock, *Letters from Snowdon*, 1770, 34

37   Baring-Gould and Fisher, The Lives of the British Saints, 1907–13, vol.4, 220; Rees, 'Ffynnon Tegla', 87–9

38   *Archaeologia Cambrensis*, 1891, 14; *Archaeologia Cambrensis*, 1846, 53

39   Jones, 'History of the Parish of Llansanffraid-yn-Mechain', *Montgomeryshire Collections*, 1871, 136

40   Tusser's *Redivivus*, 1744, 80

41   Jones, 'History of the Parish of Llansanffraid-yn-Mechain', *Montgomeryshire Collections*, 1871, iii

Chapter 5 In the Bag pages 59 to 80

1   Guest, *The Mabinogion*, 1877, 473

2   Ford, 'A Fragment of the Hanes Taliesin by Llewellyn Sion', 1975, 458

3   Ford, *The Mabonogi*, 1977, 164

4   Ford, *The Mabonogi*, 1977, 160

5   Ford, *The Mabonogi*, 1977, 160

6   Ford, 'A Fragment of the Hanes Taliesin by Llewellyn Sion', 1975, 451, fn.2

7   Ford, 'A Fragment of the Hanes Taliesin by Llewellyn Sion', 1975, 451, fn. 4

8   E. Ekwall, *Concise Dictionary Of English Place*-Names, 1936, 96

9   *Vita Merlini*, transl. J.J. Parry, 1929, 75

10   *Description of Wales*, transl. L. Thorpe, 1978, 198

11   J.C. Howson, *The River Dee*, 1875, 6

12   *Bulletin of the Board of Celtic Studies*, vol.7, 1993, 1–4

13   Rhys, in *Hibbert Lectures*, 1886, 89–92; Bromwich, *Trioedd Ynys Prydein*, 1961, 327

14   *Metrical Dindshenchas* vol.4, 91; *Revue Celtique*, vol.15, 461–2

15   *Folklore,* Vol.4, 479–80

16   *Y Cymmrodor*, 28, 1918, 49–50

17   Fifth century BC

18   Morris, *Bulletin of the Board of Celtic Studies*, 29, 1980, 290

19   *Eriu*, 8, 1916, 1–63

20   Jones and Jones, *The Mabinogion,* 1993, 30

21   Dafydd ap Gwilym, transl. Hughes, T., in *The Rattle Bag*, vol.2 18–19, 32

22   Eliade, *Images and Symbols*, 1961, 152

23   Guest, *The Mabinogion,* 1877, 476

24   B. Colloms, *Charles Kingsley*, 1975, 113

25   Dee Estuary Conservation Group, *Report,* 1976, 16–17

26   Chester Miracle Play, MS. of 1592, in Pollard, *English Miracle Plays,* 2003

27   Pollard, *English Miracle Plays,* 2003, vol.2 29–35

28   F.J. Utley in *Speculum*, vol.16, 1941, 426–451

29   Bartrum, *A Welsh Classical Dictionary,* 1993, 593

30   A. Wade-Evans, *Archaeologia Cambrensis*, 85, 1930, 332–3

31   Graves, *The Crane Bag and Other Disputed Subjects*, 1969, 4–5

32   Bromwich, *Trioedd Ynys Prydein*, 1961, Appendix 2, 238–9

33   T. Jones in *Proceedings of the British Academy*, vol.53, 1967, 97–137

34   Bromwich, *Trioedd Ynys Prydein*, 1961, 166

35   Jones, 'The Stanzas of the Graves', 1967, st. 23, and 133

36   M.E. Byrne in *Eriu,* vol.11, 1932, 97

37   Quoted in Ford, *Ystoria Taliesin*, 1992, 16

38   Ford, *Ystoria Taliesin*, 1992, 16, quoting Martin's *Description of the Western Isles*, 1703, 8

39   G. Grigson, *The Englishman's Flora*, 1987, 224

40   *Archaeologia Cambrensis*, 1867, 346

41   Bromwich, *Trioedd Ynys Prydein*, 1961, 13

42   *Metrical Dindshenchas* IV, 184 and 286; also *Revue Celtique*, vol. 16, 60

43   D.W. Nash, *Taliesin,* 1858, 156

44   Baring-Gould and Fisher, *The Lives of the British Saints,* 1907–13, vol.1, 217

45   G.C. Boon, *Bulletin of the Board of Celtic Studies*, 25, 1973, 347–358

46   G.C. Boon, *Bulletin of the Board of Celtic Studies*, 25, 1973, 358

47   F. Simpson, *The River Dee*, 1907, 99–100

48   Skene, *Book of Taliesin,* 1868, poem 15

49   Skene, *Book of Taliesin,* 1868, poem 10

50   *RCAHM Flintshire*, 40; Pennant, *Tours in Wales, 1778–1781, 1883 edn.,*vol.2, 207

51 Skene, *Book of Taliesin,* 1868, poem 30 stanza 7
52 W. Stephens, *Collected Poems,* 1984, 102
53 W. Stephens, *Collected Poems,* 1984, 13
54 Deptartment of Transport, *International Code of Signals,* 1991, 28–9
55 *The Double Vision of Mananaan,* eighth century, trans. J. Montague
56 Jones and Jones, *The Mabinogion,* 1993, 28
57 North, *Sunken Cities,* 1957, 78
58 J. Steers, *The Coasts of England and Wales,* 1964, 151
59 Meyrick, *History and Antiquities of the County of Cardiganshire,* 1907, 78
60 J. Steers, *The Coasts of England and Wales,* 1964, 151
61 P. Edwards in *Archaeologia Cambrensis,* vol.15, 1849, 156–7
62 Skene, *Book of Taliesin,* 1868, poem 17
63 P. Edwards in *Archaeologia Cambrensis,* vol.15, 1849, 154
64 *Black Book of Carmarthen,* vol.38, st. i.
65 Rowlands, *Early Welsh Saga Poetry,* 1990, st.2
66 Skene, *Book of Taliesin,* 1868, 302, stanza 3
67 Rhys in *Folklore,* vol.4, 1893, 69
68 Skene, *Book of Taliesin,* 1868, poem 30, stanza 2
69 B. Moon in *ER,* vol.11, 224–5
70 Rhys, *Celtic Folk-Lore, Welsh and Manx,* 1901, vol.2, 383

Chapter 6 Mayday Changes pages 81 to 102

1   Guest, *The Mabinogion,* 1877, 475
2   Eliade, *Images and Symbols,* 1961, 152
3   Morris, *Celtic Remains,* 1878, 234
4   *Cambrian Magazine,* vol.5, 1833, 198–241
5   Guest, *The Mabinogion,* 1877, 473
6   Ford, *The Mabonogi,* 1977, 165
7   Guest, *The Mabinogion,* 1877, 473
8   Ford, *The Mabonogi,* 1977, 165
9   Guest, *The Mabinogion,* 1877, 473–4
10 Ford, 'A Fragment of the Hanes Taliesin by Llewellyn Sion', 1975, 459
11 Ford, *The Mabonogi,* 1977, 165
12 Evans, 1764, Vol.10, 56 and vol.11, 49
13 Skene, *Book of Taliesin,* 1868, poem 28
14 *Black Book of Carmarthen* vol.5; Skene, *Book of Taliesin,* 1868, vol.1, 504
15 W. James in *Hibbert Lectures,* 1909, 169
16 Lynch, *Prehistoric Wales,* 2000, 38
17 *Archaeologia Cambrensis,* 1924, 295–8
18 Bromwich, *Trioedd Ynys Prydein,* 1961, 241
19 Jones and Jones, *The Mabinogion,* 1993, 104–5
20 Guest, *The Mabinogion,* 1877, 475
21 Guest, *The Mabinogion,* 1877, 475
22 Guest, *The Mabinogion,* 1877, 475
23 Guest, *The Mabinogion,* 1877, 475
24 Guest, *The Mabinogion,* 1877, 475

25   Guest, *The Mabinogion,* 1877, 475
26   Skene, *Book of Taliesin,* 1868, vol.7 pt 2, 240–5
27   Skene, *Book of Taliesin,* 1868, poem 17
28   Skene, *Book of Taliesin,* 1868, poem 7
29   Meyrick, *History and Antiquities of the County of Cardiganshire,* 1907, 158
30   North, *Sunken Cities,* 1957, 147
31   Ross, *Pagan Celtic Britain,* 1967, 282
32   Condry, *The Natural History of Wales,* 1981, 180
33   Graves, *The Crane Bag and Other Disputed Subjects,* 1969, 5
34   Skene, *Book of Taliesin,* 1868, poem 18
35   T.W. Potter and C. Johns, *Roman Britain,* 1983, 34
36   Mack, *The Coinage of Ancient Britain,* 1964, 63, 68, 82–4
37   Guest, *The Mabinogion,* 1877, 483
38   Baring-Gould and Fisher, *The Lives of the British Saints,* 1907–13, vol.2, 243
39   C. Saxton, *Map of Cardiganshire,* 1575
40   Bromwich, *Trioedd Ynys Prydein,* 1961, 375
41   Rowlands, *Early Welsh Saga Poetry,* 1990, *Mi a wum,* st.5
42   Skene, *Book of Taliesin,* 1868, poem 11
43   Rowlands, *Early Welsh Saga Poetry,* 1990, 509, stanzas 2–5
44   Rowlands, *Early Welsh Saga Poetry,* 1990, 509, stanza 1
45   Dames, *Merlin and Wales,* 2002, 96–99
46   Owen, *The Customs and Traditions of Wales,* 1991, 71
47   *Archaeologia Cambrensis,* 1858, 334
48   See examples in London Museum and from Wilderspool, Lancs., now in Grosvenor Museum, Chester
49   Jones and Jones, *The Mabinogion,* 1993, 69
50   Simpson, *Folklore of the Welsh Border,* 1976, 149
51   D. ap Gwilym, in Clancy, *Medieval Welsh Lyrics,* 1965, 26–7
52   Owen, *The Customs and Traditions of Wales,* 1991, 72
53   Owen, *The Customs and Traditions of Wales,* 1991, 70
54   *Folklore,* vol.4, 53
55   Dames, *Merlin and Wales,* 2002, 171–2
56   F.W.J. Schelling, *Philosophy of Art,* 1–15
57   Ross, *Pagan Celtic Britain,* 1967, 215 and 368
58   I. Richmond in *Journal of Roman Studies,* 1945, plate I; 27
59   National Museum of Wales
60   Jones and Jones, *The Mabinogion,* 1993, 104–5
61   Owen, *The Customs and Traditions of Wales,* 1991, 71–3
62   Macrobius, *The Saturnalia,* transl. P.V. Davies, 1969, 126–130
63   *Archaeologia Cambrensis,* 1960, 136–156
64   *Encyclopedia of Religion,* vol.13, 408
65   Guest, *The Mabinogion,* 1877, 474
66   Ford, 'A Fragment of the Hanes Taliesin by Llewellyn Sion', 1975, 459–60
67   See Corinium Museum, Cirencester; and Toynbee, *Art in Britain Under the Romans,* 1964, plates 76, 84
68   *Cardigan County History,* vol.1, 389; Baring-Gould and Fisher, *The Lives of the British Saints,* 1907–13, vol.2, 263

69 Ford, *The Mabonogi,* 1977, 167
71 Guest, *The Mabinogion,* 1877, 476

Chapter 7 King Maelgwn pages 103 to 123

1   Guest, *The Mabinogion,* 1877, 476–7
2   Guest, *The Mabinogion,* 1877, 477
3   Guest, *The Mabinogion,* 1877, 477
4   Guest, *The Mabinogion,* 1877, 478
5   Ford, *The Mabonogi,* 1977, 168
6   Guest, *The Mabinogion,* 1877, 478
7   Guest, *The Mabinogion,* 1877, 478
8   Guest, *The Mabinogion,* 1877, 479
9   *Bulletin of the Board of Celtic Studies,* vol.18, 1958, 57–8
10 Guest, *The Mabinogion,* 1877, 479
11 Guest, *The Mabinogion,* 1877, 480
12 Gildas, transl. Giles, 1891, paras. 33–5, 318–20
13 Snyder, 'Sub-Roman Britain, AD 400–600', 1996, 8
14 Morris-Jones, 'Taliesin', 1918, 172–3
15 Guest, *The Mabinogion,* 1877, 481
16 Guest, *The Mabinogion,* 1877, 481–2
17 Guest, *The Mabinogion,* 1877, 482
18 Guest, *The Mabinogion,* 1877, 482–3
19 Guest, *The Mabinogion,* 1877, 483
20 Else, *Aristotle's Poetics,* 1963, 303–5
21 Guest, *The Mabinogion,* 1877, 481
22 Guest, *The Mabinogion,* 1877, 489
23 Guest, *The Mabinogion,* 1877, 483–4
24 Guest, *The Mabinogion,* 1877, 485–6
25 Guest, *The Mabinogion,* 1877, 487
26 Guest, *The Mabinogion,* 1877, 487
27 Guest, *The Mabinogion,* 1877, 490
28 Guest, *The Mabinogion,* 1877, 490
29 T. Williams, *Map of Llandudno, circa* 1840
30 Guest, *The Mabinogion,* 1877, 490
31 H.N. Savory in *Archaeologia Cambrensis,* 1958, 14–15
32 *Archaeologia Cambrensis,* 1909, 382
33 *Archaeologia Cambrensis,* 1908, 116–117
34 Jones and Jones, *The Mabinogion,* 1993, 15–16
35 *Encyclopedia of Religion,* vol.3, 157
36 Bromwich, *Trioedd Ynys Prydein,* 1961, *Triads, nos. 7, 25, 33*
37 Bromwich, *Trioedd Ynys Prydein,* 1961, *Triads, nos. 7, 25,269*
38 G. Sievking, *British Museum Quarterly,* vol.35, 1971, 232–240
39 Bartrum, *A Welsh Classical Dictionary,* 1993, 579
40 *Archaeologia Cambrensis,* 1873, 210–214
41 *Archaeologia Cambrensis,* 1873, 214
42 Baring-Gould and Fisher, *The Lives of the British Saints,* 1907–13, vol.2, 474–5

43 Morris, *Celtic Remains*, 1878, 175
44 Bartrum, *A Welsh Classical Dictionary*, 1993, 260
45 Lynch, *Prehistoric Wales*, 2000, 96–9
46 Guest, *The Mabinogion*, 1877, 485
47 National Museum of Wales
48 *Archaeologia Cambrensis*, 1952, 4
49 Morris (ed.), *Welsh Annales*, AD 547
50 Pennant, *Tours in Wales, 1778–1781*, vol.3, 138
51 Rhys, in *Archaeologia Cambrensis*, 1921, 168
52 Evans, in *Panton MS* 51, fols. 110v–111v
53 Rhys in *Y Cymmrodor*, 1888, 184–5
54 Guest, *The Mabinogion*, 1877, 491–4
55 Ford, *Ystoria Taliesin*, 1992, 38–9

Chapter 8 Trek to Llyn Geirionydd pages 124 to 145

1 G.M. Trevelyan, *A Shortened History of England*, 1989, 171
2 T. Gray, *The Bard*, 1754, st. 3, ll.20–21
3 M. Arnold, *Letters*, (ed. Russell, G.), 491
4 M. Arnold, *Letters*, (ed. Russell, G.), 491
5 Bartrum, *A Welsh Classical Dictionary*, 1993, 440
6 Skene, *Book of Taliesin*, 1868, poem 1
7 Jones and Jones, *The Mabinogion*, 1993, 47–52 and 54–58
8 Bartrum, *A Welsh Classical Dictionary*, 1993, 408–9
9 Dyer, *Prehistoric England and Wales*, 1980, 346
10 Rowlands, *Early Welsh Saga Poetry*, 1990, 507, st.6 and 11
11 Gildas, trans. Giles, 1891, para. 4, 300
12 W.E. Griffiths in *Archaeologia Cambrensis*, 1956, 73–76
13 Ford, *The Mabonogi*, 1977, 172–3
14 Ford, *Ystoria Taliesin*, 1992, 10
15 *RCAHM Carnarvonshire*, I, 72
16 Guest, *The Mabinogion*, 1877, 475
17 Guest, *The Mabinogion*, 1877, 492
18 Guest, *The Mabinogion*, 1877, 482
19 M. Arnold, *Letters*, (ed. Russell, G.), 491
20 Skene, *Book of Taliesin*, 1868, poem 7
21 Baring-Gould and Fisher, *The Lives of the British Saints*, 1907–13, vol.1, 288
22 Ford, *The Mabonogi*, 1977, 165
23 Ross, *Pagan Celtic Britain*, 1967, 362
24 Rhys, *Hibbert Lectures*, 1886, 77
25 Bernard, J. H., (ed.), in *Hibbert Lectures*, 1897, 39–40
26 J. Delaney, *Dictionary of Saints*, 1982
27 *New Catholic Encyclopedia*, 1967, vol.9, 1015
28 Owen, in *Folklore*, 1973, 242–3
29 Owen, in *Folklore*, 1973, 244–5
30 Owen, in *Folklore*, 1973, 244
31 Dames, 1992, 252

32 Owen, in *Folklore,* 1973, 248
33 *Archaeologia Cambrensis,* 1865, 278
34 Dyer, *Prehistoric England and Wales,* 1980, 231, 292
35 Owen, in *Folklore,* 1973, 243
36 *Archaeologia Cambrensis,* 1882, 333; RCAHM, Denbighshire, no.542
37 Baring-Gould and Fisher, *The Lives of the British Saints,* 1907–13, vol.1, 284
38 Lhuyd, 'Additions to the Welsh Counties', 1695, 670
39 Jones and Jones, *The Mabinogion,* 1993, 72
40 P.K. Baillie-Reynolds, in *Archaeologia Cambrensis,* 1927, 292–305
41 Rivet and Smith, *The Place-Names of Roman Britain,* 1979, 297
42 Grosvenor Museum Chester; inscriptions
43 The British Ordivician tribe
44 A geological order named by C. Lapworth 1879
45 *Archaeologia Cambrensis,* 1936, 246, no. 496
46 Lynch, *Gwynedd,* 1995, 101
47 W.F. Grimes, in *Y Cymmrodor.,* 1930, 136–7; fig.58, no. 2
48 Ross, *Pagan Celtic Britain,* 1967, 215, 368
49 Morris-Jones, 'Taliesin', 1918, 211, ll. 29–32
50 *Archaeologia Cambrensis,* 1925, 321
51 Edwards and Blair, in *Antiquaries Journal,* 1982, vol.75, 80
52 *RCAHM Carn.,* vol.1, no.178, 37
53 *RCAHM Carn.,* vol.1, no. 176, 37
54 Lowe, *The Heart of Northern Wales,* 1912, vol.1, 22–3
55 Lowe, *The Heart of Northern Wales,* 1912, vol.1, 57
56 Jones and Jones, *The Mabinogion,* 1993, 84
57 *RCAHM Carn.,* vol.1, 100
58 *Cambrian Magazine,* vol.3, 1831, 73
59 Ward, *The Lakes of Wales,* 1931, 125; E. Ekwall, *English River Names,* 1929, 268–9
60 Ward, *The Lakes of Wales,* 1931, 72
61 G. Webster in *Proceedings of the Dorset Natural History and Archaeological Society,* 1960, 104–6
62 Toynbee, *Art in Britain Under the Romans,* 1964, pl. 34, cat. no.12
63 Pennant, *Tours in Wales, 1778–1781,* 1883, vol.2, 268
64 Dames, *Mythic Ireland,* 1992, 97
65 L. Adkins, *Roman Religion,* 2001, 161
66 Skene, *Book of Taliesin,* 1868, poem 7; Guest, *The Mabinogion,* 1877, 475
67 Bromwich, *Trioedd Ynys Prydein,* 1961, Triad no. 7
68 Skene, *Book of Taliesin,* 1868, poem 52

Chapter 9 'Lake Language' pages 146 to 163

1 *Bulletin of the Board of Celtic Studies,* vol.29, 291
2 *Red Book of Hergest,* col.1049
3 Quoted in Hyde-Hall, *A Description of Carnarvonshire, 1809–1811,* 1952, 128
4 McCumsey, 'Silence', 321–4
5 *Etude Celtique,* vol.12, 178–9

6   Gildas, transl. Giles, 1891, para. 3, 300
7   Ford, *Ystoria Taliesin*, 1992, 39
8   Skene, *Book of Taliesin*, 1868, poem 52 stanza 2
9   Guest, *The Mabinogion*, 1877, 475
10   Teignmouth, *Memoire of Sir William Jones*, 1807, vol.2, 128
11   K.H. Schmidt in *Bulletin of the Board of Celtic Studies*, 1991, 1–19
12   P. Sims-Williams in *Bulletin of the Board of Celtic Studies*, 1991, 20–86
13   P. Sims-Williams in *Bulletin of the Board of Celtic Studies*, 1991, 26
14   M. Henderson in *The Times*, 17th Feb 2003, 7
15   Guest, *The Mabinogion*, 1877, 475
16   Trevelyan, *Folklore and Folk-stories of Wales*, 1909, 172
17   Gerald of Wales, *The Journey Through Wales*, (trans. L. Thorpe 1978), 246
18   *Black Book of Carmarthen*, vol.3 pt.2, I–4
19   Guest, *The Mabinogion*, 1877, 483; Skene, *Book of Taliesin*, 1868, vol.7 pt.2, 86–91
20   Skene, *Book of Taliesin*, 1868, poem 7
21   Dames, *Mythic Ireland*, 1992, 168–7
22   Skene, *Book of Taliesin*, 1868, poems 1 and 2
23   Skene, *Book of Taliesin*, 1868, poem 8
24   Hyde-Hall, *A Description of Carnarvonshire, 1809–1811*, 1952, 128
25   Bennett, *The Pedestrians Guide Through North Wales*, 1838, 322
26   *Archaeologia Cambrensis*, 1855, 114; RCAHM *Carn*. vol.1, no. 573
27   Skene, *Book of Taliesin*, 1868, vol.1, 275; vol.2, 11–12
28   Skene, 1868, vol.1, 275; vol.2, 41–2
29   Dames, *The Silbury Treasure*, 1976, 52–4, 73
30   Skene, *Book of Taliesin*, 1868, poem 16
31   Skene, *Book of Taliesin*, 1868, poem 19
32   Skene, *Book of Taliesin*, 1868, poem 73
33   Skene, *Book of Taliesin*, 1868, poem 1
34   Skene, *Book of Taliesin*, 1868, poem 15
35   Skene, *Book of Taliesin*, 1868, poem 14
36   Bromwich, *Trioedd Ynys Prydein*, 1961, 363; Pennant, *Tours in Wales, 1778–1781*, 1883, vol.1, 331
37   Dyer, *Prehistoric England and Wales*, 1980, 220
38   Skene, *Book of Taliesin*, 1868, poems 19 and 55
39   Skene, *Book of Taliesin*, 1868, poem 8
40   Skene, *Book of Taliesin*, 1868, poem 7
41   Skene, *Book of Taliesin*, 1868, poem 4
42   J. Stephens, *The Mead of Poetry*, 259–66
43   Skene, *Book of Taliesin*, 1868, poems 7 and 8
44   Skene, *Book of Taliesin*, 1868, poem 55
45   Skene, *Book of Taliesin*, 1868, poem 55
46   Lynch, *Prehistoric Wales*, 2000, fig.3.12, and p.115
47   Skene, *Book of Taliesin*, 1868, poem 7
48   Skene, *Book of Taliesin*, 1868, poem 19
49   Skene, *Book of Taliesin*, 1868, poem 8
50   R. Palmer, *Folklore of Gloucestershire*, 2001, 114

51 Skene, *Book of Taliesin,* 1868, poems 6 and 55
52 Skene, *Book of Taliesin,* 1868, poem 7
53 Skene, *Book of Taliesin,* 1868, poem 3
54 Skene, *Book of Taliesin,* 1868, poem 15
55 Skene, *Book of Taliesin,* 1868, poem 7
56 Skene, *Book of Taliesin,* 1868, poem 3
57 G.G. Davies, *The Life of Gwilym Cowlyd,* Cardiff, 1976
58 Stephens, *The Oxford Companion to the Literature of Wales,* 1986, 231
59 Stephens, *The New Companion to the Literature of Wales,* 1998 , 651
60 R. Prior, *Anglo-Welsh Review,* 1977, 11
61 Skene, *Book of Taliesin,* 1868, poem 3
62 Guest, *The Mabinogion,* 1877, 483
63 F.J. North, *Mining For Metals,* 1960, 140–2
64 Guest, *The Mabinogion,* 1877, 476
65 Skene, *Book of Taliesin,* 1868, poem 9
66 J.G. Davies, in *Transactions of the Honorable Society of Cymmrodorion,* 1957, 141
67 J.G. Davies, in *Transactions of the Honorable Society of Cymmrodorion,* 1957, 141
68 Knappert, *Indian Mythology,* 1991, 220
69 Knappert, *Indian Mythology,* 1991, 254
70 Guest, *The Mabinogion,* 1877, 483
71 A. Mookerjee, *The Tantric Way,* London 1977, 133
72 *Encyclopedia of Religion,* vol.6, 242 and vol.7, 134
73 Teignmouth, *Memoire of Sir William Jones,* 1807, vol.2, 128
74 Skene, *Book of Taliesin,* 1868, poem 8
75 Skene, *Book of Taliesin,* 1868, poem 56
76 Ford, *The Mabonogi,* 1977, 180
77 Skene, *Book of Taliesin,* 1868, poem 2 stanza 2, 11.6–7

Chapter 10 Gold and Grave pages 164 to 182

1   Dyer, *Prehistoric England and Wales,* 1980, 347
2   Skene, *Book of Taliesin,* 1868, poem 46
3   Skene, *Book of Taliesin,* 1868, poem 53 stanza 2
4   Johnson, *The Complete Poems of Emily Dickinson,* 1975, poem 569, 1–2
5   Emerson, *Essays,* 1855, 435
6   K. Smith and J. Bromley, *Frank Lloyd Wright: Taliesin and Taliesin West,* New York 1997.
7   Guest, *The Mabinogion,* 1877, 484
8   Bromwich, *Trioedd Ynys Prydein,* 1961, 140, 427–8
9   Bromwich, *Trioedd Ynys Prydein,* 1961, 140, 427
10 Gwynn-Jones, *Welsh Folklore and Folk Customs,* 1929, 157
11 Stephens, *The New Companion to the Literature of Wales,* 1998, 174
12 Bromwich, *Trioedd Ynys Prydein,* 1961, 439–40
13 Rhys, *Celtic Folk-Lore, Welsh and Manx,* 1901, 417

14 R. G. Gruffydd, in *Transactions of the Honorable Society of Cymmrodorion,* 1995, 9–21
15 Condry, *The Natural History of Wales,* 1981, 131–2 and 200
16 Skene, *Book of Taliesin,* 1868, poem 1
17 Stephens, *The Oxford Companion to the Literature of Wales,* 1986, 98
18 Condry, *The Natural History of Wales,* 1981, 202
19 Jones, *Chwedl yr Anifeiliad Hynaf,* 1951–2, 62–6
20 E. Isaac, *Coelion Cymry,* 1938, 42–4
21 Bartrum, *A Welsh Classical Dictionary,* 1993, 175
22 Skene, *Book of Taliesin,* 1868, poem 4
23 Jones and Jones, *The Mabinogion,* 1993, 112
24 Baring-Gould, and Fisher, *The Lives of the British Saints,* 1907–13, vol.2, 243–4
25 R.G. Gruffydd, in *Transactions of the Honorable Society of Cymmrodorion,* 1995, 18
26 Baring-Gould and Fisher, *The Lives of the British Saints,* 1907–13, vol.2, 224
27 G.H. Jenkins, in *Cardigan County History,* vol.3, 1998, 160–8
28 G.H. Jenkins, in *Cardigan County History,* vol.3, 1998, 160
29 *Mining Journal,* vol.58, 1888, 47
30 *Mining Journal,* vol.58, 1888, 1315
31 *Mining Journal,* 22nd Dec 1888
32 G.H. Jenkins, in *Cardigan County History,* vol.3, 1998, 168
33 C.G. Brooke, in *Archaeologia Cambrensis,* 1931, 75–7
34 Meyrick, *History and Antiquities of the County of Cardiganshire,* 1907, 321
35 Burnham, 'Roman Mining At Dolaucothi', 335
36 *Mem. Geological Survey,* 1922, 22; O. Davies in *Archaeologia Cambrensis,* 1931, 51–2
37 *Bulletin of the Board of Celtic Studies,* 28, 1980, 719–729
38 Sansbury, *Megalithic Monuments of Cardiganshire,* 1936, 26
39 Skene, *Book of Taliesin,* 1868, poem 3
40 *Bye-Gones,* 3rd Nov. 1909, 13
41 Lhuyd, 'Additions to the Welsh Counties', 1695, 647
42 C.S. Briggs, in *Cardigan County History,* vol.1, 1994, 177–9
43 Lynch, *Prehistoric Wales,* 2000, 122
44 D.K. Leighton, in *Proceedings of the Prehistoric Society,* 50, 1984, 334
45 Trevelyan, *Folklore and Folk-stories of Wales,* 1909, 254
46 Wyndham, *A Tour Through Monmouthshire and Wales in July 1771,* 1781, 160
47 National Library of Wales, Llanstephan MS. 193
48 Lhuyd, 'Additions to the Welsh Counties', 1695, 647
49 Dames, *The Silbury Treasure,* 1976, 28–30
50 *Archaeologia Cambrensis,* 1847, 356–7
51 M. Williams, in *Cardiganshire Antiquaries Society Transactions,* 1931, 39–44
52 Davies, *Folk-lore of West and Mid-Wales,* 1911, 326
53 T. Rees, *Topographical Description of South Wales,* 1819, 154
54 J. Wood, in *Ceredigion,* vol.8, 1976–9, 414–6
55 S. Scott, *Art and Society in 4th Century Britain,* 2000, 120
56 Hutchinson, 'Bacchus in Roman Britain', 1986, 18–19

57 Costello, *The Falls, Lakes and Mountains of Wales*, 1845, 169
58 Guest, *The Mabinogion*, 1877, 499
59 Skene, *Book of Taliesin*, 1868, poem 3
60 *Y Cymmrodor*, 21, 1908, 119

Chapter 11 Five Lights to Home pages 183 to 199

1   Skene, *Book of Taliesin*, 1868, poem 1
2   Skene, *Book of Taliesin*, 1868, poem 53
3   Skene, *Book of Taliesin*, 1868, poem 56
4   Skene, *Book of Taliesin*, 1868, poem 7
5   Skene, *Book of Taliesin*, 1868, poem 1
6   Lhuyd, 'Additions to the Welsh Counties', 1695, 647
7   Skene, *Book of Taliesin*, 1868, poem 13 stanza 18
8   Skene, *Book of Taliesin*, 1868, poem 8
9   Skene, *Book of Taliesin*, 1868, poem 16
10 Guest, *The Mabinogion*, 1877, 482
11 Guest, *The Mabinogion*, 1877, 482; Skene, *Book of Taliesin*, 1868, poem 16;
    Dames, *The Silbury Treasure*, 1976, 161–4
12 Meyrick, *History and Antiquities of the County of Cardiganshire*, 1907, 320
13 Skene, *Book of Taliesin*, 1868, poem 56
14 Wood, 'Bedd Taliesin', 1979, 416
15 Meyrick, *History and Antiquities of the County of Cardiganshire*, 1907, 320
16 J.C. Boon in *Antiquaries Journal*, 41, 1961, pl. 12
17 Toynbee, *Art in Britain Under the Romans*, 1964, pl. 34, cat. no. 12
18 *Archaeologia Cambrensis*, 1847, 357
19 'J.H.S.E.' in *Archaeologia Cambrensis*, 1873, 292–3
20 'J.H.S.E.' in *Archaeologia Cambrensis*, 1873, 292
21 E. Owen, in *Archaeologia Cambrensis*, 1867, 106–7
22 Dyer, *Prehistoric England and Wales*, 1980, 75
23 Skene, *Book of Taliesin*, 1868, poem 30 stanza 2
24 Jones and Jones, *The Mabinogion*, 1993, 90
25 Bromwich, *Trioedd Ynys Prydein*, 1961, 354
26 Bromwich, *Trioedd Ynys Prydein*, 1961, Triad 78; Cirencester Museum,
    'Seasons' mosaic, figure of 'Spring'
27 British Museum, Lansdown MS., vol. 3, fol. 10
28 T.G. Jones, *History of Llansanffraid-ym-Mechain*, 1902, 138–9
29 *RCAHM Montgomomery*, no.592, 190
30 T. Harper, in Lhuyd, *Parochialia*, vol.3, 1699, 40
31 *Montgomeryshire Collections*, 35, 1908–9, 183
32 J.F.C. Wilde, *Ancient Legends of Ireland*,1888, 102–3
33 T. Harper, in Lhuyd, *Parochialia*, vol.3, 1699, 40
34 Skene, *Book of Taliesin*, 1868, poem 3
35 Dames, *Mythic Ireland*, 1992, 208–9
36 *Archaeologia Cambrensis*, 1946, 112–14; Pennant, *Tours in Wales, 1778–
    1781*, 1883, vol.2, 296
37 Caradoc of Llancarfan, *The Historie of Cambria*, 1584, 21

38 *RCAHM Montgomomery*, no. 419; Grid ref. SJ 105 044
39 By June 2005 it had collapsed.
40 *RCAHM Montgomomery*, no. 423
41 *Montgomeryshire Collections,* 16, 1883, 339
42 *Montgomeryshire Collections,* 16, 1883, 324
43 *Montgomeryshire Collections,* 48, 1848, 151
44 *Montgomeryshire Collections,* 17, 1884, 321, 339; Phillips, *A View of Old Montgomeryshire,* 1997, 175
45 Trevelyan, *Folklore and Folk-stories of Wales,* 1909, 167
46 J.I. Davies, in *Montgomeryshire Collections,* 1984, 42–4
47 *Archaeologia Cambrensis,* 1885, 150–1

Chapter 12 Magic Arts pages 200 to 210

1   Welsh National Eisteddfod, Bala, 1997, Fine Art Catalogue, Welsh Arts Council
2   www.bbc.co.uk/walesnorthwest, 15th August 2005
3   Skene, *Book of Taliesin,* 1868, poem 33
4   W.J. Gruffydd in *Bulletin of the Board of Celtic Studies,* 1934, 1–4
5   E. Ekwall, *English River Names,* 1929
6   Rhys, *Hibbert Lectures,* 1886, 89–90
7   Pennant, *Tours in Wales, 1778–1781,* 1883, vol.2, 208
8   J. Fisher in *Archaeologia Cambrensis,* 1915, 381; Skene, *Book of Taliesin,* 1868, vol.6 pt 2, 1 and 71
9   Guest, *The Mabinogion,* 1877, 482
10 Skene, *Book of Taliesin,* 1868, poem 19
11 C.H. Drinkwater, in *Archaeologia Cambrensis,* 1888, 26–7
12 Ross, *Pagan Celtic Britain,* 1967, 230
13 *Bye-Gones,* 1873, 147
14 Jones and Jones, *The Mabinogion,* 1993, 32–3
15 Skene, *Book of Taliesin,* 1868, poem 30 stanza 4
16 Skene, *Book of Taliesin,* 1868, poem 30 stanza 2, transl. Haycock
17 Skene, *Book of Taliesin,* 1868, poem 30 stanza 2
18 Guest, *The Mabinogion,* 1877, 483
19 Skene, *Book of Taliesin,* 1868, poem 3
20 Skene, *Book of Taliesin,* 1868, poem 38
21 trans. J.E.C. Williams
22 Skene, *Book of Taliesin,* 1868, poem 8 .
23 Skene, *Book of Taliesin,* 1868, poem 7
24 Skene, *Book of Taliesin,* 1868, poem 9
25 Skene, *Book of Taliesin,* 1868, poem 56
26 Skene, *Book of Taliesin,* 1868, poem 3
27 Skene, *Book of Taliesin,* 1868, poem 8
28 Skene, *Book of Taliesin,* 1868, poem 9
29 Bromwich, *Trioedd Ynys Prydein,* 1961, 214
30 Skene, *Book of Taliesin,* 1868, poem 30 stanza 3

Bibliography

Arnold, M., *A Study of Celtic Literature*, London, 1905.

Alcock, L., 'Excavations at Deganwy', 1961–6; *Antiquaries Journal*, 124, 1967, 190–201.

Allen, D.F., 'Coins of the Iceni', in *Britannia*, 1, 1970, 1–33.
— 'Cunobelin's Gold', in *Britannia*, 4, 1975, 1–19.

Allen, W.B., '*The Origins of the Red Dragon*'; in *Archaeologia Cambrensis*, 79, 1924, 216–7.

Armstrong, E.A., *The Folklore of Birds*, London, 1958.

Ashby, T., 'Excavations at Caerwent', In *Archaeologia* 58, 1902, 119–152.

Aver Falk, N.E., '*Feminine Sacrality*', in *Encyclopedia of Religion*, 5, 1986, 302–5.

Axon W.E., '*Welsh Folklore of the Seventeenth Century*'; *Y Cymmrodor*, 21, 1908, 113–131.

Baillie-Reynolds, P.K., '*Roman Caerhun*', *Archaeologia Cambrensis*, 85, 1930, 74–102; and *Archaeologia Cambrensis*, 91, 1936, 210–245.

Baring-Gould, S. and Fisher, J., *The Lives of the British Saints*, 4 vols., London, 1907–13.

Barnwell, E., '*South Wales Cromlechs*', in *Archaeologia Cambrensis*, 1874, 59–96.

Bartrum, C.A., *A Welsh Classical Dictionary*, Aberystwyth, 1993.

Bartrum, P.C., 'Fairy Mothers', in *Bulletin of the Board of Celtic Studies*, 19, 1961, 6–8.

Bowen, E.C., *History of Merionethshire*, vol. 1, 1967, Dolgellau.

Bennett, J., *The Pedestrians Guide Through North Wales*, London, 1838.

Bingley, W., *North Wales*, 2 vols., 1804, London.

Blight, J.T., '*Cromlech at Llansantffraid, near Conway*'. *Archaeologia Cambrensis*, 11, 1865, 278–80.

Birley, E., '*Roman Garrisons in Wales*', in *Archaeologia Cambrensis*, 102, 1952, 9–19.

Birrell, A., *Chinese Myths*, London, 2000.

Blamires, D., *David Jones, Artist and Writer*, Manchester, 1971.

Bolle, K.W., '*Myth*', in *Encyclopedia of Religion*, 10, 1987, 261–2.

Boon, G.C., 'Backhall Street Mosaic, Caerleon', in *Bulletin of the Board of Celtic Studies*, 19, 1961–2, 348–354.
— 'A Temple of Mithras at Segontium', in *Archaeologia Cambrensis*, 109, 1960, 136–172.
— 'Roman Antiquities at Welshpool', in *Antiquaries Journal*, vol.41, 1961, 13–31.

Boon, G.C. and C. Williams, '*The Dolaucothi Drainage Wheel*', in *Journal of Roman Studies*, 56, 1966, 122–5.

Bowen, E. C., *History of Merionethshire*, Vol. 1, Dolgellau, 1967
— (ed.), *Wales; Historical Geography*, Cardiff, 1965.

Bram, J. R., 'The Sun in Religion', in Encyclopedia of Religion, 14, 1986, 132–143.

Brand, J., Popular Antiquities of Great Britain, 3 vols. London, 1870.

Breatnach, L., 'The Cauldron of Poesy', in Eriu, 32, 1981, 45–67.

Bromwich, R., (ed. and transl.), Trioedd Ynys Prydein, 'Triads of the Isle of Britain', Cardiff, 1961.

Brooke, G.C., 'A Find of Gold Nobles at Borth', in Archaeologia Cambrensis, 86, 1931, 75–79.

Briggs, C.S., 'The Bronze Age in Cardiganshire', in Cardigan County History, 1, 1994

Bulleid, A. and Gray, H. The Glastonbury Lake Village. 2 vols., Glastonbury, 1911–1917.

Burnham, B.C., 'Roman Mining At Dolaucothi', in Britannia, 28, 1977, 335–60.

Burnham, H., Clwyd and Powys, (A Guide to Ancient and Historic Wales), London, 1995.

Burnwell, E.L., 'On Some Ancient Welsh Customs', in Archaeologia Cambrensis, 1872, 329–338.

Bushe-Foxe, J. P., Excavations at Wroxeter. 1913–16. London, 1942.

Caerwyn Williams, J., (transl.), The Poems of Taliesin, Dublin, 1968.

Chadwick, N.K., Celt and Saxon. Cambridge, 1963.

— The Druids. Cardiff, 1966.

Challinor, J. and Bates, D., Geology Explained in North Wales. London, 1973.

Cicero, De Natura Rerum, transl. Rackman, H., Cambridge Mass., 1972.

Clancy, J.P., Medieval Welsh Lyrics, London, 1965.

— The Earliest Welsh Poetry, London, 1970.

Clara, P., 'Dinas Penmaen', in Y Cymmrodor, 5, 1882, 155–8.

Clark, J.W., and T.M. Hughes, Life and Letters of Adam Sedgwick. 2 vols; Cambridge, 1890.

Collingwood, R.G., The Roman Inscriptions of Britain, 2 vols., Oxford, 1965.

Condry, W., Exploring Wales, London, 1965.

— The Natural History of Wales, London, 1981.

Costello, L.S., The Falls, Lakes and Mountains of Wales, London, 1845.

Craddock, J., Letters from Snowdon, London, 1770.

Cunliffe, B., The Temple of Sulis Minerva at Bath, 2 vols., Oxford, 1988.

Curtis, T., (ed.), Wales: The Imagined Nation, Bridgend, 1980.

'Cyffin', 'Llyn llun-caws', in   Bye-Gones, March 22nd, 1899.

Dakin, A., Calvinism, London, 1949.

Dames, M., The Silbury Treasure, London, 1976 (revised edn 2004).

— The Avebury Cycle, London, 1977

— Mythic Ireland, London, 1992 (revised edn 1996).

— Merlin and Wales; A Magician's Landscape, London, 2002.

Daniel, H., Medieval Welsh Manuscripts, Cardiff, 2000.

Davies, C., Welsh Literature and Classical Tradition, Cardiff, 1993.

Davies, D., Welsh Place-Names and their meanings, Aberystwyth, (no date; circa 1970).

Davies, E., The Mythology and Rites of the British Druids, London, 1809.

Davies, E., The Prehistoric and Roman Remains of Denbighshire, Cardiff, 1929.

Davies, E., 'Hendre and Hafod in Merionethshire', in *Journal of the Merioneth Historical and Record Society*, 7, 1973, 22.

Davies, J., *A History of Wales*, London, 1993.
— *The Welsh Language*, Cardiff, 1993.

Davies, J.C., *Folk-lore of West and Mid-Wales*, Aberystwyth, 1911.

Davies, J.G., 'Cambria, Wisconsin', in *Transactions of the Honorable Society of Cymmrodorion*, 1957, 136–141

Davies, J.L., and Kirby, D.P., (eds.), *Cardigan County History*, vol.1, Cardiff, 1997.

Davies, O., 'Finds at Dolaucothy', in *Archaeologia Cambrensis*, 91, 1936, 51–5.

Davies, T., 'Welsh Bird Names', in *Nature in Wales*, vol.1, 1955, 77.

Davies, T.R., *A Book of Welsh Place-Names*, London, 1952.

De la Bedoyere, G., *The Golden Age of Roman Britain*, Stroud, 1999.

Department of Transport, *International Code of Signals*, London, 1991.

Detienne, M., '*Dionysus*', transl. Weeks, D. M., in *Encyclopedia of Religion*, 4, 1897, 358–361.

Dornier, A., (ed.), *Mercian Studies*, Leicester, 1977.

Douglas, M., *Purity and Danger*, London, 1966.
— *Natural Symbols*, London, 1970

Drinkwater, C.H., 'Ancient British Hut-dwellings near Bala', in *Archaeologia Cambrensis*, 1888. 26–28.

Dyer, J., *Prehistoric England and Wales*, London, 1980

Edwards, G., 'Cantre'r Gwaelod, or the Lowland Hundred', in *Archaeologia Cambrensis*, 4, 1849, 155–61.

Edwards, I, and Blair, C., *Welsh Bucklers*, in *Antiquaries Journal*, 1982, 56–85.

Eliade, M., *Images and Symbols*, transl. P. Mairet, London, 1961.
— *Myth and Reality*, London, 1963.
— *Myths, Dreams and Mysteries*, transl. P. Mairet, London, 1968.

Einzig, P., *Primitive Money*, Oxford, 1966.

Eliot, T.S., *The Use of Poetry*, London, 1933.

Ellis, R.G., *Flowering Plants in Wales*, Cardiff, 1983.

Else, G.F., *Aristotle's Poetics*, Cambridge Mass., 1963.

Emerson, R.W., *Essay*, 1855, 309

Evans, E., 'Bucket from Ty'r Dewin, Caernarfonshire', in *Archaeologia Cambrensis*, 60, 1905, 255–6.
— *Some Specimens of the Poetry of the Ancient Welsh Bards*, London, 1764.

Evans-Lloyd, E., 'Rhiwaedog, Merioneth', in *Archaeologia Cambrensis*, 39, 1884, 309–314.

Evans, T.C., 'Folklore of Glamorgan', in *Cofnodion Eisteddfod*, Aberdaw, 1885.

Falk, C., *Myth, Truth and Literature*, Cambridge, 1989.

Fenton, R., *A Tour in Wales*, London, 1811.

Fisher, J., 'Bardsey Island and its Saints', in *Archaeologia Cambrensis*, 78, 1923, 225–42.
— 'The Welsh Calendar', in *Transactions of the Honorable Society of Cymmrodorion*, 1894–5, 99–145.
— (ed.), 'The Wonders of Wales', Cardiff MS. 50, pp. 53–65, in *Archaeologia Cambrensis*, 1915, 377–381.

Fleure, H.J., 'Problems in Welsh Archaeology', in *Archaeologia Cambrensis,* 78, 1923, 225–42.

Ford, P.K., (ed.), *The Early Cultures of Northwest Europe*, Cambridge, 1950.

—   *The Poetry of Llywarch Hen*, Los Angeles, 1974.

—   'A Fragment of the Hanes Taliesin by Llewellyn Sion'; in *Etude Celtique,* 14, 1975, 451–460.

—   *The Mabonogi*, Los Angeles, 1977; includes *The Tale of Gwion Bach and The Tale of Taliesin*, pp.159–181; transl. from E. Gruffydd, *Chronicle of the World*, 1548.

—   *Ystoria Taliesin*, Cardiff, 1992.

Fox, Sir C., *Pattern and Purpose*, Cardiff, 1958.

Fox, G.E., 'Uriconium', *Archaeologia*, 54, 1897, 123–173.

Frye, Northrop *Fables and Identity*, New York, 1963.

—   *Creation and Recreation,* Toronto, 1980

Geoffrey of Monmouth, *The History of the Kings of Britain*, transl. L. Thorpe London, 1966.

Gerald of Wales, *The Journey Through Wales*, transl. L. Thorpe, London, 1978.

—   *The Description of Wales*, transl. L. Thorpe, London, 1978.

Gildas, *The Ruin of Britain*, transl. M. Winterbottom, London, 1978.

Gimbutas, M., *Gods and Goddesses of Old Europe*, London, 1974.

—   *The Language of the Goddess,* London, 1989.

Gittins, E. P., 'Llanfair Caereinion Folklore', in *Montgomeryshire Collections,* 17, 1884, 321–3.

Green, M, J, *Animals in Celtic Art*, London, 1992.

—   'A Carved Head from Steep Holm', in *Britannia,* 24, 1993, 241–2.

—   *Dictionary of Celtic Myth and Legend*, London, 1992.

—   *Symbol and Image in Celtic Religious Art,* London, 1989.

—   (ed.), *The Celtic World*, London, 1995.

Griffiths, W.E., 'The Hill-fort on Conway Mountain', in *Archaeologia Cambrensis,* 105, 1956, 49–80.

Gwyndaf, R., 'The Welsh Narrative Tradition', in *Folk Life,* 26, 1987, 76–81.

Gwynn-Jones, T., *Welsh Folklore and Folk Customs*, London, 1930.

Graves, R., *The Crane Bag and Other Disputed Subjects*, London, 1969.

—   *Difficult Questions, Easy Answers*, London, 1972.

Griffiths, B., (ed.), *The Welsh Academy English-Welsh Dictionary*, Cardiff, 1995.

Gruffydd, E., 'Hanes Taliesin', in *A Chronicle of the World from Creation to the Present Day,* 1548. MS. 5276D, fol. 358–9, and 369–383v., National Library of Wales.

Gruffydd, W.J., 'Donwy', in *Bulletin of the Board of Celtic Studies,* 7, 1933, 1–4.

—   'Mabon ab Madron', in *Revue Celtique,* 33, 1911–12, 452–461.

—   *Rhiannon*, Cardiff, 1953.

Guest, Lady C., (transl.), *The Mabinogion*, 2nd edition, London, 1877; with *Taliesin,* pp.471–494.

'Gwenddolau', 'Manners of the Welsh Peasantry', in Cambrian Magazine, 2, 1829, 413–14.

Gwyn-Jones, T., *Welsh Folk-lore and Folk Customs*, London, 1929.

Hamel, A.G. Van, 'Gods, Skalds and Magic', in *Saga Book of Viking Society*, 11, 1934, 136–8.

Hancock, T.W., 'Llanrhaiadr-yn-Mochnant', in *Montgomeryshire Collections*, 4, 1871, 201–248; *Montgomeryshire Collections*, 5, 1872, 303–28; *Montgomeryshire Collections*, 6, 1873, 319–331.

Harding, F.J.W., 'Matthew Arnold and Wales', in *Transactions of the Honorable Society of Cymmrodorion*, 1963, 251–272.

Harley, J.B., and R.R. Oliver, *Old Series Ordnance Survey Maps, vol. 6, Wales,* London, 1992.

Harries, E.E.F., 'The Tressilt Idol, St Nicholas', in *Archaeologia Cambrensis,* 55, 1900, 237–8.

Haycock, M., '*Preiddeu Annwn* and the Figure of Taliesin', in *Studia Celtica,* 18, 1983, 52–77.

Haywood, B., *Novalis and The Veil of Imagery,* S'Gravenhage, 1959.

Hemp, W.J., 'Merionethshire Cairns and Barrows in Llandrillo', in *Bulletin of the Board of Celtic Studies,* 14, 1951, 155–165.

— '*Some unrecorded Sheela-na-Gigs in Wales*', in *Archaeologia Cambrensis,* 93, 1938, 136–139.

Henig, M., '*A Gold Votive Plaque from East Anglia*', in *Britannia,* 15, 1984, 246.

— and G. Soffe, '*The Thruxton Mosaic*', in *Journal of the British Archaeological Association,* 146, 1993, 1–28.

Henry, P.L., 'The Cauldron of Poesy', in *Studia Celtica,* 14, 1979, 110–123.

H.L.T., 'Early British Remains in Wales', in *Archaeologia Cambrensis,* 11, 1855, 114.

H.L.W., 'The Yellow Plague Prophecy of Taliesin', in *Y Cymmrodor,* 5, 1882, 157.

Hobbs, R., *British Iron Age Coins in the British Museum,* London, 1996.

Horst Schmidt, K., 'Latin and Celtic', in *Bulletin of the Board of Celtic Studies,* 38, 1991, 1–19.

Howells, W., 'Cambrian Superstitions', in Cambrian Magazine, 3, 1831, 71–73.

Hughes, W., 'Llanuwchllyn', in *Archaeologia Cambrensis,* 40, 1885, 183–191.

Humphries, C.H., 'Llanfair Caereinion in the early 19th century', in *Montgomeryshire Collections,* 48, 1943, 151–176.

Hutchinson, V.J., '*Bacchus in Roman Britain*', in *British Archaeological Reports (British Series),* 151(1), 1986, 1–572.

Hyde-Hall, E., *A Description of Carnarvonshire, 1809–1811,* Carnarvon, 1952.

James, W., 'A Pluralistic Universe', in *Hibbert Lectures,* New York, 1900.

— *The Varieties of Religious Experience,* London, 1952.

Jarman, A.O.H., and G. Rhys-Hughes, *A Guide to Welsh Literature,* 2 vols., Swansea, 1976–9.

Jenkins, D.E., *The Reverend Thomas Charles of Bala,* 3 vols., Denbigh, 1908.

Jenkins, G.H. and I.G. Jones, *Cardigan County History,* vol. 3, Cardiff, 1998.

Johnson, T.H., *The Complete Poems of Emily Dickenson,* London, 1975

Jones, D., *Anathemata,* London, 1955.

Jones, E., *A Relation of Apparitions and Spirits in Wales,* Newport, Mon., 1813.

Jones, E., *Chwedl yr Anifeiliad Hynaf, vii,* Cardiff, 1951–2.

Jones, F., *The Holy Wells of Wales,* Cardiff, 1954.

Jones, G., and Jones, T., — (transl.), *The Mabinogion,* London, 1993.

Jones, O.T., *Lead and Zinc Mining in North Cardiganshire*, London, 1922.

Jones, T., (ed. and transl.), 'The Stanzas of the Graves', in *Proceedings of the British Academy*, 53, 1967, 97–137.

Jones, T.G., 'History of the Parish of Llansanffraid-yn-Mechain', in *Montgomeryshire Collections*, 4, 1871, 136–9.

Kendrick, T.D., 'Portion of a basalt hone from North Wales', in *Antiquaries Journal*, vol.21, 1941, 73.

Kerenyi, C., *Dionysus*, London, 1926.

Kirk, J., 'Bronzes from Wood Eaton, Oxon', in *Oxonia*, 14, 1949, 1–45.

Knappert, J., *Indian Mythology*, London, 1991.

Knight, H.H., 'Methods Employed by the Ancients in working Gold Mines', in *Archaeologia Cambrensis*, 1856, 132–138, and 224–8.

Knight, J.M., 'Excavations at Montgomery Castle', in *Archaeologia Cambrensis*, 143, 1994, 139–203.

Leach, E., *Rethinking Anthropology*, London, 1961.
— *The Structural Study of Myth and Totemism*, London, 1967.
— *Culture and Communication*, Cambridge, 1976.

Leach, M. (ed), *Funk and Wagnalls Standard Dictionary of Folklore, Mythology and Legend*, 2 vols., New York, 1949–50.

Leighton, D.K., 'Structured Round Cairns', in *Proceedings of the Prehistoric Society*, 50, 1984, 319–350.

Lewes, E., 'The Goredi near Llanddewi, Aberarth', in *Archaeologia Cambrensis*, 79, 1924, 379–399.

Lewis, S., *A Topographical Dictionary of Wales*, 2 vols., London , 1848.

Lhuyd, E., 'Additions to the Welsh Counties', in Camden, W., *Britannia*, ed. Gibson, E., 1695.
— *Parochialia*, 3 vols., 1698–1710, Cardiff, 1910–11.

Lloyd-Griffiths, '17th century Bestiary Ware from Buckley, Clwyd', in *Archaeologia Cambrensis*, 129, 1980, 162–4.

'Llywarch Hen', '*Welsh Astrologers and Sorcerers*', in   Bye-Gones, 1888, 177–9.

Lones, T. F., and A.R. Wright, *British Calendar Customs*, 3 vols., London, 1936–1940.

Loomis, R.S., *Arthurian Literature in the Middle Ages*, Oxford, 1956.
— *Wales and the Arthurian Legend*, Cardiff, 1956.

Lowe, W. Bezant, *The Heart of Northern Wales*, 2 vols., Llanfairfechan, 1912–1927.

Lukis, J.W., 'St Lythans and St Nicholas Cromlechs', in *Archaeologia Cambrensis*, 30, 1875, 171–185.

Lynch, F., 'Culture and Environment in Prehistoric Wales', in Taylor, J. A., (ed.), *British Archaeological Reports (British Series)*, 76, 1980, 238–9.
— *Gwynedd, (A Guide to Ancient and Historic Wales)*, London, 1995.
— *Prehistoric Wales*, Stroud, 2000.
— 'Report on the re-excavation of Bedd Branwen, Ynys Mon', in *Archaeologia Cambrensis*, 120, 1971, 11–83.

Mack, R.P., *The Coinage of Ancient Britain*, London, 1964.

Marr, J.E., *The Classification of Cambrian and Silurian Rocks*, London, 1883.

Matonis, A.T.E., 'The Concept of Poetry in the Middle Ages', in *Bulletin of the Board of Celtic Studies,* 31, 1989, 1–12.

McCumsey, E., 'Silence', in *Encyclopedia of Religion*, 13, 1987, 321–4.

Merrifield, R., *The Archaeology of Ritual and Magic,* London, 1987.

Meslin, M., 'The Eye', in *Encyclopedia of Religion*, 5, 1987, 236–9.

Meyrick, Sir S.R., *History and Antiquities of the County of Cardiganshire,* 2nd ed., Brecon, 1907.

Middleton, C., *Pataxanadu,* Manchester, 1977.

Miller, D.L., *The New Polytheism,* New York, 1974.

Miller, M., 'The Foundation Legend of Gwynedd in the Latin Texts', in *Bulletin of the Board of Celtic Studies,* 27, 1978, 515–30.

Moon, B., 'Pearl', in *Encyclopedia of Religion,* 11, 1987, 224–5.

Morgan, P., *Iolo Morganwg,* Cardiff, 1975.

Morgan, T.J. and P. Morgan, *Welsh Surnames,* Cardiff, 1985.

Morinis, E.A., *Pilgrimage in Hindu Tradition,* Oxford, 1984.

Morris, L., *Celtic Remains* (1700–1765), ed. D.S. Evans, London. 1878.

Morris-Jones, J., 'Taliesin', in *Y Cymmrodor, 28, 1918, 1–290.*

Morrison, T.A., 'Gold Mining in Western Merionethshire', in *Journal of the Merioneth Historical and Record Society,* 7, 1973, 30–32.

Nash-Williams, V.E., 'Roman Stations at Neath and Caer Gai', in *Bulletin of the Board of Celtic Studies,* 13, 1950, 239–45.

— 'The Roman Gold Mines at Dolaucothi, Carm., in *Bulletin of the Board of Celtic Studies,* 14, 1950, 79–84.

Negri, E., *Julian the Apostate,* London, 1905.

'Nemo', 'Llyn llun-caws', in　　　　　　*Bye-Gones,* 1878, 110.

Nennius, *British History and the Annales of Wales,* ed. J. Morris, London, 1980.

Norberg-Schulz, C., *Intentions in Architecture,* Oslo, 1963.

North, F.J., *Sunken Cities,* Cardiff, 1957.

'N.W.S.', 'Llyn llun-caws', in　　　　　　*Bye-Gones,* 1873, 146 and 235.

O'Rahilly, T.F., *Early Irish History and Mythology,* Dublin, 1946.

Otto, W.F., *Dionysus, Myth and Cult,* transl. R.B. Palmer, Bloomington, 1965.

Owen, E., *Old Stone Crosses of the Vale of Clwyd,* London, 1886.

Owen, T.M., 'The Celebration of Candlemas in Wales', in *Folklore,* 84, 1973, 238–251.

— *The Customs and Traditions of Wales,* Cardiff, 1991.

— *Welsh Folk Customs,* Cardiff, 1959.

Owen, W., (Pughe), *The Cambrian Biography,* 1803; ed. B. Feldman, London, 1979.

Ovid, *Metamorphosis,* transl. H. King, London, 1871.

Parry-Jones, D., *Welsh Children's Games and Past-times,* Denbigh, 1964.

Peake, H.J.E., 'Roman Bronze Cupid found at Segontium', in *Archaeologia Cambrensis,* 1894, 77.

Peate, I.C., 'Flint Arrow-heads found at Bugeilyn, Mont.', in *Archaeologia Cambrensis, ,* 80, 1925, 342–5.

— 'Mari-Lwyd and Lair Bhan', in *FL,* 1, 1963, 95–6.

— *The Welsh House,* London, 1940.

Pennant, T., *Tours in Wales, 1778–1781,* 3 vols., ed. J. Rhys, Caernarvon, 1883.

Phillips, P., *A View of Old Montgomeryshire*, Swansea, 1997.

Pinker, S, *The Language Instinct*, London, 1994.

Pollard, A.W.F., *English Miracle Plays*, London, 2003

Puhvel, J., *Comparative Mythology*, London, 1987.

Ordnance Survey, *Cadair Idris and Bala Lake*, map no.O.L.23, Southampton, 1998.

— *Snowdon and Conwy Valley*, map no.O.L.16, Southampton, 1998.

Radford, E. and M.A., *Dictionary of Superstitions*, London, 1961.

Rainey, A., *Mosaics in Roman Britain*, Newton Abbot, 1973.

Readwin, T.A., 'Gold Mining in Wales', in *Mining Journal*, 58, 1888, 47.

Rees, A.D., 'Ffynnon Tegla', in *Bulletin of the Board of Celtic Studies,* 8, 1935, 87–90.

Rhys, Sir John, 'The Lady of Llyn y Van Fach', in *Y Cymmrodor*, 4, 1881, 164–70.

— 'Welsh Fairy Tales', in *Y Cymmrodor*, 4, 1881, 163–216

— 'Welsh Fairy Tales', in *Y Cymmrodor*, 5, 1882, 45–143

— 'Welsh Fairy Tales', in *Y Cymmrodor*, 6, 1888, 159–198.

— *Celtic Folk-Lore, Welsh and Manx*, 2 vols, Oxford, 1901.

— 'Sacred Wells in Wales', in *FL*, 4, 1893, 1–25.

Rhys, S.D., 'Welsh Giants', transl. Owen, H., in *Y Cymmrodor*, 27, 1917, 124–152.

Rivet, A.L.F., *The Roman Villa In Britain*, London, 1969.

Rivet, A.L.F. and C. Smith, *The Place-Names of Roman Britain*, London, 1979.

Ross, A., *Pagan Celtic Britain*, London, 1967.

Rogers, R.J., 'The Norse Element in Celtic Myths', in *Archaeologia Cambrensis,* 53, 1898, 312–344.

Rowlands, J., *Early Welsh Saga Poetry*, Cambridge, 1990.

Rown, P., '*Black Luck'*, in *FL*, 71, 1960, 188–193.

Royal Commission on Ancient and Historical Monuments, Wales, *Carnarvonshire*, London, 1956–64.

— *Cardiganshire*, vols. 1–3, Cardiff, 1998.

— *Denbighshire*, London, 1913.

— *Glamorgan*, vol. 1, parts 1 and 2, London, 1976.

— *Merionethshire*, London, 1921.

— *Montgomeryshire*, London, 1911.

— *Radnorshire*, London, 1913.

Ruddy, T., *'Flint chips at Bala',* in   Bye-Gones, 1898, 423.

Salway, P., *Roman Britain*, Oxford, 1981.

Sansbury, A.R., *Megalithic Monuments of Cardiganshire*, unpublished, Aberystwyth, 1936.

Saunders Lewis, 'The Taliesin Tradition', in *Transactions of the Honorable Society of Cymmrodorion,* 1968, 293–8.

Savory, H.N., *'Bronze spear head from Bala',* in *Bulletin of the Board of Celtic Studies*, 21, 1966, 371–3.

— 'New Hoard of La Tene Metal Work from Merionethshire', in *Bulletin of the Board of Celtic Studies*, 20, 1964, 449–75.

— 'The Late Bronze Age in Wales', in *Archaeologia Cambrensis,* 107, 1958, 3–63.

— 'Votive arrowheads on Pumlumon', in *Bulletin of the Board of Celtic Studies*, 23, 1969, 4–5.

Scott, R.D., *The Thumb of Knowledge in Legends of Finn, Sigurd and Taliesin*, New York, 1930.

Scott, S., *Art and Society in 4th Century Britain*, London, 2, 000.

Sheppard, T., 'The Parc-y-Meirch Hoard, Denbighshire', in *Archaeologia Cambrensis*, 96, 1941, 1–10.

Sieveking, G.de G., 'The Kendrick's Cave Mandible', in *British Museum Quarterly*, 35, 1971, 230–245.

Sikes, W.W., *British Goblins*, London, 1880.

Simpson, J., *Folklore of the Welsh Border*, London, 1976.

Sims-Williams, P., 'The Emergence of Old Welsh, Cornish and Breton Orthography, AD 600–800', in *Bulletin of the Board of Celtic Studies*, 38, 1991, 20–86.

Skene, W.F., *Book of Taliesin*, in *The Four Ancient Books of Wales*, 2 vols., Edinburgh, 1868.

Snyder, C.A., 'Sub-Roman Britain, AD 400–600', in *British Archaeological Reports (British Series)*, 247, 1996.

Soulsby, I., *The Towns of Medieval Wales*, Chichester, 1983.

Stead, I.M., 'The Cerrig-y-Drudion Hanging Bowl', in *AntJ*, 62, 1982, 221–223.

Stephens, M., *The Oxford Companion to the Literature of Wales*, Oxford, 1986.
— *The New Companion to the Literature of Wales*, 1998

Stevens, W., *Collected Poems*, London, 1984.
— *Opus Posthumous*, ed. S.F. Morse, London, 1959.
— *The Necessary Angel*, London, 1960.

Stokes, W., (ed.), 'Ben Boirche', of the Edinburgh Dindshenchas, in *FL*, 4, 1893, 471–97.

Stukeley, W., *Itinerarium Curiosum*, London, 1724.

Suppe, F., 'Decapitation in High Medieval Wales', in *Bulletin of the Board of Celtic Studies*, 36, 1989, 149–162.

'Taffy', 'Bala is Gone, Bala will Go', in Bye-Gones, 1873, 187.

T.R., 'Popular Superstitions of the Welsh', in *The Cambro-Briton*, 1, 1819–20, 172.

Teignmouth, Lord, *Memoire of Sir William Jones*, London, 1807,

Thomas, R., *Antiquae Linguae Britannicae, Thesaurus*, London, 1753

Thomas, R. J., (ed.), *Geiriadur Prifysgol Cymry*, (A Dictionary of the Welsh Language), Caerdydd, 1950–2002.

Thompson, F.H., *Roman Cheshire*, Chester, 1965.

Thompson, M.W., *The Journeys of Sir Richard Colte Hoare*, Gloucester, 1983.

Torrance, T.F., *Calvin's Doctrine of Man*, London. 1949.

Tolstoy, N., *The Quest for Merlin*, London, 1985.

Toynbee, J.C.M., *Art in Roman Britain*, London, 1962.
— *Art in Britain Under the Romans*, Oxford, 1964.

Trevelyan, M., *Folklore and Folk-stories of Wales*, London, 1909.

Trueman, A.E., *Geology and Scenery in England and Wales*, London, 1949

Turville Petrie, *Myth and Religion of the North*, London, 1972.

Waddelove, E., 'The Roman Road between Rug and Caer Gai', in *Studia Celtica*, 21, 1995, 31–52.

Waddington, H.M., 'Games and Athletics in Bygone Wales', in *THCS*, 1953, 84–100.

Ward, F., *The Lakes of Wales*, London, 1931.

Ward, J., 'St Nicholas Tumulus, Glamorgan', in *Archaeologia Cambrensis,* 70, 1915, 253–320.

Wait, G., 'Ritual and Religion In Iron Age Britain', in *British Archaeological Reports (British Series)*, 149 (I), 1983, 1–431.

Webster, G., *The Cornovii,* Stroud, 1991.

Wedd, C.B., *Geology of the Country around Oswestry,* London, 1929.

Westwood, J.O., 'Early Inscribed Stones in Wales', in *Archaeologia Cambrensis,* 10, 1855, 154–5.

Wheeler, R.E.M., 'Llynfawr … Bronze Age Hoard in Wales', in *Archaeologia* 71, 1921, 133–140.

— *Prehistoric and Roman Wales,* Oxford, 1925.

Wheelock, W.T., '*Sacred Language*', in *Encyclopedia of Religion,* 8, 1987, 439–446.

Wheelwright, P., *Poetry, Myth and Reality,* London, 1942.

Williams, A., 'Clegyr-boia, St Davids, Pemb., ' in *Archaeologia Cambrensis,* 102, 1952, 20–47.

Williams, C.J., *The Great Orme Mines,* Cardiff, 1995.

Williams, G., 'Poets and Pilgrims in 15th–16th century Wales', in *Transactions of the Honorable Society of Cymmrodorion,* 1991, 61–75.

Williams, Sir I., 'Chwedl Taliesin', in *O'Donell Lectures,* 1957, 18–24.

— 'Lectures in Early Welsh Poetry', in *O'Donell Lectures,* 1944, 49–63.

— *The Beginnings of Welsh Poetry,* Cardiff, 1972.

— 'The Poetry of Llywarch Hen', in *Proceedings of the British Academy,* 18, 1932, 275–99.

Williams, J., 'Ogham Inscriptions at Kenfegge, Glamorgan', in *Archaeologia Cambrensis,* 1, 1846, 413–6.

Williams, M., 'Bedd Taliesin', in *Cardiganshire Antiquaries Society Transactions,* 8, 1931, 39.

Williams, O. and I. Jones, *Geirlyfr Cymraeg,* Llanfair Caereinion, 1831–5.

Williams, W., *A Survey of the Ancient and Present State of the County of Caernarvon,* National Library of Wales, MS 821, 1806.

Willoughby Gardner, The Little Orme's Head Hoard of Roman Coins, in *Archaeologia Cambrensis,* 107, 1958, 64–71.

Wood, J., 'Bedd Taliesin', in *Ceredigion,* 8, 1979, 414–418.

— 'The Elphin section of Hanes Taliesin', in *Etude Celtique,* 18, 1981, 229–244.

— 'Versions of Hanes Taliesin by Owen John and Lewis Morris', in *Bulletin of the Board of Celtic Studies,* 29, 1980, 285–95.

Wright, R.P. and I. A., *The Roman Inscribed Stones in the Grosvenor Museum, Chester,* Chester, 1955.

Wyndham, H.P., *A Tour Through Monmouthshire and Wales in July 1771,* London, 1781.

'Zefu', 'Reverence for Fairies in Wales' in *Bye-Gones,* 1886, 209.

Index

Bold indicates illustrations

Sources of illustrations

t = top, c =centre, b = bottom, l = left, r = right

Antiquaries Journal: 30tr, 104tr, 104bl, 139tr. *Archaeologia*: 25tl, 56tr, 56bl, 108c. *Archaeologia Cambrensis:* 20c, 25tr, 25cl, 25cr, 28r, 30tl, 30bl, 33l, 51c, 51tr, 60tl, 60br, 60bl, 85bl, 96tr, 104br, 108cr, 112cr, 119c, 119tr, 129bl , 129br, 136, 152t, 152c, 154tr, 156br, 161r, 176br, 180bl, 191r, 194cr. Armagh Museum: 96tl Ashmolean Museum: 32b, 94,l. Ben. Stone Collection: 66t. Bowen E. G.: 205r. *British Museum Quarterly:* 73br, 119b. Bulletin of the Board of Celtic Studies: 56br, 73tr, 187tr. Bulleid, A., 33b. Carmarthen Museum: 53br. Chester Archaeological Society: 25bl, 25br, 114c, 114r. Corbridge Museum: 30cl. Council for British Archaeology: 33c, 87t. Drayton, M.: 16r, 63br. Fleure, H. J.: 20, l. Geoffrey Clements: 41t. Gloucester City Museum and Art Gallery: 85cl. Gooders, J.,: 28l. Grimes, W. F.: 53bl. Gwynedd Archives: 16l, 18, 19, 37r, 41b, 96b, 154tl. Gwynedd Museum and Art Gallery: 51br. Hoare, R.,: 56tr. Holland, K., 37b. Hone W.,: 45b. Hughes H.,: 62t. Iwan Bala: 206. Lancaster Museum: 187tl. Llandudno Museum: 139tl. Llangollen Library: 63cr. Lubke, W., :90tl, 90tc. Mack, R.: 90tr, 112c. Jeremy Moore: 208b. Museum of English Rural Life: 129tr. Museum of London: 36l. Museum of Welsh Life, St Fagans: 108b, 112tl, 112tr. National Library of Wales/Llyfrgell Genedlaethol Cymru: 85r, 180br. National Museums and Galleries of Wales: 32t, 53tl, 60tr, 63bl, 73tl, 73bl, 85tl, 114cl, 121b, 143br, 156l, 156tr, 194bl. Newport Museum: 48br, 53tr, 96tl, 108cl, 154bl. Oxoniensia: 51tl, 51cl, 51bl, 143c. Reading Museum: 36r, 90c. RCAHM Wales: 25tr, 152br. Rhyl Library: 73tl. Royal Irish Academy; 108c. Sikes, W.: 20r. Somerset County Museum and Glastonbury Antiquarian Society: 133br. Sonia Halliday: 128bl. Stukeley, W.: 63t. Tullie House Museum and Art Gallery, Carlisle: 33r. Wroxeter Museum: 101t.

M. Dames cover, viii, 2, 6, 8, 11, 13, 16, 30 (bottom right), 34, 16 (bottom), 45 (top left and top centre), 48 (top left), 56 (bottom right), 62 (bottom), 82, 83, 95 (top and bottom right), 101 (bottom), 104 (top left and bottom right), 108 (top), 112 (bottom left and bottom right), 114 (top and bottom), 116, 117, 118, 119 (left), 121 (top and centre), 125, 126, 128 (top left, top right, bottom right), 133 (top left, top right, bottom left), 140, 143 (top left), 145, 147, 150, 152 (bottom left), 154 (bottom right), 159, 161 (left), 166 (centre and bottom), 169, 170, 174, 176 (top and bottom left), 180 (top and centre), 185, 188, 190, 192, 194 (top left, top right and bottom right), 196, 198, 202, 204 (top left, centre and bottom), 208.

Anne Tarver maps on pages vii, 76, 119, 166.

Sacred Places
Prehistory and popular imagination
Bob Trubshaw

Sacred Places asks why certain types of prehistoric places are thought of as sacred, and explores how the physical presence of such sacred sites is less important than what these places signify. So this is not another guide book to sacred places but instead provides a unique and thought-provoking guide to the mental worlds – the mindscapes – in which we have created the idea of prehistoric sacred places.

Recurring throughout this book is the idea that we continually create and re-create our ideas about the past, about landscapes, and the places within those landscapes that we regard as sacred. For example, although such concepts as 'nature', 'landscape', 'countryside', 'rural' and the contrast between profane and sacred are all part of our everyday thinking, in this book Bob Trubshaw shows they are all modern cultural constructions which act as the 'unseen' foundations on which we construct more complex myths about places.

Key chapters look at how earth mysteries, modern paganism and other alternative approaches to sacred places developed in recent decades, and also outline the recent dramatic changes within academic archaeology. Is there now a 'middle way' between academic and alternative approaches which recognises that what we know about the past is far less significant than what we believe about the past?

Bob Trubshaw has been actively involved with academic and alternative approaches to archaeology for most of the last twenty years. In 1996 he founded *At the Edge* magazine to popularise new interpretations of past and place.

> '*Sacred Places*... is a very valuable addition to the small body of thoughtful work on the spiritual landscapes of Great Britain and therefore recommended reading.' Nigel Pennick *Silver Wheel*

> 'One of the best books in the field I have ever read.'
> D J Tyrer *Monomyth Supplement*

ISBN 1 872883 67 2. 2005. 245 x 175 mm, 203 + xiv pages, 43 b&w illustrations and 7 line drawings, paperback. **£16.95**

Stonehenge:
Celebration and Subversion

Andy Worthington

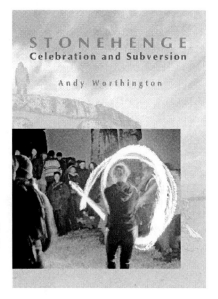

This innovative social history looks in detail at how the summer solstice celebrations at Stonehenge have brought together different aspects of British counter-culture to make the monument a 'living temple' and an icon of alternative Britain. The history of the celebrants and counter-cultural leaders is interwoven with the viewpoints of the land-owners, custodians and archaeologists who have generally attempted to impose order on the shifting patterns of these modern-day mythologies.

The story of the Stonehenge summer solstice celebrations begins with the Druid revival of the 18th century and the earliest public gatherings of the 19th and early 20th centuries. In the social upheavals of the 1960s and early 70s, these trailblazers were superseded by the Stonehenge Free Festival. This evolved from a small gathering to an anarchic free state the size of a small city, before its brutal suppression at the Battle of the Beanfield in 1985.

In the aftermath of the Beanfield, the author examines how the political and spiritual aspirations of the free festivals evolved into both the rave scene and the road protest movement, and how the prevailing trends in the counter-culture provided a fertile breeding ground for the development of new Druid groups, the growth of paganism in general, and the adoption of other sacred sites, in particular Stonehenge's gargantuan neighbour at Avebury.

The account is brought up to date with the reopening of Stonehenge on the summer solstice in 2000, the unprecedented crowds drawn by the new access arrangements, and the latest source of conflict, centred on a bitterly-contested road improvement scheme.

> '*Stonehenge Celebration and Subversion* contains an extraordinary story. Anyone who imagines Stonehenge to be nothing but an old fossil should read this and worry. [This book is] ... the most complete, well-illustrated analysis of Stonehenge's mysterious world of Druids, travellers, pagans and party-goers'. Mike Pitts *History Today*

ISBN 1 872883 76 1. 2004. Perfect bound, 245 x 175 mm, 281 + xviii pages, 147 b&w photos, **£14.95**

The Enchanted Land

Myths and Legends of Britain's Landscape

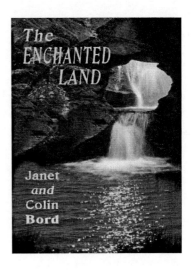

Revised, fully illustrated edition

Janet and Colin Bord

Britain's landscape is overlain by a magic carpet of folklore and folktales, myths and legends. Enchantment and legend still lurk in places as diverse as hills and mountains, rivers and streams, caves and hollows, springs and wells, cliffs and coasts, pools and lakes, and rocks and stones.

The dramatic stories woven around these places tell of sleeping knights, beheaded saints, giants, dragons and monsters, ghosts, King Arthur, mermaids, witches, hidden treasure, drowned towns, giant missiles, mysterious footprints, visits to Fairyland, underground passages, human sacrifices, and much more.

The 'Places to Visit' section locates and describes in detail more than 50 sites.

This revised edition is fully illustrated, with around 130 photographs and illustrations.

Janet and Colin Bord live in North Wales, where they run the Fortean Picture Library. They have written more than 20 books since their first successful joint venture, *Mysterious Britain* in 1972.

From reviews of the first edition:

'Janet's own enthusiasm for a number of the sites is conveyed vividly and lends credibility to the notion that Britain is still an enchanted land.' *Mercian Mysteries*

ISBN 1 872883 91 5. March 2006. 245 x 175 mm, over 200 illustrations, paperback **£16.95**

Footprints in Stone

The significance of foot- and hand-prints and other imprints left by early men, giants, heroes, devils, saints, animals, ghosts, witches, fairies and monsters

Janet Bord

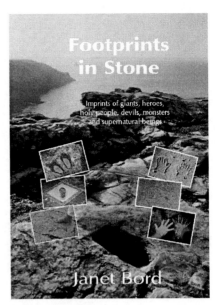

'A delightful exploration of a truly mysterious subject. 9 out of 10'
Bob Rickard *Fortean Times*

'Fascinating stuff and highly recommended.' Mike Howard *The Cauldron*

'... a good and wide-ranging first step into investigating the significance of the foot imprint.' John Billingsley *Northern Earth*

From the earliest humans to the present day, there has always been a compulsion to 'leave one's mark': early cave art includes thousands of hand outlines, while many churches in Britain have foot outlines inscribed in lead and stone. These two extremes span almost 30,000 years during which time all kinds of persons, real and legendary, have left visible traces of themselves. But 30,000 years ago seems almost recent, when compared with the finding of some (admittedly controversial) fossilized human footprints in rocks apparently contemporary with dinosaur footprints that are tens of millions of years old.

Most of the footprints – and hand-prints, knee-prints, and impressions of other body parts – are clearly not real, having allegedly been impressed into rocks around the world by such high-profile figures as the Buddha, Vishnu, Jesus Christ, and the Virgin Mary, as well as a vast panoply of saints, whose footprint traces and associated stories occupy two chapters. Their horses also left hoof-prints, and other animals are represented too. Not surprisingly, the ubiquitous Devil has a whole chapter to himself – but giants, villains and heroes, such as King Arthur, also feature strongly. Witches, fairies, ghosts and assorted spirits have made their mark: there are many modern instances of phantom hand- and foot-prints, the latter often bloodstained and indelible.

Hundreds of imprints are described in this book, which concludes with location details for more than 100 imprint sites all around the world.

ISBN 1 872883 73 7. 2004. 245 x 175 mm, 263 + x pages, 112 b&w photos, 26 line drawings, paperback. **£14.95**

Mystery Big Cats

Merrily Harpur

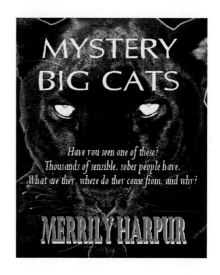

In the past twenty years every county in Britain, from Caithness to Cornwall, has had recurrent sightings of 'big cats' – described as being like pumas or panthers. These anomalous big cats sightings are now running at an estimated 1,200 a year.

Farmers, gamekeepers, ornithologists, policemen and even parents on the school run have all been thrilled – or terrified – to see what they assume is a big cat escaped from a zoo. Yet these big cats are neither escapees from zoos nor, as this book conclusively argues, the descendants of pets released into the countryside by their owners in 1976 when the Dangerous Wild Animals Act made it too expensive to keep big cats.

The questions therefore remain, what are they and where have they come from? With the orthodox explanations overturned, Merrily Harpur searches for clues in the cultures of other times and places. She discovers our mystery felines have been with us for longer than we imagine, and throws unexpected light on the way Western civilisation looks at the world.

Mystery Big Cats is the first serious and comprehensive book on the subject. From the drama of eyewitnesses' verbatim accounts to the excitement of new perspectives and insights into a strange and often terrifying experience – it gets to grips with what is now the commonest encounter with the unknown in Britain.

Merrily Harpur is a cartoonist and writer. She has published three books: *The Nightmares of Dream Topping, Unheard of Ambridge* and *Pig Overboard.* She divides her time between Dorset and Ireland, where she founded the Strokestown International Poetry Festival.

ISBN 1 872883 92 3. March 2006. 245 x 175 mm, illustrated, paperback.**£16.95**

*Winner of the Folklore Society
Katherine Briggs Award 2005*

Explore Fairy Traditions

Jeremy Harte

We are not alone. In the shadows of our countryside there lives a fairy race, older than humans, and not necessarily friendly to them. For hundreds of years, men and women have told stories about the strange people, beautiful as starlight, fierce as wolves, and heartless as ice. These are not tales for children. They reveal the fairies as a passionate, proud, brutal people.

Explore Fairy Traditions draws on legends, ballads and testimony from throughout Britain and Ireland to reveal what the fairies were really like. It looks at changelings, brownies, demon lovers, the fairy host, and abduction into the Otherworld. Stories and motifs are followed down the centuries to reveal the changing nature of fairy lore, as it was told to famous figures like W.B. Yeats and Sir Walter Scott. All the research is based on primary sources and many errors about fairy tradition are laid to rest.

Jeremy Harte combines folklore scholarship with a lively style to show what the presence of fairies meant to people's lives. Like their human counterparts, the secret people could kill as well as heal. They knew marriage, seduction, rape and divorce; they adored some children and rejected others. If we are frightened of the fairies, it may be because their world offers an uncomfortable mirror of our own.

> '... this is the best and most insightful book on fairies generally available... ' John Billingsley *Northern Earth*

> '*Explore Fairy Traditions* is an excellent introduction to the folklore of fairies, and I would highly recommend it.' Paul Mason *Silver Wheel*

ISBN 1 872883 61 3. Published 2004. Demy 8vo (215 x 138 mm), 171 + vi pages, 6 line drawings, paperback. **£9.95**

The Princess Who Ate People

The psychology of Celtic myths

Brendan McMahon

Childhood, adolescence, courtship and death. Personal identity and madness. These are the key themes of many myths in traditional Celtic literatures. Although written many centuries ago, their narratives still reflect and define our essential humanity.

Many Celtic tales of exile and loss anticipate modem dilemmas of alienation but offer ways of understanding such difficulties without pathologising them. Individuals are seen in their social context and, in contrast, madness is identified with loneliness and isolation. The traditional stories describe how appropriate narratives help restore integrity and identity. These life-cycle narratives and concepts of identity are more complex and less fixed than psychoanalytic narratives which, by comparison, seem contrived or impoverished.

Psychotherapy assists people to construct a narrative which makes sense of their lives. However psychoanalysis too often relies on outdated and limited assumptions. By learning from the poets who created the Celtic myths, therapists can help their patients develop more appropriate personal narratives.

However this is not a book written only for psychotherapists. The stories considered here speak to all of us. McMahon helps us to fully understand these life cycle narratives and thereby helps us to understand ourselves. We need these myths now more than ever before.

Brendan McMahon is a practicing psychotherapist in Derbyshire who has written many articles and papers on therapy and Celtic myth. He is also a poet and university teacher.

ISBN 1 872883 88 5. January 2006. Demy 8vo (215 x 138 mm), 102 + viii pages, 5 specially commissioned illustrations from Ian Brown, paperback **£9.95**

Leicestershire Legends

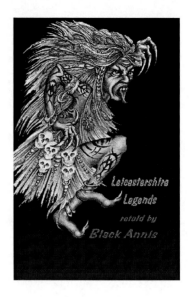

retold by Black Annis

'Let's you and I get a thing or two straight. The name's Black Annis, but you may call me 'Cat Anna' between yourselves – but not to my face, if you value the appearance of yours. There've been days when the aches and pains make me a bit awkward at times, I'll admit as much myself. I've been known to get a bit upset when silly little kids used to play around outside my cave and shout rude remarks like me being an old witch.'

But is she or isn't she? Just an old woman with an attitude problem or actually more of a witch? Herself one of Leicester's best-known legends, Black Annis never quite lets on if she really knows more than she is prepared to say about the Old Ways. But in her direct manner, and with a bit of help from some of her friends, she retells some of the tales of Leicestershire in a way they've never been heard before, with local phrases and dialect rather than written out all posh.

Phantom black hounds, weird goings on where saints were murdered, very odd ways of finding water, pipers who enter underground tunnels and are never seen again, stories about stones, strange lights in the sky, and any number of ghosts – it's all happened in Leicestershire and much more besides, at least if these legends are to be believed.

Specially illustrated by Jenny Clarke, one of Britain's leading tattoo designers.

> 'I really enjoyed reading this collection. The stories are so well told and the printing is so well done that you can feel you are actually there listening to conversations about ghosts, UFOs, old Leicestershire witch trials, phantom hounds, silent sentinels, and so much more. There's just enough of local dialect to add to the reality... Highly recommended.' Francis Cameron *Pentacle*

ISBN 1872883 77 X. 2004. Demi 8vo (215 x 138 mm), 99 + xiv pages, 10 line drawings, perfect bound. **£6.95**

Also published by Heart of Albion Press

Explore Phantom Black Dogs

edited by Bob Trubshaw

Contributors: Jeremy Harte, Simon Sherwood, Alby Stone, Bob Trubshaw and Jennifer Westwood.

The folklore of phantom black dogs is known throughout the British Isles. From the Black Shuck of East Anglia to the Moody Dhoo of the Isle of Man there are tales of huge spectral hounds 'darker than the night sky' with eyes 'glowing red as burning coals'.

The phantom black dog of British and Irish folklore, which often forewarns of death, is part of a world-wide belief that dogs are sensitive to spirits and the approach of death, and keep watch over the dead and dying. North European and Scandinavian myths dating back to the Iron Age depict dogs as corpse eaters and the guardians of the roads to Hell. Medieval folklore includes a variety of 'Devil dogs' and spectral hounds. Above all, the way people have thought about such ghostly creatures has steadily evolved.

This book will appeal to all those interested in folklore, the paranormal and fortean phenomena.

'I think this must be the best entry in the Explore series I have seen so far... ' **Aeronwy Dafies** *Monomyth Supplement*

'This is an excellent work and is very highly recommended.' **Michael Howard** *The Cauldron*

ISBN 1 872883 78 8. Published 2005. Demy 8vo (215 x 138 mm), 152 + viii pages, 10 b&w half-tones, paperback. **£12.95**

Explore Folklore

Bob Trubshaw

'Highly Recommended'
by the Folklore Society's
Katharine Briggs Folklore Award 2003

**'A howling success, which plugs a big
and obvious gap'**
Professor Ronald Hutton

There have been fascinating developments in the study of folklore in the last twenty-or-so years, but few books about British folklore and folk customs reflect these exciting new approaches. As a result there is a huge gap between scholarly approaches to folklore studies and 'popular beliefs' about the character and history of British folklore. *Explore Folklore* is the first book to bridge that gap, and to show how much 'folklore' there is in modern day Britain.

Explore Folklore shows there is much more to folklore than morris dancing and fifty-something folksingers! The rituals of 'what we do on our holidays', funerals, stag nights and 'lingerie parties' are all full of 'unselfconscious' folk customs. Indeed, folklore is something that is integral to all our lives – it is so intrinsic we do not think of it as being 'folklore'.

The implicit ideas underlying folk lore and customs are also explored. There might appear to be little in common between people who touch wood for luck (a 'tradition' invented in the last 200 years) and legends about people who believe they have been abducted and subjected to intimate body examinations by aliens. Yet, in their varying ways, these and other 'folk beliefs' reflect the wide spectrum of belief and disbelief in what is easily dismissed as 'superstition'.

Explore Folklore provides a lively introduction to the study of most genres of British folklore, presenting the more contentious and profound ideas in a readily accessible manner.

ISBN 1 872883 60 5. Perfect bound, demi 8vo (215x138 mm), 200 pages, **£9.95**

Also from Heart of Albion Press

Explore Mythology

Bob Trubshaw

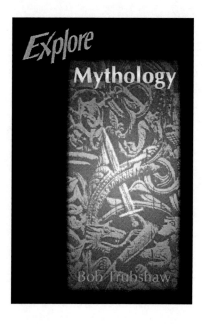

Myths are usually thought of as something to do with 'traditional cultures'. The study of such 'traditional' myths emphasises their importance in religion, national identity, hero-figures, understanding the origin of the universe, and predictions of an apocalyptic demise. The academic study of myths has done much to fit these ideas into the preconceived ideas of the relevant academics.

Only in recent years have such long-standing assumptions about myths begun to be questioned, opening up whole new ways of thinking about the way such myths define and structure how a society thinks about itself and the 'real world'.

These new approaches to the study of myth reveal that, to an astonishing extent, modern day thinking is every bit as 'mythological' as the world-views of, say, the Classical Greeks or obscure Polynesian tribes. Politics, religions, science, advertising and the mass media are all deeply implicated in the creation and use of myths.

Explore Mythology provides a lively introduction to the way myths have been studied, together with discussion of some of the most important 'mythic motifs' – such as heroes, national identity, and 'central places' – followed by a discussion of how these ideas permeate modern society. These sometimes contentious and profound ideas are presented in an easily readable style of writing.

> 'Here's another brilliant volume, an account of mythology such as you are unlikely ever to have seen before. This is no mere collection of mythological stories. It's a thoughtful, well researched exposition which really gets down to the deep structure of the narratives which encode the consciousness of groups and societies.... Buy it! If you follow up even a fraction of the leads, there's enough here to keep you occupied for many a month to come.' Francis Cameron *Pentacle*

> '... this book is... a useful introduction to literature that many would find hard to come by, and offers a challenging perspective that does not let assumptions rest easy.' John Billingsley *Northern Earth*

ISBN 1 872883 62 1. Perfect bound. Demi 8vo (215 x 138 mm), 220 + xx pages, 17 line drawings. **£9.95**

Ymir's Flesh

North European
creation mythologies

Alby Stone

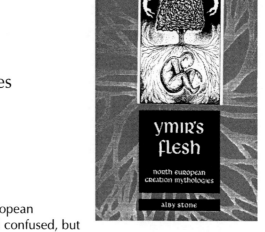

In isolation the pre-Christian north European
creation myths appear fragmented and confused, but
a thematic cohesion is apparent when they are taken as a whole and compared to
their counterparts in Vedic India, ancient Greece and Rome, medieval Ireland,
ancient and medieval Iran, and so on. From this arises a wider significance that
would not otherwise be apparent.

This wider significance includes the recognition of a distinctive social structure,
formally defined in the institutions, myths and religion. The myths of creation have a
pivotal r le in the construction of this system. A vast and complex mythical scenario
describes the spontaneous generation and subsequent dismemberment of a primal
humanoid being and the manufacture of the features of the cosmos from parts of his
body.

Ymir's Flesh gathers together the distorted fragments of this mythology and provides
an original and inspiring insight into the complex inter-weaving of mythological
themes.

> 'Alby writes in a clear way about a complex subject, injecting an
> occasional glimpse of humour. For anyone interested in Germanic
> mythology, Indo-European culture and shamanism this book is an
> essential addition to your reading lists.' *White Dragon*

> 'Fascinating seems too simple a word to describe this book; yet it is,
> and partly because it has a style that makes the content easy to read
> - no small achievement with densely interwoven material like this.
> *Northern Earth*

> 'The scope of research and analysis in the book would at first
> appear to beckon an extremely dense read, however the style and
> verve of the text does much to enliven the highly involved subject
> matter.' *3rd Stone*

ISBN 1 872883 45 1. 1997. A5, 240 pages, illustrated, paperback **£12.95**

Myths of Reality

Simon Danser

'This liberal author's knowledge of contemporary society is amazingly broad. He exposits the mythic depths (and appearances) of everything from 'the myth of science' to superhero attitudes of contemporary American nationalism.

'Along the way he challenges many superficial trivialities about myths functioning in culture. He regards the mythic as a primary, highly effective agent of social ideology, and is never hesitant about demanding that the garments of our truly mythological capitalism are ill-fitting and socially harmful.

'This is the best book I know in terms of disclosing the pragmatic functioning of myth in society.'

William Doty, Professor Emeritus, The University of Alabama and author of *Mythography: The study of myths and rituals*

Simon Danser asks us to think of myths as like the lenses in spectacles – we see the world through them, but rarely see them in their own right. He then systematically focuses on the myths at the core of the belief systems which create every aspect of what we take to be reality: religion, politics, commerce, science, knowledge, consciousness, self-identity, and much else that we take as 'given'.

This book reveals how reality is culturally constructed in an ever-continuing process from mythic fragments transmitted by the mass media and adapted through face-to-face and Internet conversations.

'And now, in 2005, there is a powerful new voice from outside American culture to motivate the old symbol and myth chasing posse. This time it comes from England and author Simon Danser in his short but brilliant book *Myths of Reality*.' John Fraim *Jung Pages*

Published by Alternative Albion, an imprint of Heart of Albion Press.
ISBN 1 872883 80 X. 2004. 215 x 175 mm, 205 + xiv pages, paperback. **£12.95**

Heart of Albion

The UK's leading publisher of
folklore, mythology and cultural studies.

Further details of all Heart of Albion titles online at
www.hoap.co.uk

All titles available direct from Heart of Albion Press.

Please add 80p p&p (UK only; email
albion@indigogroup.co.uk for overseas postage).

To order books or request our current catalogue
please contact

Heart of Albion Press

2 Cross Hill Close, Wymeswold
Loughborough, LE12 6UJ

Phone: 01509 880725
Fax: 01509 881715
email: albion@indigogroup.co.uk
Web site: www.hoap.co.uk